ECONOMIC RACISM

MEMOIR OF A HEROIC NONCONFORMIST

I0113960

MARTIN KUSH

Revised Edition

Library of Congress Cataloging-in-Publication Data

Name: Martin Kush, author

Title: Economic Racism: Memoire of a Heroic Nonconformist /

Martin Kush. —1st ed. | Atlanta: Red Hill Media, [2022] | Includes bibliographical references. Identifiers: LCCN 2022920332 | ISBN 9798985933307 (Paperback)

Subjects: Nonfiction–Business & Economics–Corporate & Business History–Social Science–Ethnic Studies–African American Studies–Discrimination–Colonialism–Corporate America–Bigotry–Policy–Politics & Government–Prejudice–Race

ISBN: 979-8-9859333-0-7

Red Hill Media

DEDICATION

To my best friend and daily inspiration, Alecia. Also, to my children, Rosita, Xaine, and Xavier. May you continue to grow wiser in dealing with this world.

CONTENTS

ACKNOWLEDGMENTS

When I started this work, I was writing as a form of therapy to have somewhere to store my deep emotions from the real world. I thought that if I wrote it down, I would dissipate the anger and be able to cope with what I was feeling. Besides, polite people should not talk about racism. As a result, I wrote a very angry first draft, and I hope that the remainder still has some residue of the anger but that I have shown some calm to give me the distance to come up with solutions. People close to me kept me grounded, helping me cope while I wrote this, often with dismay as I searched for a solution to a complex and long-standing global dilemma of Economic Racism.

I want to thank the following people for their inspiration and encouragement:

My soulmate and partner, the woman I met on a trial and whim, who encouraged me daily to finish this book, despite my many distractions like my day job and other projects;

To my extended family spread throughout the world, for their unbridled feistiness, brilliance, integrity, and laughter even when times seem dire, for their unwavering candor, ambitions, upliftment, and love;

To my children, who have been an encouragement in their resiliency, brilliance, strength, and relentlessness toward life. I hope that this book becomes a toolkit for public and private policy, as well as citizens, to use to eradicate racism incrementally over time sufficiently so we can enjoy more equality than I did and suffer from less racism than we all experience;

To my friends, colleagues, and business associates—sometimes all-in-one—worldwide, from whom I have learned statecraft, to be adventurous, curious, and passionate about the world and its many cultures, peoples, economies, ideals, and histories;

To all my former managers, particularly the good ones who taught me how to be the best leader that motivates and inspires all people I encounter, recognizing that the individuals that work with you are human beings with real lives; and to the bad managers who, through their exhibition of low self-esteem and destructive ways, taught me and the people around them what the qualities are of a poor manager and the ultimate results of such. I thank them for their unintended inspiration for this book.

And finally, I thank the lowest persons in our society: the unhoused, the beggar, the prostitute, the cleaner and janitor, and those whom society considers invisible people we should forget but human beings who help us remember our humanity, and whom all come from a history that does not seal their future unless they allow it. All are equally important. It's been a great life so far. Thank you for sharing it with me.

INTRODUCTION

Warning, dear reader: this book will be uncomfortable, but that is okay. You will not die from reading it. We all need thick skin on our journey to discovering the ways of the world. Like it or not, it's your world. You have the responsibility to make it better. Even allowing everything to burn and start renewed will require action on your part. I hope the following pages will open your mind and give you my perspective on how we got here.

I started off writing a book about my life and family. It was supposed to be mainly life lessons to my children—part of my legacy of sorts to them and whoever else benefited. When I got to the chapter on workplace experiences, I recalled numerous stories about navigating strange, borderline unprofessional behavior specific to the USA. At work, I went through an in-your-face type of racism, of the kind that made you wonder whether that remark from a boss was a weird compliment or an insult because of their racial upbringing and socialization.

This experience was like being punched in the face by Mohamed Ali in a 15-round boxing match. Even then, I staggered but remained standing. At first, the pain and humiliation from the blatant disrespect caused me to burn with anger. I recognized the cancerous behavior but did not accept the racism I faced. Consequently, I never internalized it as my fault. Yet, I realized many people who grew up in America, including my family, accepted it. It was how they survived.

I decided the book on my family, life adventures, and lessons had to wait. Instead, I would write about racism. When I moved to the United States of America, the capital city of racial hate groups like the Ku Klux Klan in Atlanta, Georgia, I became interested in economic racism. My novel community experiences led me to read just about anything I could find on the topic written from the brown and white peoples' perspectives. I observed people more at work and in society. I took breaks between reading some books on race because I was dismayed, depressed, and angered that people could treat their species with such horror. I asked people about their racial experiences and heard some heartbreaking stories of oppression against black and brown people.

I grew up mainly in the Caribbean, where most people were brown and black. While there are class dynamics surrounding white people, most islanders, to some extent, are intolerant of white racists. We had our regional form of racism—known as colorism. But it did not manifest itself as Economic Racism, at least not in my lifetime. The impact on the economic distribution of benefits was more prevalent in my grandmother's and mother's time. You see, I considered myself a novice to the pursuit of whiteness, that is, American racism. For the last decade, I have lived in Switzerland. While it is predominantly white there, people are not so openly dogmatic about whiteness as they are in the United States and are generally ashamed of being called a racist in public.

In America, white people usually ignore any suggestion of their racial prejudice and simply deny the reality of their bias. They get emotionally defensive, faux insulted, and seek to create distractions by asking for proof like it's a scientific experiment. Then, when they don't get their ironclad proof or they offer some of the usual defenses, they presume it will go away. Brown people are expected to accept the status quo.

The defensiveness of white people is not strange. A friend of mine explained it this way: "They must be depicted as 'good' people. Racism seems terrible and uncomfortable. It reminds them of the kidnapping and enslavement of Africans and other such atrocities; stuff they want to pretend did not happen. When confronted, they hear the other person say, 'you are a bad person, not worthy of what you have.'"

I know this will be painful for white people reading this book who have racist tendencies, and I do not assume that all white people are racists. I will go more into this later. I commend you for reading this far. It is comforting to know that you want to leave the world better than when you found it. You care about humanity. Those of you who have already quit reading, well, as I said, you live here too. Good luck if you think the status quo is working.

I know that it's easy for some brown people to sit back and accept it or just try not to bring racism up. Many brown people get worn down from the constant racial knife slashes on one's emotional skin. To keep from constantly exploding with anger from all my racial wounds and sores, I wrote about it.

This allowed me to calm my nerves and understand, from a social scientist's point of view, the context surrounding the white premise of superior human beings to anyone with brown skin. Many books look at this idiocy, but I have yet to find literature on the topic by a person of Caribbean origin who has lived and traveled globally. Working in the United States came later in my professional career after exposure to Europeans, Asians, and Africans in their native countries. It gave me a different perspective and expectations for behavior, placing me in direct conflict with white American immigrants who have forgotten their history.

It must be caustic to live a life in which one abuses people they consider inferior. Racist behavior perpetuates a racist system among both educated and non-educated people. They think whiteness and their assumed privilege are somehow natural.

My expectations for success, equal opportunity, and respect are considered arrogant, while their desire for power and domination is trumpeted as a strength of character and even God-given. What has this privilege, or white affirmative action, caused? Significant cultural problems and ruination of the growth potential of millions of non-white people across the world. What irreversible and generational harm has been done to young brown people? These are some of the questions I will answer.

What hope do brown people have when racist white people still think that non-white people should solve white racism on their own, without them involved? White people see it as a "black" problem. They often say, "This is the past and should have no effect on your present or future." Or "pull yourself up from your bootstraps." Or "look at the Asians, or look at how the Italians, Polish or . . . (another fill-in-the-blank-minority-group) have been successful." They conveniently neglect reality. These "others" were not recently enslaved and did not have the stigma of people who believed in propaganda, like minstrelsy. Years of old-fashioned colonialism and new forms of modern hegemonic domination and imperialism have caused incalculable damage. This oppression affected interactions we had during our formative years and can remain burned into our psyche even when we don't actively remember. It will continue to leave fingerprints on our parenting and influence our children for generations to come. The cumulative result is a difference in the quality of life experienced between most black and white people.

Dave Chappelle, a famous American stand-up comedian, actor, and producer, said in one of his television shows, "Poor white people and poor black people are the same." He meant they suffer the same economic challenges, exploitation from rich people, educational deficiencies, and are deprived of opportunities for financial advancement and independence. The only difference is that poor white people believe something is wrong with their lives, and usually, their economic challenges are someone else's fault.

Brown people need to be reminded, as do white people, of the main culprit for the racial mess in which we find ourselves. For over 400 years, European countries' decision to branch out into the world to prosper and grow rich, in competition with each other, brought damnation to multiple civilizations worldwide.

Today, the remnants of imperialism are stark: to justify slavery, the separation of people by skin color and origin, simplified down to "black" and "white," resulted in significant disparities in life success. Then there is the persistent conditioning that continued in everything from books, culture, language, media, politics, law enforcement, entertainment, pseudo-science, and religion, all to ensure that one myth is continuously perpetuated to preserve power in one group of people.

It's all about power. A group of people searching for ways to dominate another group convince themselves of absurd myths such as anything black is bad, dark is evil: there's the black sheep of the family, black market, dark web, dark skin tones, dark eyes, black eyes, and skin is dark, as is Satan and other demonic personages from other non-Christian religions. This is all while asserting that anything white is pure, angelic, and positive.

A white lie is a neat little unharmful lie, and there are white angels with white feathered wings. Even Jesus is supposedly white. Churches exhibit white religious effigies everywhere, even though Jesus was, according to the Holy Bible, born in Bethlehem. Bethlehem is a desert city where people's skin is naturally sand-colored because it is blazingly sunny. Religion plays a vital role in the assumption of racial domination and messages of superiority.

Even in the Christian churches in the global south, images of the stations of the cross depict Jesus Christ on the day of his crucifixion and other people all as white. This is even though most of their congregation is brown. They believed in Palestine, Jesus' community of origin, where there were no white people.

The film industry and popular culture have their contribution too. Most comic book superheroes are white—Superman, Batman and Robin, Spiderman, Thor, most of the X-Men, and so on. Only recently have there been moves to introduce some brown superheroes on the big screen. When "black" movies portray brown people in a positive light on the big screen, many of my white friends would decry the production as poor quality. They were never specific in their criticism, probably because they, with many years of deep racial bias conditioning, could not explain it. These friends were supposed to be progressive, non-racial white people. They could not come right out and say that the movie was terrible because it portrayed a black hero and black civilization with a life other than enslavement or servitude. Some African productions, like the series on Netflix's Queen Sono, showcase a black action heroine and her team, who are also intelligent and humane, while fighting the impact of white colonizers' slash-and-burn approach to wealth hoarding.

Accordingly, we have yet to see a proliferation of movies or other heroes from the African continent, Arab world, Asia, or an indigenous people group. The message is clear: the protector, champion, rescuer, guardian, and world's savior can only be white, usually a white man. The Chinese film industry now portrays heroes as Asian people and British and American white men as villains. One famous example is the Wolf Warrior series, which features a Chinese macho, action-adventure hero starring Wu Jing (Jacky Wu). They distribute these productions globally to counter the "great white hope" propaganda. The hope is that they also displace other Asian movies made in the west with white actors who painted their faces yellow, wore eye prosthetics, and portrayed Asians using some established white stereotypes.

We still need more positive role model films, in both fiction and non-fiction, of African, First Nations people from everywhere, Middle Eastern, and Latin American origin. Brown people are starving for television with positive content about them. I am tired of media portrayal of starving kids in Africa and half-naked women in traditional tribal costumes from native tribes in Africa or South America. These images are often thirty to fifty years old but are replayed to maintain a global perception that Africa is underdeveloped.

When I visit Africa, I usually am worried about getting to my destination in a reasonable time, not because of hungry people but because of the plethora of cars on the multi-lane highways and traffic jams. I marvel at the high-rise buildings, sophisticated metropole, diversity, and success of professional people dressed in suits and fancy clothes. Despite the social challenges that originated with colonialization, these countries are thriving. Imagine what they would be like today without foreign interference and its resulting destabilizing effects.

Why, in popular media, can't I see the successes and developments in Africa, and other countries, instead of only poverty? Admittedly, Netflix and other forums are starting to show brown heroes and white villains— closer to the real history of Africa. Part of the challenge is that the mechanisms to showcase other non-white cultures lack access to money and power. Consequently, they may not be as good at marketing a pro-brown agenda.

White culture attracts money. White culture and history, especially among similar classes, generate trust between them so that the opportunities gifted to their economic class are almost expected. Middle- and upper-class white people do not worry about being poor because other white people will help them. Recall what Dave Chapelle said: they don't see white poverty as a natural course of life. If they are poor, they believe and act like it's temporary. Underclass brown people think it's a natural course of life. Yet both groups, often unwittingly, contribute to the white class's growth in power and money (Oluo 2018). The exception may be the Appellation Hill people, or what some authors call "rednecks," the poor white people, referred to as "trailer trash," who come from the poor peasant class of Europe (Sowell 2005).

We take for granted the meaning of poorly chosen words and the negative influence they have on our psyche, as with "black" and "white," descriptors used to describe people of African origin and those of European descent, respectively. Words and phrases such as "slaves" versus "enslaved people" are profoundly different—the former falsely depicts an independent entity that chose to be, and the latter truthfully point to the direction of the oppressor over the oppressed.

Today's underclass, whether brown or poor white, contains many people. Native people across the world suffered genocide at the hands of their invaders and colonizers. This includes brown people who were kidnapped from their homelands, enslaved, raped, murdered, stripped of their homeland culture and any dignity it nourished, and forced to provide free labor to enrich Europeans. All so that aristocrats could have sweeteners in their teas, wear comfortable designer cotton clothing, men could smoke quality tobacco products, or have servants at their beck and call, including for satisfying sexual urges.

The underclass includes people murdered and left without rights because of their choice of religion. Then there are women of all cultures, considered subjects for rape and plunder, then discarded. We forget that women, as the species that reproduce us, are the reason we still exist. They deserve complete respect from more of us. Some people are born with diverse sexual orientations or desires, unlike most of the population. Yet, others try to destroy anything that seems different. What arrogance makes white culture, religion, skin color, or sexuality more civilized than black or brown culture? Why does white culture distort the definition of "civilized" when they condone or participate in other people's systematic, generational, physical, and economic racialism in the name of culture, religion, and skin color? That behavior is not *civilized*.

In this book, I will explore my experiences with some of these issues and how I suggest dealing with them. My pain and abuse forged the premise of this book. Like many professional brown men and women, I have been overlooked for promotions and raises, interviewed to prove that they tried to hire a minority candidate, had my intelligence insulted, my background disbelieved, and on some occasions, been potentially life-threatening situations, like being nearly kidnapped.

At first, I believed it was just white ignorance. When I lived outside America, I always heard that the primary and secondary school quality of education was below many other Global North and Global South countries. The disparity is multiplied many times over for children in many economically depressed school districts. I later came to realize that it was ignorance of a different type. It was one of ideology. Racism guided many of those interactions.

Yet I know others have suffered far more than I could imagine. I am still on a journey to learn about America's racism and the damage it has caused that erupts now and again into protests like a puss-filled sore creeping toward betterment. In the end, all this need for domination is unnecessary. Therefore, I hope readers can combat racism wherever they encounter it to improve our world.

I am a trained economist. My work has always been to examine scarcity and to find ways to spread prosperity for all citizens of a city, region, state, or country. In economics, human beings are differentiated based on their strength of character and abilities, talents that contribute to personal and universal prosperity. We learn that resources will flow naturally, like gravity, to where it's most productive. For example, a highly qualified man or woman will get a job over a lower-skilled woman or man regardless of their complexion, origin, accent, name, or sexual orientation.

In economics, a firm and its representative hiring manager will hire the best candidate to join their company because they rationally and consistently want to preserve the long-term profits and prosperity of the stockholders. When racism disrupts natural economic rational behavior, people suffer due to inaccessibility to the tools and cooperation required to achieve and enjoy wealth. The damage ripples like a wave in a pond from a single stone of racism thrown in the middle. Each tide is a generation that encounters injury from losing its predecessor's prosperity. The ripples are a manifestation of Economic Racism. The result of each successive wave of civilization in the long term is economic murder.

Chapter 1

HOW RACISM ERODES SOCIETY

"No one is born hating another person because of the color of his or [her] skin, background, or religion. People must learn to hate, and if they can learn to hate, they can be taught to love, for love comes more naturally to the human heart than the opposite."

~ NELSON MANDELA, South African anti-apartheid revolutionary, political leader, and philanthropist.

First, let me make my position clear on "white" and "black" as descriptions for any distinction between human beings. It is crucial to draw my lines in the sand early. I believe racial differentiation between black and white is a fiction conjured to fulfill a narrative needed when Europeans decided to obtain free labor by enslaving Africans for their newly appropriated lands, also known as colonialism.

As a child, I could not understand why white people were called "white" and brown-skinned people "black." In primary school, I remember assuming one of my white friends was wearing pink socks when in fact, he had no socks on at all. He laughed when I remarked, "I thought you were white, so why does your ankle look pink?" Even with decades of education and life experience, the terminology still makes no sense to me as an adult. So-called "white" people are cream, red, pink, brown, tan, and various colors, none of which is close to the color "white." Similarly, "black" does not come close to describing brown, tan, pink, red, cream, and the array of shades encompassing people with African, Asian, or other indigenous heritage. The colonialists aimed to make one dominant color and its associated "race" pure while justifying the subjugation and animalization of the other that was enslaved, using the color "black."

History belies the narrative that claims all enslaved people were "black." Thousands of Europeans enslaved by North Africans from the 1700s to 1800s had barely sun-kissed complexions. Were they also black because they were enslaved? What about the penal settlements supplied with peasants, the poor, the homeless, and convicted criminals from Europe? Their treatment by the monarchy, military, and bourgeoisie was also brutal, and many found themselves sold into slave-like indentureship. They were not "black," yet they were also enslaved and abused, as with generations of new immigrants to the United States.

I prefer to say brown-skinned people or brown people instead of "black." This is for the following reasons. At five years old, my eldest son, during our after-school car ride home, informed me that a white female classmate had licked his skin to determine whether he tasted like chocolate. Disgusting! As a germaphobe friend used to say, "Do you know how many germs are in someone's mouth?" I never researched a definitive answer, but I know it is more than zero. My son wisely reasoned she must be foolish since there was also white milk chocolate. He was not inclined to reciprocate, saying her skin was nasty. "Plus," he added, "I would never do that because it's uncivilized behavior." Neither did he understand why she called him "black," yet she likened his complexion to chocolate. Most chocolate is brown, never black. My son said to her he has brown skin and, well, he does. As a tribute to him, I will continue along that vein.

My son has the most beautiful, smooth, chocolate-colored, even-toned skin I have ever seen. He has symmetrical features and could easily be a model if he wanted to use his body more than his brain to earn a living. Yet, he also has a brilliant mind, so he is one of those who got all the gifts. He, like so many others, has a dark brown complexion. Their skin tone does not include the color black. Children are authentic that way and, to be frank, often more intelligent than the average adult. Since then, I have been fighting the need to interchange "brown" and "black" depending on my audience.

I hope you understand why I hesitate to use "black" as a unique signifier for such a culturally broad base of people. I do this because I am also protesting the invented notion of being "black" with all the negative connotations given to it. Recognizing that the African and European diaspora has embraced this concept as a descriptor is essential. It creates a separation for the colonial cause. Usage of the term "black" also serves as a divide-and-conquer tool. They separate "black" from indigenous people, Hispanics, North Africans, Asians, or Middle Easterners. These categorizations prompt groups to behave as crabs-in-a-barrel without collectively addressing the real problem.

There is also a very delicate, internalized racial dynamic at play. Tell any other brown person you are not "black," and they respond by telling you,

you are "playing white," or superior, or somehow denying your race and heritage. What follows is their inevitable lurking around for something tragic to befall you. If it does, those that have internalized the label won't miss their opportunity to laugh in your face. Look at the *black* community's reaction to the likes of Tiger Woods, among others. When Tiger Woods said he was a "Cablinasian," he attempted to capture all his parents' origins, a mixture of white, black, Native American, and Asian. Yet he was castigated for trying to hide his blackness. Brown people were hurt because they thought this man had finally dominated a sport previously only open to whites, denying the notion of a black man succeeding in this field. As a result, they felt robbed. The federal census office created that one-drop approach to subscribe one to the *black* or African American club. Perhaps those celebrities were trying to use their platform to even the playing field and remove this colonial-created description. Since they know there is no black or white blood, they can recognize their entire heritage without being ridiculed. Maybe they were too progressive for the times and appeared to disassociate themselves from the subjugated class.

Before you object, I know some brown people try to shun the "black" label and its implications so much that they offend others. They acquire money and fame. The money and fame attract a group of freeloaders who suckle on the teat of affluence. These fortunate brown people, for a while, fly on top of the world until the day white people either say something racist or withdraw their support as quickly as the wealth evaporates.

A friend of mine recalled feeling chic because he had a gaggle of white friends while living in the Caribbean. If asked, he would have labeled them progressive until the day they described another associate as a "black monkey." My friend suddenly realized something horrible. When he was not around, his friends probably talked about him like that too. These people didn't think of themselves as racist because they had a brown friend among them, seemingly laughing at their racist remarks. It was also a predominantly brown country.

Throughout the book, I refer to *black* people as brown. I use the term "black" or black in italics to signify how the research presented the text for distinction or to relay a direct quote. I don't like the term people of color, because it signals our struggle (as I find myself here) to either accept the white people's racist description or find our own, hopefully, less racist human categorization. Besides, everyone has color. It still perpetuates the idea that white is pure and everyone else is of color, which is suggestively unpure. In some instances, because ruthless white economics affects all non-white people, brown can include indigenous people, people of African descent, and any non-white oppressed group who cannot pass as white due to their skin color, religion, culture, language, or origin.

The question remains, what is "white" in terms of race? As I said, this is still confusing to me. Most Americans self-select their race. They often consider themselves white because that is where the power base in this society resides. For our purposes, white is regarded as a description of white people, particularly those who chose whiteness. Many books discuss race invention and its subsequent damage to those in the lower echelons of classification.

Notwithstanding the above, when I refer to "white," I mean white racist people. I mean, white people who thrive on the existence of a great imagination kept in what I call a minstrelsy box. Contrastingly, some white people are not racist. You usually know them when you meet them. You hear mutual respect in their speech, see it in their body language and feel it from their interactions with you as a person. They are not insecure and, therefore, don't exhibit it. Let's dive into what racism is and why it exists at all.

According to Dr. Audrey Smedley, Professor of Anthropology at Virginia Commonwealth University and author of Race in North America: Origin and Evolution of a Worldview, race is "any action, practice, or belief that reflects the racial worldview, that is the ideology that human beings can be divided into separate and exclusive biological entities called races" (Smedley 2004).

The word "race" grew in usage with the growth of European imperialism. As Europeans ventured out into the world and found new lands inhabited by other civilizations, they created this term to show differences and distinct features, habits, and cultures from theirs. Still, later as they dominated and conquered these lands and displaced or murdered these people, they justified their actions again using "race" coupled with religion to show their efforts were just and in their interest (Cruz 2017).

They developed a causal link between people's physical characteristics and traits of personality, intellect, and morality based on doctrine, normally Christianity, and other cultural and behavioral features. They explained to European society that some races were innately superior to others. The ruse gained popularity in the 17th century when the Europeans started to enslave people from west-sub-Sahara-African coastal countries (Ogusola 2015).

Ironically, the North Africans, primarily the Muslim people from countries today referred to as Morocco, Algeria, Tunisia, and Libya, themselves had enslaved people from European and other nearby countries. While the African slave trade supported European trade and made Europe rich with the free lands in the Americas and labor from west Africa, the Volga trade was ongoing between North Africa and Russia. While they traded all varieties of enslaved peoples from the 15th century until the middle of the 18th, writers used the term "white slavery" to denounce the slavery of European Christians (Grabmeier 2004).

The North African slave markets traded in European enslaved people kidnapped by pirates in slave raids on ships and incursions on coastal towns from Italy to Spain, Portugal, France, England, the Netherlands, and as far afield as the Turkish abductions in Iceland. The Ottoman Empire financed and supported these seizures. They captured men, women, and children and decimated seacoast towns, just as the Europeans did to African coastal cities and villages. According to Robert Davis, Barbary pirates captured between one million and 1.25 million Europeans. They sold them as enslaved people in North Africa and the Ottoman Empire between the 15th and 19th centuries (Mahmood 2019).

Since the late 20th century, the notion of a biological race has been recognized as a cultural invention, entirely without a scientific basis. *Black* people are said to be racially *black*, but their skin is not black, nor is the premise of race correct. The same is true for white people (Y. Williams 2018).

The biological trait argument for a race is based on pseudoscience circular logic that one group is oppressed because the hegemonic group—white people in this theory—are dominant because of natural superiority. The logic of racism is that it's an efficient economic strategy; humans can only survive and, indeed, strive by oppressing another group for resources. Yet, anthropoidal studies reveal that groups, including ten million Native Americans, have lived here for 12,000 years without annihilating or persecuting each other to control resources (History.com 2020).

The Malthusian theory stated, in summary, that the planet will run out of food as the population grows, causing people to starve. He was wrong. Ingenuity in agricultural production, the use of technology to increase the productivity of land and crop yield, and declining birth rates as countries became more successful all proved that we could make enough resources to survive and have a better standard of living than in the past. Planet earth has more than enough resources, but greed to hoard most of it, as expressed by any country's Gini coefficient measuring income distribution, is the factor that makes societies suffer. While the global population is just over seven billion, we have enough food and resources to feed ten billion (Holt-Gimenez 2014). So why create systems of systemic racism, class structure, and oppression to gain and hoard resources?

Racism is not a biological trait or an evolutionary result of *black* and brown people. It is a psychological contrivance created by feelings of insecurity and anxiety about their mortality. Psychologists show us that racism comes in a spectrum from mild to extreme. That's why a brown person feels uneasy when President Joseph Biden, in a Freudian slip at an Iowa speech in 2019, said, "poor kids are just as bright and just as talented as white kids"—a mild form maybe from his implicit bias (M. Stevens 2019). Then there may be extreme forms, like when a white supremacist massacred nine worshippers at the Emanuel African Methodist Episcopal Church in Charleston, South Carolina, on June 17, 2015 (Elliott 2020).

Psychologists break down racists into five groups:

People with a sense of insecurity or lack an identity may want to associate themselves with a group to bolster their feeling of self and fitting in. This could be a golf club, where members know a financial filter of high cost for membership would allow mostly their "kind." These are the people who are typically adamant that they are not racist. Yet they may believe that black people being lazy is why they are economically behind other groups. They may have a preference to hire white candidates for jobs, with a few token black lower-level candidates to prove they are not racist. They may still be concerned with being seen as "good people."

An identity that builds pride and comradery is good, but it could lead to the second form or stage, where the group exhibits hostility or enmity towards the "others." White people may move out of a neighborhood—so-called "white flight"—to escape the growing number of brown people moving into their previously only white community. They may be verbally abusive or vandalize the homes of their unwanted neighbors to encourage them to move or to simply indicate how much they do not want "others" too close to their group.

Those willing to be verbally and physically abusive may become obsessed and paranoid with their "otherness." They may take steps to withdraw any empathy for people outside their belief system. They may feel compassion only for people in their group while being cruel in actions and deeds to their perceived "outsiders." Here non-racist white people who openly go against brown oppression may also face backlash. This group may believe they are losing something by others progressing.

The growing brutality and lack of compassion can lead to an attempt to homogenize everyone in the group. All individual personalities are quashed to encourage a tighter sense of belongingness in the group. Open criticism of women wearing the hijab and even attacking them becomes possible here.

The final group is the most dangerous and destructive. They may lose a sense of reality by projecting their failures and flaws onto the other group to avoid their shame and guilt. Different groups become scapegoats and may be punished, attacked, or murdered as revenge for alleged crimes. People who cannot admit their faults, like those with narcissistic personality disorder, are prone to this stage and will demonize anyone outside their group (Taylor 2018).

Consequently, not all white people are racist or equally racist. There are many people for whom skin color or origin is not considered for human engagement. Some people judge you based on your strength of character. I know it's tough when you come from a culture where white people signal danger and criminality, like lynching and its nasty historical attachment. Still, there are lovely white people, too, as there are beautiful brown people. However, lovely white people need to be the shield of brown people against those that are racist (Blay 2015).

Throughout this book, the term "white people" mainly fits the understanding of the common language of identifying a group of people. "White," however, is a belief system more than it is a category of people. That's why you can have someone who is a Dutchman or Frenchwoman who considers themselves to be a Dutchman or a Frenchwoman. They do not think of themselves as white in their national context. They do not believe in "whiteness" and all the violence, dominance, and colonialism it stands for. Therefore, they are not racist. They can become racists to assimilate into the Western culture and to differentiate themselves from abused people. Their complexion allows them to assimilate, so they do not get abused. But keep in mind while reading that every time I refer to a 'white' person, I am referring to someone who believes in whiteness. This also explains why a German woman whom I follow on social media always talks out against racism. In the West, she would be considered white. Yet, because she is a mother to children she had with a brown man, she does not believe in whiteness.

As a result, some brown people can be racist, because they too believe in whiteness. Like most of us influenced by our society, they get induced by their implicit bias. Some brown people get caught up in a preconception that manifests itself in preference based on a gradient of complexion (Nittle, The Roots of Colorism, or Skin Tone Discrimination 2020). We call this colorism, something we face in the Caribbean along with some other brown societies.

I aim to educate people about race by sharing my experiences and stories. My best advice for everyone is to travel. While doing so, be open to meeting people from all backgrounds. Cultural contrast will shed light on the destruction implicit bias has caused our societies. You may want to move or be inspired to write, publicizing the mess racism has caused. Either way, I encourage everyone, brown and white alike, to see the world and expose their mind to the possibilities.

Now to get a little radical. In my opinion, the words "black is no less derogatory than the last century's words "nigga" or "negro." They should not be used in polite company because of the hate and suffering these words evoke. When the words nigga or negro are used, especially by someone white towards someone brown, it directs a subdermal sting of remembrance that, "Hey, be careful, I once owned your body and mind, plus your children, even your destiny, and can do so again!" There is a debate about whether white people should have the right to use the word in the presence of brown people without repercussions. I believe white people, who want to be racially sensitive, should never use the word. However, I get that brown people can use the word in the sense of brotherhood or comradery, whether in speech or music. Admittedly, I prefer someone brown, if they must, to call me their brother rather than their nigga. I will not respond well to someone white calling me by that word.

Consequently, the requirement to identify any race or ethnicity by the U.S. national census and all formal documents often feels like it's for a perverse objective. This data collection accompanies almost every form, from your medical records to an application for a job or college. They all come with a request for you to pause and self-identify according to some notion of race, an invented concept for segregation. The Census Bureau says it's ensuring adherence to and monitoring of discrimination laws and helping develop programs like affirmative action programs aimed at social justice. They collected this data in 1790 when brown, enslaved people were considered three-fifths of a man.

The agency was required then to undercount enslaved people. Today, despite the monitoring and reporting on discrimination, bigotry continues. The disadvantaged group can't help the impression that the agency is a tool to support rather than prohibit discrimination through no fault of its own. When a brown person applies for a job in a company run by white people, they don't excitedly say, "Finally, we have some qualified racially *black* applicants to choose from."

The understanding is that they dump a resume with a brown-sounding name in the bin regardless of discrimination laws. Being brown relegates you to menial jobs rather than top leadership roles. Credit accessibility and rates are higher for blacks, despite discrimination laws and the monitoring of the Census Bureau data, which shows that brown people are discriminated against in housing, education, jobs, and ownership of most valuable assets. Yet, the Bureau does not indicate how to protect brown people from jealous riotous conduct from poorer whites if a brown person owns too many assets and gets too successful.

The Bureau's reason for collecting race data remains weak and, in many cases, lacks credibility and does not hint at achieving greater social justice. My point is that measuring disparities is not enough. Racial data collection should be linked to a mechanism to rectify the negative findings toward racial equality.

While data collection should support racial equity, so should the public symbols that can be interpreted as a form of racial dominance of a particular group. For example, confederate memorial statues built during the Jim Crow era, way after the U.S. Civil War, should be removed from public places. I am not saying destroy them, but people who believe the war was for the sake of "states' rights" to enslave people and want to remember "the good ole days" via statues should erect them on their private properties. It also helps others distinguish your racism. Since I believe some people will hold on to their racist beliefs steadfastly, it's good that they identify themselves with images, flags, and statues on their private property.

Confederate memorial statues glorify the terrorization, exploitation, and genocide of a group of people. Citizens who do not believe in being enslaved themselves or enslaving others should not be forced to pay tax dollars to erect or maintain them in public view. That money could help improve people subjected to racism and implicit bias.

In addition to racialized symbolism, race dominance appears in the attempt to categorize everyone based on origin, ethnicity, or race. I am resistant to say African American, Cuban-American, or whatever-American because these terms are too narrow for the global perspective I wish to outlay. I get the rationale. When a nation spends every resource to remind you that you are more valuable to them as property to abuse and use as they see fit, brown people want to escape, to be attached to some more welcoming homeland. Some white people question brown people's patriotism when they seek out a hyphen to categorize themselves. It's hard to feel patriotic when the so-called "patriots" attack their citizens. Many brown Americans do not think that the America many whites are patriotic about includes them (Summers 2020). As the author and political activist Toni Morrison once said, "In this country, American means white. Everybody else has to hyphenate."

Bear with me. Some may take offense at my use of terms. The concept of race is still a touchy subject. Many still suffer from racism and, in some cases, have yet to experience emancipation, whether white or brown. Yes, I meant that. Enslaving brown people gave birth to white racists. It wrecked our world in an all-encompassing way. It damaged the lives and future lives of millions of brown people globally—all that brainpower and the potential wealth of countless nations have been lost.

The brain drain or unneeded constraints that frustrate progress continue to the present day. I will start with a few examples of this invention's effects in modern times. I know many brown professionals with years of global experience, tertiary education, and self-confidence to climb the corporate ladder, and many of us have been to the top. Yet white managers who had none of the above surrounded us. For instance, I once had a project approval held up for three months and only sanctioned after a white associate (outside my company) wrote to the white operations manager to tell him to approve the project. The operations manager finalized the authorization documents within two hours. Despite my education and experience surpassing both, he needed another man to tell him that my project approval would impact him negatively, so he should sign.

The only commonality between the two men was that they both

believed in whiteness. Let me explain why my boss could justify trusting someone outside the organization over me. How can I reconcile that all my previous bosses, a genuinely multicultural mix, would respect and trust me even if they disliked me? Why would this boss trust, accept, and act upon an email from a guy he met for a few hours over breakfast, over me, a professional staff he engages with daily? Could it be simply because I am not white? I am an expert with over thirty years of global experience, more than the boss who got his job through his privilege of a societally accepted skin color. Since I am brown, to him, I deserve less trust equity than someone white. That's why it's difficult for brown people to progress, even when we put in ten times the effort and are far more qualified.

Trust equity is gained or lost at the beginning of the relationship. By 'trust' here, I mean the social glue that binds a group together because of commonalities such as family, cultural, and religious ties. I use the word 'equity' because I consider trust a resource, just like land, labor, capital, and intellectual property. Trust in a group allows everyone in that bubble to share ideas, be enthusiastic about collaboration, and build teams. Trust will enable us to give of ourselves without expecting much in return because we see our building of anyone in the group as automatically building ourselves. With brown skin, you are habitually judged to lose trust before you say something. For example, a white female panelist once told her colleagues that I seemed to know too much about the job I was interviewing for. She concluded I should not be hired because it seemed suspicious. After I met this woman, I decided I would not hire her for any job I had because she was what the writer and philosopher Ayn Rand referred to as a moocher. I mean it in the sense of someone who feeds off their advantage through the generosity of society while ensuring they maintain their privilege even at the expense of destroying opportunities for others. In this case, her intrinsic racial bias weakened her judgment such that she was a moocher (Rand 1957).

Fast forward years later, the same white woman requested my help with her studies. Through what I call "white solidarity," she was given a job for which she was unqualified. Her studies were supposed to help her qualify for the job after she had it. White solidarity is "the tacit agreement that we will protect white privilege and not hold each other accountable for our racism" (R. J. DiAngelo, 2018). This lady knew my skill set. She was willing to use me for her benefit. In the past, during that interview, she could not agree to support me joining the company, not because she did not know I would do a good job, but because she felt my expertise must be fake or somehow, I was given an unfair advantage. Perhaps she also worried I would bring other qualified brown people up. Getting a job based on merit is not the same for many white people.

Many of my white friends and colleagues have expressed to me how they can get a job based on their potential to do a good job. They don't need experience or even qualifications. I have noticed that brown people are often overqualified for a corporate jobs and are scrutinized by less capable white people as incompetent. Alternatively, they may be required to hide the underperformance of their white supervisor by performing both tasks. Being overqualified does not guarantee them success. How did society become so upside-down?

It begins with the disadvantages that beset all minority groups. We start with the handicap and stigma of being the most recently legally enslaved people by white Europeans. Despite legal emancipation, the mental chains and micro- or macro-aggressions continue to act as tools to perpetuate easy success for one minority group and not for others.

A white person from a "good" family can leave school and progress through life with few stumbling blocks. They can, on their journey of self-discovery, indulge in drugs. In some instances, white-collar workers have been known for their daily cocaine breaks while maintaining essential jobs that pay them at least six figures. If caught, they are ushered into some form of rehabilitation. I have even heard of predominantly white unions that have drug rehabilitation as paid service.

They can become addicts. Even after several cycles of relapse and rehab, their peers continue to accept them. They are helped to return to their high-paying productive jobs and continue climbing in their careers as if nothing ever happened. In addition, they may even write a book about their struggle, and their peers will empathize with them, rarely rejecting them. Society will support and applaud their triumph over drug or alcohol addiction, wife-beating, crime, or whatever adversity befalls them. They will praise their journey back to a successful life, often giving them a chance to start over.

If white people overdose on drugs, even then, they are remembered for their monumental efforts and achievements, no matter how minute. Their efforts are glorified even in death. There is no shame settled on their names like dust. Their remaining family often gets support and can start anew without a stigma. One of my former white bosses was alleged to be an alcoholic and often would be caught sleeping in his office. At times, I recall some of our conversations were difficult because he smelled of alcohol. He was never terminated. Eventually, he resigned to take up an even better job.

It is not the same for non-whites. Brown people with similar drug addiction problems are often demonized. They are labeled "lazy." Talking heads and politicians proclaim that "these *black* people made no efforts to break their addiction." Usually, no help is forthcoming, even though they have fewer resources. Flippantly they are told to "just say 'no!'" Any misconduct renders brown people, their families, and friends with layers of social degradation.

Besides, brown people still suffer more from drug offenses due to a lack of empathy. This is because brown people have far fewer incidences of drug use. In a 2011 Substance Abuse and Mental Health Services Administration survey, 20 percent of white people used cocaine, compared with 10 percent of brown people (Knafo 2013). Studies show that in 2016, brown people were arrested twice more than white people for cocaine. "*Black* people in 21 states [in the US] were arrested at a rate at least three times higher than white people for narcotics and cocaine offenses combined in 2016 (Equal Justice Initiative 2019)."

Their bosses would sooner fire a brown person for drug abuse. This usually triggers a downward spiral: income loss, homelessness, divorce, family displacement, depression, and all the negative impacts these situations place on the children or family they support. Many brown people turn to crime out of desperation. Imagine being caught in this quagmire, only to have it worsened with incarceration. The perception is that non-white people deserve jail rather than rehabilitation. Imprisonment without a rehabilitation objective is, in effect, enslavement. This form of detention destroys families and related communities. It is the strangulation of good role models for the younger generation to follow.

The most recent depiction of the racist differences in treatment between white and brown people is the approach to the opioid drug crisis. Today, since mainly white people are addicted to opioids, it's considered an "epidemic." An epidemic is the spread of "disease" through some means outside the responsibility of its victim. Today, white politicians and healthcare leaders say, "it's not their fault." Instead, they proclaim, "It's the fault of those who make the drugs available."

Government policies, money, and charitable organizations have suddenly appeared to help white people addicted to drugs. For brown people, police carry tasers, guns, handcuffs, and batons, all of which they eagerly use to detain, maim, and arrest, sometimes murder brown people. White people have anti-overdose medications to save them. Where were Narcan and Evzio naloxone-type brands when brown people died of heroin overdoses in the 1980s? In brown culture, addiction is seen as the fault of the brown people themselves. If you are brown, addiction is not considered a disease. And it was not considered an epidemic. It's your problem.

Without help and with condemnation, brown people become even more depressed and hopeless. Without the ability to get quality work that pays at least similar to the white equivalent, their chances of recovery are slimmer. If brown people overdose, they are not glorified and remembered for their contribution or their struggles in life. They are treated as worthless.

As experience shows, there is no equity in the treatment of human beings. We continue to perpetuate the fraud that there is parity of care. We exhibit *faux* politeness for fear of being denied work or even minimal societal acceptance. Brown people help disseminate the equity scam, claiming "you just need to try harder like the other guy." We all (yes, you too, reader) know it is false equality, but brown people also pretend, believing this is the best we can get.

The result is an uncontrollable sinking frustration. We should not overlook this false equity. It has a profound impact on all the efforts of brown people. They are denied opportunities, paid less, treated worse, trusted less, and no one believes in their hard-won expertise. Because we believe in this *false* equity, we also help white people to grow while suppressing brown people's success.

I have seen this unequal provision of opportunities in my homeland. A white guy came to the Caribbean from Canada with little to no money, almost a pauper. He put on a suit, went to a bank, borrowed a few million dollars without collateral, built and opened a shopping mall, and left the island twenty years later a multi-millionaire. Have you ever heard of this scenario working for a brown person? Perhaps, but rarely. The result is not just social class immobility but more like trying to swim in a tub of glue, leaving a trail of stickiness that passes on for generations. Just as your children inherit your wealth, when well-managed, they inherit your poverty. The only difference is that the external guardian managing brown poverty is usually a white colonialist descendant who prefers to be racist.

Even when wealthy parents don't help their kids, the kids can operate and take business risks because they know they won't starve. They have a safety net in their parents. Wealthy white parents have the means to lend and support their children to start a business. Entrepreneurial giants like Richard Branson got created on this foundation. Sure, they had the grit and guts to make it work. They also had parents to lend or give them a million dollars to start, or at least the fortitude and space from daily assaults to encourage and teach their children industrious values. Their circle of friends and family, who are most likely involved in professional jobs or entrepreneurs, provide free, trustworthy advice and financial and moral support. The environment of support, and space for trial and error, is seen as the ordinary course of their lives. They don't have to worry about failure (Branson 2007).

Conversely, children who see the struggle of their less fortunate families grow to believe it's the only way of life, and so it becomes the only way for them. They don't speak the language of wealth. There is rarely a family or friend providing moral and financial support, especially in a way that allows unjudged and repeated trial and error. They don't discuss a bull market, rental income, earnings-per-share, options, dividend earnings, mergers, acquisitions, equity swaps, returns on investment, or prime rates. The practical impacts of this wealth language are often impenetrable to brown people, forbidden from generational white members-only backrooms.

Besides, every brown financial expert I have encountered has a story of being forced out of money-powered spaces like Wall Street.

Brown people struggle to be prosperous because, with each generation, they must start over. The legacy of distrust continues to haunt their progress. They can't go to school and make trusting friendships with wealthy white children because, as I will show later, the schools are typically segregated. For many, it's not even conceivable. Most of my former white bosses, especially the Americans, did not trust me. Their kids are unlikely to trust my children because we never reconciled or cleaned up the mental remnants of enslavement. Now defunct Jim Crow laws, implicit bias, and the numerous iterations of race, gender, sexual orientation, and religious discrimination linger on and guide whom we trust and help.

This distrust is not biological. It is taught. A former colleague gave me an example of how racism imparted social behavior. She recounted her experience from primary school. For a few days, one of her best friends was a little blond, blue-eyed girl. They were enthralled with each other, walking around the school, holding hands and having little-girl conversations. Upon arriving home every day that week, they raved with the excitement of each other's wonderful friendship, much to the parents' delight that their kids were becoming well-adjusted in school and making new friends. They were happy to be in school. More importantly, they had no idea they were considered different in their society.

One day, the white girl's mother came to school to pick up her daughter. The little white girl excitedly ran up to her mother to show off her new best friend, who had made coming to school so enjoyable. The white mother discovered, to her horror, that her daughter's best friend was, in fact, a brown girl. The next day, the white girl did not speak to her brown best friend. The white girl acted as if her friend did not exist anymore. The brown lady recounted how heartbroken she was as a child to experience that—her first brush with racism.

How does a mother explain that early form of racism to her young child? How does she explain that the little white girl's mother taught her child, when she was five years old, how to be a racist in the first week of school? The seared memory of that event still hurt. Imagine the phycological impact that has on a small child on both sides. Both kids had a massive part of their future success taken from them that day. They also had the natural love shared between each other ripped from their hearts.

Enslavement's residue glazes over fair judgments, determining whom we send to jail for drugs and whom we send to rehabilitation. They determine whom we promote and give a salary increase to after only two months in office or whom we tell that salary raises require a "study" for which a white consulting company must be hired to determine if the brown people should get raises after ten years of salary freezes. It is institutionalized racism cloaked inside the question, "are you even qualified to work here?"

There are hidden messages in our subconscious that stay latent after a form of enslavement. Mentally, we must deal with the past enslavement, oppression, and the feeling that no matter how hard we work, we will always be seen as unacceptable. That has a tremendously negative effect on our psychology. Yet the past still haunts us. To add to past injustices, non-white people regularly experience micro-aggressions. If brown people are self-confident, progressive, and intelligent, people, especially white men, feel insecure. A self-confident brown man is considered arrogant. Their solution is to try to discredit and destroy him. This can come in many forms. You can be declared a sexual predator, a pedophile, a drug addict, a felon, or just someone who is vaguely corrupt and lies. Conversely, white people, especially white men, can be as egotistical as they want because they are safe knowing that for them, those traits of arrogance are perceived as competent, assertive leadership.

We have seen this phenomenon in our politics. A white president ignorant of the world and government affairs is considered a man of the people. The press and his supporters justify his gaffs and give him credibility by excusing rude and incompetent behavior. If a brown president presented similar behavior—well, they would not make it as a viable candidate. A brown leader must be perfect and precise even to be considered. Even then, he would be called elitist, a racial code for an "uppity nigga."

The yardsticks are diametrically different. Both sides need to realize that and accept it. It is the same for discrimination based on gender, religion, or sexual orientation. We must call this what it is, and all recognize that it hinders the optimal success of a company, government, city, or country. The fear and distrust created by racism have not allowed society to function optimally.

We must find a viable way to reconcile the residue of enslavement and all forms of discrimination. Part of this is allowing our countries to grow by giving all people equal opportunities and treatment white men consistently receive.

Your white boss must trust you even more than he would believe another white person who does not work with him. He must accept that regardless of your complexion, you are a professional that can add value to an organization, as you have in the past. You work hard and need to be fairly rewarded as promptly as he has for other white people. Any other behavior is racial discrimination and needs to be stamped out!

You might think; that racism seems too simple an explanation. It's true; many people face institutionalized discrimination and irresponsible behavior. Examples include a boss requesting sexual favors from a staff member for a raise or promotion, a boss accusing a known hard worker of non-performance simply to set up a wrongful termination, and anti-theft regulations leveled on everyone while the actual thieves themselves suffer no consequence because they are politically connected, or any form of abuse of power over someone perceived to be vulnerable.

Even in this arena, racism amplifies discriminatory acts. In one place I worked, black female colleagues confided in me about the harassing treatment of their white boss. He would ask them about their husbands, touch their hair, and rub their shoulders without permission. He would comment on their feet when they wore open shoes. The women felt uncomfortable but feared a backlash if they made a formal complaint to the human resources department. One of my staff confided that her former white supervisor bullied her and assumed all-*black* staff was dishonest, especially those that stood up to him. When it was time for raises, she was overlooked. Another brown colleague had to fight a white male colleague in her office. He allegedly entered her office, locked the door, and tried to kiss her. Predatory behavior and bullying of staff are an abomination and create fear and reduced productivity in an organization.

White racist people should recognize that their behavior sometimes damages communities and organizations irreparably. I have seen white bosses decimate productive company cultures with their implicit biases. It spread like cancer through the organization. Leaders need to cultivate a system that offers equal opportunity. Reader, if you are white, you already have a head start. Being white gives you a legacy of privilege that makes your trajectory from poor to rich a viable possibility. Racism makes people have righteous indignation at the devastation it causes. We must allow facts to reign over beliefs.

Brown people, please remember you have a responsibility to yourself first to accept only the facts. Racism, and therefore *blackness* and whiteness, are an invention. You should remember to guard your pride from corrosive, racially biased aggression or implicit bias. Carve out your future, but never sacrifice yourself or your tribe or allow others to destroy you.

Do not accept false narratives that use you as the scapegoat. You have a value that contributes to the world. Those less productive duds should not punish hard work and love for one's work, whether white or brown, boss or not. Reject false proclamations that attempt to diminish your esteem. White people should not be allowed to make brown people ashamed of their efforts or skin color. Don't accept attacks on your successes and achievements.

We see such attacks on success in schools. Imagine a high school where a child that gets straight A's is castigated as a nerd or is even attacked by other less scholastically-minded children. There are so many examples of children actively trying to fail, or achieve less, to prove they are not as bright as people think to stop the physical and verbal abuse. They, too, propagate fraud to survive. That is wrong, and it's an acceptance of a harmful system.

Similarly, racism and racist behavior, including implicit bias, make society suffer. Making someone feel guilty for the good they produce because of a personal and internal ideology of race is evil. Skin color, race, and origin do not dictate humanity. These optical factors do not evoke a moral differentiation among humans. Yet, there is racism. This racial system, developed by colonialism, the philosophy that supports it, and the construction of the United States, has a caste system enshrined into the fabric of its laws, culture, worship, whom we love, ownership, business, customs, and norms. I use the word 'caste', typically used to describe the top-down class structure in India. It's structural, but it's also mental. Even the subjugated sometimes accept their fate. Isabel Wilkerson delved into this idea of the American caste system much deeper than I intended (Wilkerson 2020).

In the next chapter, I will examine the history that helps create this destructive concept of race. Our biases are historically rooted and started with a need to enrich specific individuals as consumerism grew. I will illustrate the remnants of inhumanity that history left us. Later, I will discuss how that affects us today.

Chapter 2

RUTHLESS ECONOMICS

*"The question of whether one alleges the
Superiority or Inferiority of any given race is
irrelevant; racism has only one psychological
root: the racist's sense of his Inferiority."*

~ AYN RAND, writer and philosopher

Colonialization messed us up. It degraded the mentality of people from the countries involved, and while leading to the growth of wealth of an already elite class, it brought damnation to a horde of other people of all origins. That and all the previous colonization—Rome, Greece, Ottoman Empire, Moors, those of African kingdoms, and the more recent United Kingdom, France, Belgium, Spain, Portugal, and now the United States—as well as others lost to historical, archeological destruction and false storytelling, have all had mixed effects. These effects, however, result from historically ruthless economics that favors one group of people over another.

Our first black leaders in the Caribbean propelled some nations from trading in sugar made from cane to tourism—selling vacations in sun, sea, and sand, sometimes with sex implicitly included. Cotton was grown for export as raw material rather than value-added. Jamaica and other islands like Antigua and Barbados still export a long strand of premium West Indian Sea Island cotton.

The global north's trade tariffs during slavery, and still today, are designed to escalate once developing countries add value to the final product. That practice kept countries of the global south producing and exporting primary products while the real value-added was encouraged in the metropole.

Some leaders have recognized the strategy of forcing countries of the global south to produce goods at the primary stage of the supply chain, where value is lower than at the finished product side. The President of Ghana, Nana Akufo-Addo, told the French President, Emmanuel Macron, that he wants his country to stop depending on aid to finance its basic needs like healthcare for its citizens. He had the vision to produce through the value chain, selling final products to the world. For example, instead of exporting cocoa beans or pods, they could produce cocoa products for import to the global north. The value of the intermediary product will be higher than cocoa beans, thus bringing more money, technology, and knowledge transfer to Ghana (Asiedu 2017).

It's a great plan, as it would create cleaner jobs, support research and development, and bolster the nation's human capital while reducing dependency on imports and foreign aid. Pessimistically, I wondered whether President Macron would soon send troops, spies, or mercenaries into the country to create unrest around this president, making governing his vision almost impossible. There is precedent. The assassination of the first democratically elected Prime Minister of The Democratic Republic of Congo, Patrice Lumumba, and the removal of his friend, President Kwame Nkrumah of Ghana, both for similarly trying to pull away from colonialism by controlling their country's resources. Lumumba was assassinated in 1961 in a joint American - Belgian government operation. After several assassination attempts, President Nkrumah was ousted from power by a coup in 1966 (Nzongola-Ntalaja 2011).

In Ghana, the French and Swiss are the leading cocoa importers (Mesnards 2020). It's still early to judge his success in reducing dependency and making his people and country more resilient. However, President Akufo-Addo was still in power and pushing his agenda at the time of writing. They are exporting processed, and semi-processed cocoa with some struggles as the economic structure of loans makes borrowing for farming difficult, high-interest rates, and lack of viable sugar production, and the dairy sector is non-existent or weak. Thus, much of the adjacent raw material for chocolate must be imported. History suggests that European countries and America, dependent on African raw materials, will neither change their production structure nor let their industries fold due to African resistance. If diplomacy, development aid, and political interference fail to keep control of resources in their hands, they simply use their military might. The asymmetry of military power between African countries and the West suggests the West may always win in the short- to medium-term.

The trade patterns from colonialism continue today and obstruct brown people of the global south from sustainable growth. In 2016, the head of state in the East African Community, whose members are Uganda, Kenya,

Tanzania, Rwanda, Burundi, and South Sudan, concluded they needed to ban the importation of used clothes into the region within three years phase-out. This was part of their Vision 2050 to enhance the manufacturing sector so that its contribution can increase from 8.7 percent of the Gross Domestic Product to 25 percent by 2032.

In Rwanda, a friend who has been running the economic development department since 2008 helped implement the ban. Most of the used clothes arrive in Rwanda, and many other African nations, through the African Growth Opportunity Act (AGOA) from the United States. It's a trade pact that, on the surface, enhances trade and investment in selected, least-developed African countries by granting duty-free access to 6,500 exported products, typically raw materials. The flip side was they had to liberalize their markets to allow selected imports, including used clothes from the global north, mainly from America. Throughout the continent, AGOA had the unintended impact of ruining the garment sector while the used clothing sector in the U.S. prospered.

The Rwandan government acted. With the support of President Paul Kagame, the government said wearing hand-me-downs threatened the dignity of its people. Rwandans could now feel proud and create a fashion design and textile industry, thus creating jobs and technology transfer. Before the president's action, they wore used clothes that were not even from their culture. I suspect a more extensive pride of consciousness is wrapped inside this domestic industry, with nationalism stemming from citizens wearing clothes made for and by native people.

Rwanda increased tariffs on imported used clothes from $0.20 (£0.15) to $2.50 (£1.90) per kg in 2016. They aimed to phase out used-clothes imports and create jobs for their people. Therefore, the U.S. used clothing exporters had time to adjust to new markets. Unfortunately, the U.S. administration under President Trump responded with hostility. It suspended the AGOA agreement for Rwanda in retaliation, saying the United States used clothing industry would face "economic hardship" (Kariuki 2019).

In the global south, people have also been lulled into thinking foreign products are always better. Consumer preferences are manifested through spending habits. Furthermore, the belief reigns that when the white man sells it, or someone who could pass for white, it is often considered good quality. As a result, it's easy to relax and let the imports flow. Fighting them means going to war with large companies and their deep pockets and political lobbies in rich countries with centuries of financial stability and business development prowess. Don't forget that at the extreme, the governments of the global north could coordinate a coup or simply assassinate the leaders under some made-up pretext propagandized in the western press.

I have seen the "foreign-products-from-white-countries-are-better" attitude at work in former colonial countries. The "white equals high-quality" mentality is what I like to call the "mego-man syndrome." Let me explain this concept. The Caribbean islands have a small population of people of Middle Eastern descent who usually are entrepreneurs. Understandably, they come from a region and countries like Persia that, historically, once held economic wealth envied by the rest of the world. One might say entrepreneurship is culturally natural for them.

Upon emigrating to the islands, they make a living by selling new clothes, household items, and other goods on micro-credit to the villagers. You could buy a shirt and tie for that upcoming friend's wedding and pay two dollars a week or whenever you get paid. Before you finish paying off the debt of the first item, you find yourself buying more goods during their future door-to-door visits. In the first year, they did this by carrying their goods in a suitcase. They traveled on public transport and walked long distances in tropical temperatures to keep transport costs down. Their customers referred to them as "mego-man."

Their business often received credit for their start-up from established, more successful predecessors of the same region of origin. They learned the local language or dialect, the needs of each client, gathered knowledge of their families, what church they went to, their regular activities from night clubs to choir practices, parties, womanizing, working, or whatever, and provided what people needed. Their understanding of their clients was analogous to today's Amazon artificial intelligence and algorithmically managed customer profiles through data mining our computers and behaviors online.

On average, in a year, a mego-man would buy a car, often cash purchases, and sell even more items from the back of the vehicle. They had a constant income stream because they credited everyone who could not afford the full purchase price for a suit or other item they needed for that upcoming hot date. Then after about a year, they would open a store in the main town and deliver to their regular clients over the weekend until they could encourage all their loyal patrons to come to the store for any household need. By then, they are wealthy and successful, having repaid their original business start-up loan from their predecessor.

In the earlier years of my career, I learned that these paths in life were not universally applied regardless of ethnicity. Getting a start-up loan was near impossible for young brown men who tried the same progression to start selling clothes or other merchandise. They had few predecessors who trusted them to repay their debts because not many predecessors were so successful that they could lend start-up capital. The often foreign-owned banking system was run by people who knew they would not keep their cushy bank job in air-conditioned buildings lending money to risky brown businesspeople. These brown people were not considered risky because they were brown. They were risky because, through no fault of their own, they were in a racist system that believed they should not own anything. In this system, brown people often have little to no collateral. They don't have successful forerunners who would lend them money. I have a friend who buys clothes and other goods in the United States and sends them to the Caribbean to sell, incurring all the risks and employing her family back home. They may make some money, but they rarely get as prosperous as the entrepreneurial emigrants from the Persian region.

The point is, often, societies accept the tall tale that white men, or even those that were not white but may pass as white, somehow deserve riches and power more than the masses of brown people. Due to fear, squashed ambitions, and perhaps in acknowledgment of their recently enslaved ancestors, brown people are systematically sapped of the will to want, organize, and do more for the next generation. The system is designed against them so that white people can prosper. Often, they struggle to survive in the present and have no space for legacy planning.

In America, Europe, or anywhere people who have encountered both sides of colonialism suffer the same affliction. Whether they are the governments, ancestors of enslaved people, former colonizers, the colonized population, wealthy proletariat owners, or cheap feudal workers does not matter. People forget that racism negatively affects not only brown people but everyone involved.

The white-controlled organizational refrains are the same, especially in the USA, where racism is unashamedly part of life and often the cause of suffering and death. Even in the business of exchanging your skills for remuneration, racism plays a role.

"You have a great resume and are super qualified for the job," said a recruiter. I replied, "That's nice to hear, but tell me, what did the candidate that got the job have that I did not?" I got no real explanation. I got a weak answer, "I don't know." She knew but was afraid, ashamed, or, more likely, complicit in the crime of racism. I later checked on who got the job. It was a white man with less experience and qualifications.

White people are not oblivious to racial discrimination, whether producing it or watching it performed on a brown person. They know the code switches. I also knew but continued to search for data to figure out what rationality goes through their mind while they are either practicing racial bias or have just witnessed it. I realized history has stripped many white people of their humanity since they were young, and they don't care. Some argue they are complicit because they fear being sued for discrimination. However, there are many more who are taught not to care. They don't care because, as one white person pointed out to me one day, very early in life, they are taught that the plight of brown people is not the fault or action of white people. The propaganda broadcasted on television, skewed religion, white written history, not to mention pseudo-science, teach white people that they should not get involved because it is natural that brown people suffer. The radicals among white people even believe it's the will of God.

With these societal teachings, many white people can stand idly by and watch with indifference or approval at police brutality in the 1965 race riots in Selma, Alabama, and that same brutality today. Then, after the news that in many segments uses its time to denigrate brown people's credibility, they tune in to the latest sporting event and forget about the riots. They forget because they are conditioned to believe it's not their problem or their fault. Then there are the radicals and super religious eager to join a battle to abuse and murder brown people. These people, with their children, likely meet at Kennesaw Mountain in Georgia to re-enact the Civil War and relive their good old days of enslavement, complete with uniforms and bayonets (Brownlee 2016). While hiking with a friend, I saw this unforgettable spectacle with my own eyes.

White people historically ride on the backs of brown people. They steal ideas, labor, land, and money for their gain at the expense of brown people. These same behavioral patterns manifest today in the workplace. As an illustration, I was talking to my sister-in-law, who said she needed a new job. She was frustrated because she had to do her boss's job and her own. He is white with less experience and qualifications than her, and that's why she did his work. She was an MBA graduate and had an excellent work reputation but never got commensurate promotions. This organization's leaders preferred hiring white men rather than promoting a qualified, eager-to-work brown woman. As a result, the organization lost productivity and output profits. But it's not just about profits and performance. It's also about maintaining power in the hands of trusted people.

My sister-in-law lamented that she had worked at this company for over a decade. She was convinced there could be no other logical reason for the lack of promotion except her decided brownness because she had been passed over innumerable times and been required to train her bosses to do their work. Imagine her pain and that of others like her. They have the best education, work hard, are good, churchgoing, law-abiding people, articulate, often brilliant, and have unrealized potential just because of their complexion. Imagine the impact on her household income and as a mentor in her family. If a younger relative was deciding what to aspire toward, they might see her frustrations and her financial situation and conclude that education and hard work are not worth the investment. There are no rewards for these in a white-run world.

Brown young people can watch the world and conclude that even if they were extraordinary, they could still be surpassed and asked to report to a mediocre, less qualified white person. Brown people who were ordinary might struggle to be successful, but for white people, being ordinary still typically leads to success. That's partly the nature of racism. A brown man getting a Ph.D. in the 1930s was often an extraordinary person. To achieve this feat, they had to endure endless racial abuse from professors, classmates, and society, who felt this person was out of place. The abuse often included violence from white colleagues or law enforcement (McIntyre, Duncan, and Siddique 2021). In fear for their well-being, even their own family might discourage them from pursuing their dreams. Speaking up for "equal," not "superior" rights, got brown people murdered. Many white people then assume that brown people might seek revenge for these murders. By all indications from the violent nature of many white xenophobes, if the tables were turned, white people would be a menace to society and plot the downfall of brown people.

Such indications of likely violence in reaction to even a hint of brown success are seen in all the lists of terrorist attacks on brown people over time. These include the massacres of Colfax, Louisiana, in 1873; Wilmington, North Carolina, in 1898; Atlanta, Georgia, in 1906, Elaine Arkansas, in 1919; Tulsa, Oklahoma, in 1921; and Rosewood, Florida, in 1923, among other attacks, lynching and acts of violence (Cane 2020). These violent acts are not unique to the United States. They are centered on a perceived concept that, somehow, the white race (remember, "race" is imaginary, a belief system, and not biological) is endangered. The imaginary dangers include indigenous people, *blacks*, Jews, Muslims, immigrants, refugees, and leftist politicians, even when they are visually viewed as white. More recent acts of terrorism of whites against brown and non-white people include the Charleston, South Carolina church shootings in 2015 (Chen 2017), Christchurch, New Zealand in 2019 attack on two mosques (Roy and Martin 2019), Oak Creek, Wisconsin, the U.S. in 2012 attack on a Sikh temple, Trollhättan, Sweden attack on immigrants with dark skin in 2015, a Labor Member of Parliament Jo Cox shot and stabbed to death in the UK in 2016, an attacker plowing a car through a crowd of people protesting against neo-Nazi groups in Charlottesville, Virginia, the U.S. in 2018, and mass shootings in a synagogue in 2018 in Pittsburgh, Pennsylvania, U.S. (Beckett 2019). One white guy, after killing 22 and wounding 22 people at a Walmart in El Paso, Texas, in 2020, told police he was trying to kill Mexicans. In 2021 in Atlanta, Georgia, a white man drove to three spas owned by Asians and shot and killed eight people, including six Asian women (Vinopal 2021). The one in Texas that killed 22 people ranted, "I am simply defending my country from cultural and ethnic replacement brought on by an invasion." Ironically, Texas was part of Mexico from 1821 to 1836.

Texas is just one of ten such states. Before European arrival, people traversed all these lands without border restrictions. It became the 28th U.S. state in 1845 (HipLatina 2018). The cultural and ethnic replacement and invasion he speaks of happened to the original people of the same land by his ancestors. Now he attempts to start further genocide. In my research on race attacks, the list of violent acts, either to a group or individually, many of them fatal to the victims, could be the makings of volumes outside the scope of this book.

In a more humane society, my sister-in-law would move quickly up the ranks through performance-based promotions to be the director, then vice president of the region, with the requisite salary, benefits, stock options, and the authority to select her idea of a winning team. Ultimately, she would have had the space and support to make her company successful against the competition. The shareholders' profits would probably soar under her tutelage, rather than the less abled white men they keep promoting. My sister-in-law is trapped in intangible ideologies of race that erode her tangible future.

Discrimination comes in all forms that affect lives, prospects for brown people, and their offspring. Parents with no opportunity to build a legacy also have the challenge of helping their children leave a legacy. Brown parents need decent jobs that pay them what they are worth. They need to be promoted to positions of power and trust that they are qualified for. They should be supported in developing ideas and dreams when opportunities arise.

They should have equal access to opportunities at all levels. They should have equal access to financing and federal support to start businesses and corporations and build enterprises that raise all brown and white communities out of poverty. Equitable, transparent access is the only way to truly eradicate racism. Brown managers should train and support their brown staff, not support the philosophy of white managers to prevent their growth. I have had brown managers keep training, and other growth opportunities, from their brown staff because they found it difficult under the white man and did not want to make it easy for others. I recall having a black professor of accounting who had a similar colonial mindset of holding brown people back. He suffered from racism while studying for his Ph.D. in the United Kingdom during the 1950s. I often wondered how the pressure of fending off racial abuse, physical and verbal, did not make him have a nervous breakdown. Maybe he did. Yet, there are some self-confident brown leaders (or professors) that will help their brown protegees. He was not one of them.

Imagine the multiplying effect this would have on an economy if brown people earned the same as white people. Money grows more wealth and prosperity as people's incomes grow. The local and federal governments would benefit, too, with a more expansive tax collection base and societal benefits from more sophisticated people not desperate for survival.

Here is the sad reality, if you read books that seek to educate the public about racism and its impact, you would likely know this. According to the Brookings Institute, white households get ten times as much income as a similar black household in America (McIntosh et al. 2020). The wealth gap between brown and white families shows an accumulation of inequality and racial discrimination.

This disparity is true even in self-described *"black* meccas" like the city of Atlanta. The result is less power for brown people and more for whites since they are paid more. This has happened since the United States was formed, so it's no surprise that we are still in the state we are in today with an ever-growing wealth gap between brown and white.

Pay equity creates empowerment. It stimulates the economies of communities and helps lift the people around the paid brown person out of poverty. It allows brown families to pay for their children's education to enroll them in after-school programs for languages, arts, sports, and other extra-curricular activities. Primary education of high quality makes for a well-structured individual. Eliminating the wealth gap could ensure their children access top-quality schools early, thus instilling a rhythm of anticipated success during their formative years. They don't leave college riddled with a debt they can never repay, because a white-controlled system pays their income. Such parents can finance their children's first homes or even the deposit, thus allowing them to start their work-life debt-free. This simple formula, on aggregate, will lead to legacy wealth growth from one generation to the next. Although this is mainly adding brown people to the real economic progress, it will benefit the nation.

A lack of pay equity deprives brown families of property and wealth inheritance needed to pass on to the next generation to give them a head start. Brown families rarely have solid estate planning because they can't find enough certified accountants, financial specialists, risk specialists, and lawyers they can trust to help and advise them on how to manage their wealth, however meager it may be. Often brown wealth dies with the same or the next generation because of a lack of financial education and the entire system mentioned above.

Economic racism caused by the pay gap is no accident. Lack of pay equity is a means of control. It keeps brown families on the fringes, as consumers, able to afford their present needs (sometimes), with no actual surplus to save for investment in themselves, prepare for retirement, enjoy life with their own vacation home, and invest in their children. Being on the fringes creates desperation. Desperation encourages mistakes, criminal behavior, mental depression, family breakups, and hopelessness. The income blockage is worse for black and Hispanic women. In my mind, it is tantamount to murdering the *black* economy and often leads to physical

41

death due to desperation. The even bigger dilemma is that economic murder is not only happening to the present generation but also to the future generations of that deprived group of people.

According to the Institute for Women's Research Policy, a think-tank to stimulate dialog, policy, and advance prospects for women of varied backgrounds, 2018 salaries were ranked in order from white men at the top to white women, *black* males, Hispanic males, *black* females, and then Hispanic females at the bottom. They did not even bother to study Native Americans. Remember them? They are the group that lost entire continents of land and millions of their people to genocide thanks to white Europeans with guns and their novel diseases. Some researchers refer to this as the Indigenous Holocaust in the Western Hemisphere. Their research revealed that the population of Native Americans declined by seventy million from 1492 to 1900 in the U.S. and over 170 million in the entire Hemisphere. These figures do not include the number of Indigenous people who died because of war, disease, subjugation, racism, and harsh conditions of life due to a legacy of colonialism and contemporary institutionalized racism (D. M. Smith 2016).

Women suffer from a lack of paid leave or subsidized childcare, discrimination in compensation, and recruitment. In some European countries, like Switzerland, the price of childcare is a percentage of household income. Having a third child triggers a series of government subsidies to assist mothers, especially if they are single mothers. They recognized the value of women in something fundamental, the continuation of the human species. Such policies are prevalent in Singapore and many European countries with aging populations. They recognize that economic growth is only sustainable when the population grows and adds more producers and consumers. Brown men suffer when they cannot get paid the same as white men and have to scramble to make ends meet, often even taking on a second or third job, also known as "the hustle," just because they cannot see a way out (Hegewisch 2020).

Despite all this, women who, in frustration, complain about the injustice are further victimized. When she was consistently passed over for promotion, one of my brown female friends asked her boss's boss for an explanation. She had the academic qualifications and experience to take on more responsibility and was more competent than any of the people they kept hiring above her. Rather than right their racism, they faked discomfort with her question because she was asking them to explain their repeated racist actions. They quickly exercised white solidarity to protect their sensibilities from her question. She was a young brown woman they considered "feisty" for questioning their normal business flow. They realized, despite her age, that she understood their racism and did not want to train her white managers anymore. They laid her off: "We are having cutbacks and have to let you go." When she left, they hired two white replacements. I don't think they even worried about a lawsuit for racial discrimination.

Despite employment non-discrimination laws, she, and many brown people, contend with underemployment, less pay, poor treatment, bullying, or even sexual harassment. Why? Because calling too much attention to your suffering puts you on a no-hire list. Referees will say you are a problematic staff member and prevent you from getting a job in the future.

Most brown people know how quickly this can lead to becoming one of the desperate classes mentioned above. If you lose a job, can't pay bills, and can't find work, you end up on the street, which could get you killed by a police officer who interprets your tenseness as suspicion of a crime. Pretty soon, you are "accidentally" shot dead to ensure the protection of affluent white families from your desperation. This scenario could happen to any brown woman, man, teenager, or even a child in America, no matter your social status, education, income level, or socio-political connections. You can go from superstardom to being shot dead by a police officer or white supremacist in the blink of an eye. Between those events, they assassinate your character and decimate your family on the road to your demise.

Even in writing this book, I have wondered how employers will look at it and judge me rather than listen to the message. They may only see a brown man wanting what a white man has, something colonialism says we should never aim for because it's not brown people's place to be as successful or wealthy as white people.

Sometimes you suck it up and leave that workplace. Laws against racial discrimination, often written by white lawyers or legislators who haven't experienced racism, or those who think their political connections or money will protect them, never account for the victimization that occurs when you sue for discrimination. The rewards are too evasive and risky.

It reminds me of a man who appeared on *The Daily Show with Trevor Noah* trying to equate white people losing their jobs due to artificial intelligence (AI) and the need for reparation for their loss of work in the future, with brown people wanting reparations for being enslaved.

They blamed trade agreements for the loss of their jobs when evidence shows that about eighty percent of replaced jobs are due to automation, machine learning, and AI. The rest is due to factories moving overseas to produce often American-designed goods using cheaper labor. They equate that with brown people wanting reparations for being enslaved!

I loved Trevor Noah's response. He said you could not equate these different levels of injustice. When white people forcibly enslaved *black* people, the *black* people had no options to purchase their freedom. They were not paid. Furthermore, they were treated worse than animals. *Black* families' social structures were destroyed. This is not the same as white people losing a paid job because of AI. Reparation means to repair. Being enslaved not only resulted in a genocide of the native people, but lands, labor, and raw material resources were taken by force and given to white people for centuries. They made money for generations from this free land stolen from native people. They prevented the *black* enslaved people from voting, so they had no political or economic power to determine their future.

White people in the United States tried to reintroduce a form of continuous slavery when they introduced Jim Crow laws that enforced racial segregation during the 1950s. Later, during the next fifty years, white politicians fostered the creation of industrial prison businesses and incarcerated and forced the free labor of 2.2 million *black* people and almost one million Hispanics compared to 380,000 whites (Prison Policy Initiative 2019).

Critics of organizations like the Prison Policy Initiative worry that the statistics exaggerate the numbers to make America look bad. Besides, they believe that even if the numbers were correct, "*black* people are lazy and just need to stop killing each other!" Here, the white critics wriggle their way out of culpability by avoiding the history that led to these prison systems. To be fair to some white people, many don't appreciate the accurate and comprehensive chronicle of the country and the world, so they genuinely believe the propaganda that tells them the suffering of brown people is their fault.

However, the companies that manufacture guns and ammunition are not owned or run by brown people. No brown person has ever started or owned a missile company. Some suggest that white people profit from brown people buying weapons and shooting each other in crimes of desperation. Just as we label the opioid crisis an epidemic caused by the manufacturers of drugs, perhaps we should also label the gun crisis an epidemic and go after the manufacturers.

There is a different type of epidemic in the corporate world. This epidemic destroys brown families just like the opioid crisis does to white families. The problem occurs when brown people are obstructed from working meaningful jobs. White people use seemingly innocent phrases to justify not hiring a black person for a job. This includes, "Well, you are very smart, but I don't know what you can do," and "you are overqualified for this job. I don't think you will stay," "you may get bored," "you are a great candidate, but not the best fit among all other candidates," or "you are underqualified." Or sometimes they look at you, and you can tell they know you would be perfect, but their hands are tied. I had this experience when I interviewed for a federal job over a decade ago. The hiring manager, a white man, was very apprehensive about not hiring me. My research later revealed that he hired a white person familiar with people in the department.

Inexperienced white people are provided on-the-job training and a big salary to motivate them to stay. It explains why white people stay in jobs longer than brown people. Despite inexperience, they are likelier than black or Latino people to have "good" jobs (Fottrell 2019).

White xenophobe rules say that white solidarity must keep power away from brown people, including women of color. Equal access to financing, ownership of capital and land, and political authority or influence over political authority are the most important forms of power. Most brown people are outside these spheres of power, owning only their labor for sale. To support this behavior against brown people and remove culpability, white people also create psychological narratives to diminish brown intelligence and the value of willpower.

In a University of Missouri's School of Journalism study in 2015, the professor focused on implicit bias in sports broadcasting in the U.S. For those still unsure what this term means, implicit bias is the inclination to believe or demonstrate prejudice against particular groups or characteristics in people—partly because of negative societal propaganda. The podcast's theme was how sports newscasters described the success of white athletes as the result of their brains and intellect. They used words related to strategy like "smart," "intellectual," "hard work," "practice," "lots of effort," "strong-willed," "dedication to the game and team," "sense of purpose," "supportive family," and "practice since he/she was a child." These statements signified that success came from inside the person due to their efforts and smarts. The success of white athletes is judged to come from their actions, and the larger society mirrors these opinions (DeCapua 2015). Similar research in the U.K. found the same implicit bias among news commentators (Nakrani 2020).

The same study showed that for brown-skinned people, the phrases used correlated with strength, such as "he is built like a tank," "natural ability," "brute strength," "he/she is a natural," and "his body is built for this sport." In other words, brown athletes don't need to put in much effort, be intelligent and strategic, have intellect, and dedication, practice to perfection, have a sense of purpose, or come from a supportive family. It's innate to their race. They can't help but be good at that "no-brain-needed" approach they have to sport. It's all muscle memory. The conclusion to support the belief in race marketing is that brown people have minimal cognitive credibility and are constantly asked to prove themselves capable.

Sometimes, these stereotypes are ridiculous. Usain Bolt is a former sprinter, a world record holder in the 100 meters, 200 meters, and 4 x 100 meters relay, an eight-time Olympic gold medalist, and the only sprinter to win Olympic 100- and 200-meters titles at three consecutive Olympics. White people said he achieved all this because he ate a special yellow yam only grown in Jamaica, plus chicken nuggets (Armstrong and Fletcher

2012). The Jamaican government and farmers cashed in on this ignorance and exported more yellow yams and derivative products.

Similarly, Kenyan runner, Eliud Kipchoge, was the first person to complete a marathon in under two hours. His time was one hour, fifty-nine minutes, and forty seconds. Reports claimed he had an advantage because he wore a special Nike shoe dubbed the Alphafly. The sports regulatory body deemed the shoes and others like them non-compliant and banned them from future races (Hodgetts 2020). In yet another example, Tiger Woods has played golf since he could walk under the tutelage of his father. He trained incessantly, yet he was said to have a "natural talent" for golf.

Furthermore, brown athletes and celebrities are much more likely to have addictive media coverage of their foibles while covering up those of their white counterparts (Rogers 2017). A simple Google image search for "O. J. Simpson" revealed many photos of him in court, trying on gloves, looking shocked or disheveled, with bloodshot eyes, and in court prison jumpers. Sure, he was suspected of murder, but he was also a National Football League legend. Even a search for "O. J. playing football" still shows some negative images instead of the football glory days.

On the contrary, according to an article in The Guardian, the case of Roman Polanski, a self-declared rapist, and pedophile present a grotesque example of white solidarity. Search for him online, and you will find his many accolades, Oscar winnings, and high praise from many movie stars who have worked with him since his conviction and admittance that he is sexually attracted to 'young girls' in interviews and his autobiography. He continued to work, so his film success never wavered because he was a fugitive. He continues to live a comfortable, wealthy life in France, away from U.S. incarceration, while film stars defend him as a victim of gossip and a corrupt U.S. justice system (Freeman 2018). The same Guardian newspaper, three years earlier, portrayed attempts to extradite Polanski to the U.S. as a violation of the victim's appeal for the "legal machine to stop." The article praised his achievements as a filmmaker (Smith and Walters 2015). The negative imagery of brown people, including the famous among them, and positive images of white people are often burned into our minds so that it consistently governs the embedded prejudices of white and brown people.

One of my former bosses became a CEO because they needed a white guy to appease a larger political scandal related to race in America. I interpreted him, wrongly or rightly, as a typical white guy who would not exert the energy to think outside his small world. He once said to me, "we think alike." I thought that was incredulous. Why on earth would we think alike? His experience was comprised of growing up in an America, where images of people that look like me were demonized, and people that look like him were glorified, often deified. Yet, this image differential is similar abroad.

Beyond the U.S., even in brown-governed countries where the population is mainly brown people, there is an implicit bias against their people in support of white people. The propaganda machine, operational for over 400 years, in some instances, created self-hate among brown people. Luckily, this is changing as more people discover their history and the beauty and resilience of their people. However, where the blotch remains, the result of all this subliminal racialism was that he was hired for a job my boss was not qualified for without even trying hard to get it. Meanwhile, I had to be overqualified to get into the room for consideration for most of my U.S.-based jobs. From my perspective, we could not think alike because we experienced life through different prisms.

Notwithstanding, I worked hard to understand the environment that raises people with his mentality. It's better than becoming angry at social injustice. Like the sports newscasters, he could not believe a brown-skinned person, especially a recent immigrant, could be as experienced as I claimed.

Like so many white people in leadership positions, my boss suffered from a crisis of distrusting his brown staff. He lacked empathy towards them, the rigor of his reasoning, and authenticity towards his true team expectations. My boss trusted other white people of a similar class structure more than brown people. His discomfort was engaging with brown people, particularly males of any considerable intellect, was also telling of his crisis of trust. Driven by his biases, he would ignore any recommendations from his brown staff and immediately turn to his white male staff for advice, even after the brown-skin expert had given him a recommendation. Often the white male staff had no idea of the correct answers but would either make an erroneous recommendation or parrot the information heard from the brown team. The lack of recognition for brown expertise made the organization suffer and caused many blunders.

Remember, I said that implicit bias affects both white and brown people. While my boss ignores all his brown experts and only promotes and listens to his white staff, the brown people are also fighting against their group. Enslavement and discrimination have taught many brown-skinned people to distrust each other. I've often witnessed race-based betrayals for the white promise of a few material gifts, like a salary increase or just being able to stay in the same job with less abuse. Brown people need to understand that in the prejudiced work environments described above, no brown-skin person is safe from discrimination.

Much of the negative imagery that governs the implicit bias or outright racism of people like my boss is rooted in history. He learned racism from society, his parents, and the past behavior of others. Education with false content and without integration of all stakeholders is a significant tool for racism. Religion can be a tool for relieving people's suffering but is more used as a vital instrument against self-determination. Religion is used to soften resistance, followed closely by wonton capitalism backed by a military force to promote the ideology of race. All this effort is for power and profit. The point is that there are many influences on race and the game of acquiring and keeping control. The next chapter examines how brown people are stereotyped to encourage *black* and white people to distrust, lack empathy, and even excuse cruelty and terrorism.

Chapter 3

STEREOTYPES, MYTHS, AND MARKETING

"It is well known that in war, the first casualty is truth – that during any war truth is forsaken for propaganda."

~ Harry Browne, writer, politician, and investment advisor

A solid marketing plan helps to mold beliefs (U. Johnson 2016). To murder innocent people in war, a publicity campaign is needed to sell the idea that [insert random adversary here] is somehow evil. They say, "Hey, my paying public/fellow citizens, those people over there are not like us. They are out to commit harm," or worse, "they are less than human." In this plan, there is a need to conjure as much indifference leading to hate as possible because it reduces people to being called derogatory names and reduces the adversary to sub-humanity. We have all seen and maybe used these words ourselves. Phrases like wetbacks, spicks, rednecks, cockroaches, savages, thugs, gangsters, hoodlums, dingoes, snakes, monkeys, and many other less-than-human creatures are designed to incite fear and hatred using repeat propaganda.

The same holds for racism. The most potent propaganda, among the European and American versions, strongly justifies the subjugation of brown people because of some mythical superiority bestowed upon white people. Pictures in books, magazines, and anything people can emotionally consume portray the target, anyone with a tan or darker complexion, as some blindly fierce or docile animal with supposedly no intellect or a deficient one.

I want to step back and discuss minstrelsy, one of the earliest vehicles for spreading this white elitist propaganda. Minstrelsy is an entertainment art form where white people paint black paint on their faces and hands, make their lips red or white, and pretend to be what they consider *black* people. Starting in the 1800s, minstrelsy was an extremely popular entertainment medium designed to simplify and stereotype brown people as clowns, comical caricatures with a comical accent devoid of English syntax, and unintelligent banter. There was a white, dignified person in the midst to explain real life to the hapless *blacks* and be their savior. Just as white people today are often curious about how black people's hair feels or how they live, they were equally curious during enslavement about how brown people behaved and lived outside of their hours of white servitude. So, this medium of propaganda disguised as entertainment spread like an infection in the hearts and minds of people as they consumed this brainwashing in theaters all over America.

Minstrelsy taught white people that brown people were empty intellectual vessels. Stories were and still are today reinforced by repetition that brown people were wasteful and only played, like rascals, without a cause. On stage, brown people—really white people pretending to be brown people by dressing in *"black*face"—played the fool, frolicked, cavorted, danced, exhibited animalistic erotic prowess, sang, and jested. Based on these teachings and beliefs, many white people were appalled by the notion that brown people could be surgeons, scientists, politicians, writers, philosophers, psychologists, leaders, strategists, professors, entrepreneurs, real estate moguls, lawyers, engineers, or participate in any complex profession. Today, brown people who exhibit any apparent intellectual capacity are considered exceptional. Once when one of my white male American bosses told me I was smart, I told him I was pretty ordinary and many others where I came from were just like me. He doubled down that that could not be true. I was indeed exceptional.

With the advent of television, now in about seventy percent of American homes by the mid-1950s, programmers broadcasted even more propaganda and minstrelsy into every American home, including those of brown people.

Today, many tropes of brown people are depicted as silly-looking caricatures or tricksters who ultimately only think of the present and succumb to easy temptations with no self-restraint. Cartoon series, live-action movies, books, print ads, and the good-old-fashioned rumor mill invent stories that ignite the imagination and equate brown human beings to vermin who will stop at nothing until they infect the alleged pure, Christian, uncontaminated white society.

A modern-day version of this negative propaganda is the use of the derogatory term "welfare queen." This describes a woman who allegedly collects welfare payments through fraud, child endangerment, and manipulation for wasteful expenditures (Urban Dictionary 2014). President Ronald Reagan popularized the term in 1976 when he gave an unverified example of a woman on welfare earning "tax-free cash income" of $150,000 per year. Since then, welfare policies have been designed around this mythical welfare queen, usually a brown person (Black and Sprague 2016).

This fosters the idea that the targeted inferior races, like pests, must be controlled or exterminated to ensure they do not blight the white family. The control must be thorough, with no space for even a tiny amount of power. Not only do they subjugate the parents, but racist white people find ways to control the brown children too because if left unchecked, they may also grow up and infect a white home. Worse still, they may wise up and realize how imprisoned the world richer white people created for brown people is and fight back to gain power. Hiding past crimes and the brutal murder of entire civilizations entails rewriting and remodeling a historical narrative that must constantly be reinforced. Today, you see pushback from white people when an attempt is made to tell history, even if told from a fictional perspective. Despite its success, I often wonder why the HBO and HBO Max one-season blockbuster, Lovecraft Country, was canceled. Could it be because it portrayed the brutality of Jim Crow-era America? It showcased brown people beating the evil of racism in a complex fictional world of demons, ghosts, and monsters (Abdulbaki 2021).

An interesting example is how America was colonized. Native Americans' lands were taken by forcibly removing them from their land, eradicating their language, culture, and food, and separating them from their children, so the customs and memories of extermination die with the previous generation. This type of annihilation is designed to destroy their way of life so they cannot rise again and re-grow—the code for taking back the land/wealth stolen from them.

This marketing campaign uses two of the greatest promotional gambits—fear and sex. Fear works because everyone wants to be safe from death and harm for their legacy: commonly children, their ideas, and property. Security is one of our greatest needs as human beings. Sex works because human ideas stay immortal by recreating their culture, values, and language through children's heritage.

Fear makes the average white racist think the enemy could eat them or rape their women if they were not decimated. The rape could result in monster (mixed-race) babies taking over the white-run world. I once overheard a private conversation between two distinguished white politicians in which one was explaining to the other why the metro rail had not developed in Atlanta past its embryonic state. The local Atlantan explained that the white people feared brown boys would come to their white neighborhood and date their daughters. Early colonialists called this miscegenation—the mixing of races through marriage and sexual relations.

They took something as imaginary as race and enforced, through anti-miscegenation laws passed during the 17th century, a legal construct to forbid interracial coupling of any kind.

These anti-interracial hook-up laws only formally ended in 1967 after the landmark case Loving v Virginia. In this landmark case, the plaintiffs, Richard and Mildred Loving, a white man and black woman marriage were judged unlawful under the Virginia state law. They were exiled from Virginia to Washington, D.C. With support from the American Civil Liberties Union (ACLU), the Lovings appealed to the U.S. Supreme Court, which ruled unanimously that anti-miscegenation laws were unconstitutional under the 14th Amendment. Hirschkop, one of the ACLU lawyers, argued that Virginia's interracial marriage law, among others similar to it, was governed by racist ideologies and white supremacy. "These are not health and welfare laws," he contended. "These are slavery laws, pure and simple." The decision is often cited as a tipping point in the disassembling of Jim Crow race laws (History.com 2019). However, as I have pointed out in this book, despite having interracial relationships and friends in interracial marriages and partnerships, such couples still receive disapproving looks in certain conservative societies, especially in America. States like Alabama started upholding the Supreme Court decision in 2000 after a referendum in which only fifty-nine percent of voters supported interracial marriages, which means forty-one percent favored miscegenation laws. Polls in the U.S. deep south reveal that people still support anti-miscegenation laws (Head 2020).

Comparable legislation was passed and enforced in Nazi Germany under the Nuremberg laws in 1935 (United States Holocaust Memorial Museum 2019) and South Africa's Apartheid system in 1948 (Hall 2020). The U.S. government goes deep into its citizens' private lives, attempting to govern things like marriage and abortion. These laws, being produced by fragile white men, or any delicate people, were fighting, expanding resources, and making people suffer so they could go against the law of nature. White plantation owners and those at the top of that food chain regularly had sex with their nubile enslaved women, often producing mix-raced babies. In Germany and South Africa, the same interracial relationships happened. These relationships were probably more attractive because of their illegal nature. It was taboo sex, complete with all its illicit joys, plus natural attraction with no ideology, just real biological urges.

I imagine most were power plays to destroy brown families. Others were a means of avoiding infidelity charges when a married man satisfied his sexual urges with a sexy, young, enslaved woman or a brown child if the white plantation owner or his henchmen were pedophiles. However, sometimes these white men fell in love with their brown enslaved women. They would make them house slaves to hide the relationships, which was a silly practice because the mulatto kids could not be hidden.

People's purest physical attractions did not consider race in their choices. People are attracted to people, and even racist people can be attracted to someone of another complexion. When a white supremacist gets a southern urge while looking at a brown woman, he does not conclude that the devil has infected him with an attraction to these women. He does not go to church to pray away his sexual urges. He succumbs to them because they are honest and natural.

These legalities have intruded into what is essentially someone's private preferences. Laws should never dictate two adults' consensual relationship. In these cases of adult consent, people should follow their natural inclination toward whomever they are attracted to. No set of legislators should be allowed to dictate with whom someone should have sex.

How many cross-racial relationships have been destroyed thanks to people's wild imaginations? Unfortunately, I heard first-hand accounts from a friend of a Latin American teenager physically attacked by white boys for dating a beautiful, blond, white woman in Fayetteville, Georgia, in 2015. There was also the case of Trayvon Martin, who was fatally shot in 2012, in Sanford, Florida, by a white-aspired vigilante who later got off by claiming self-defense from a weaponless 17-year-old teenager. These are just some recent examples of the impact of brainwashing by the white propaganda machine.

The major challenge is that this propaganda machine, while based on a fantasy of superiority, has real-life damage to people and their heritage. In many cases, it means the death of innocent people. After the U.S. Civil War, veteran confederate soldiers were used to attack brown families and instill a subservient fear. America's system of policing comes from that era when its role was to control enslaved people, capture runaway slaves, and enforce enslavement while protecting the rich from insurrection. Police officers are universally used as a paramilitary group and equipped with a barrage of military gear. Then they are asked to solve social problems like domestic violence, or drug-induced episodes, with a limited skill set for de-escalating a potentially volatile situation.

I link the increase in police shootings of brown men today to the constant stream of television shows with the notion of a "black criminal" element in its content. *Cops*, the longest-running reality television show, commonly features brown people, especially men, being arrested for committing petty crimes. The police on the show seem more willing to point out the crimes of blacks over whites (Paul 2020). The show paused due to a global outcry against police brutality after a viral video of George Perry Floyd Jr, a brown man from Fayetteville, North Carolina, tortured and eventually murdered on May 25, 2020. As of October 2020, it's back on air (Slisco 2020). Langley Production is owned and run by a white family.

Cops is their globally syndicated cash cow (Taberski 2020). In the entertainment industry, the heroes are often white, whether the human hero in a real story or the superhero in a fantasy world. With this stereotypical propaganda in heavy rotation, it becomes easy to kill a brown person without legal ramifications; after all, the police, juries, lawyers, and judges consume the same propaganda, just like the white residents of suburbia in the properties they are protecting.

The existence of this narrative creates a vicious cycle that affects every aspect of a brown person's life. A brown kid who dreams of becoming an engineer cannot live in a neighborhood with good schools because his parents cannot afford the real estate prices. They can't afford to send him to a good private school with teachers motivated by their training, a decent salary and benefits, resources in the school, and students who already have a great life supported by wealth. That teenager then goes to a poor-quality school where the teachers are exasperated with deprived children. The teachers may also be so indoctrinated in the propaganda of shows like *Cops*, they see all brown kids, especially boys, as delinquents. A brown boy may struggle and get good enough grades and have self-confidence, despite everyone telling him he is pretending to be a white person by having an ambition, to get accepted into tertiary education after passing the racially biased SATs (D. A. Love 2010). The next fiery hoop is tuition fees and living expenses. If he passes that using, say, a student loan, he spends the rest of his life repaying this loan. He will constantly get overlooked for promotions and pay raises much more than his white counterparts because of a white belief in minstrelsy, and so never really make enough money to pay off his loans and take care of his family.

When the child sums up this life of failure and struggle, he may decide it's better to cut out all of that and turn to crime. Why not give up just as the society and system that not only gave up on him did while actively seeking to destroy him? Why not sell some drugs to the very white people who oppress him and his family? Perhaps they should sell to anybody who will buy. Why discriminate? Money is money. They will lock him up anyway, whether wearing a tie and suit headed to the corporate office or wearing low-waisted pants with his colorful boxers showing like others in his community.

Sometimes, as a young brown person, you experience something unsettling but can't quite put your finger on it. You can't explain what it is, but you just know you don't like it. I experienced some of what such a child would have gone through, albeit later in my career. One day, my white boss told me, "Martin, you are smart." That's code for being an "uppity nigga." He did not mean it as a compliment. He meant I defied the stereotype—the lies served him like a muddy cup of dirty tea since he was a baby. His mother and father, the family, television shows, and cowboy and Indian movies all told him I should not be wise. Remember, minstrelsy also says brown people are tricksters. So, I must be "playing" smart or pretending to be an "uppity negro" because it's impossible to be genuinely intelligent. My boss regularly tried to prove to himself that I was just playing witty in his white fantasy world and any seeking or proud brown person that might be emulating me. Just as the athletes and famous *black* people have had their credibility attacked, my boss attacked mine.

He went after my integrity and character and opposed me in every work I completed to prove his point. In other chapters, I spoke about how frustrated black people get with these types of white racists as they aggravate the work and the progress of the organization just to prove their point. Their point is important to them because proving it, even dishonestly, gives them back power. They see it as a loss to admit a brown person, or anyone who merits it, is knowledgeable, not pretending, and should be listened to, rewarded, and promoted. White racists must believe the myth of minstrelsy.

I had a white boss that tried to prove I stole a few hundred dollars from a business travel trip. I told him he either did not understand the system we had for travel, including the approval system, or he was setting these things in play to prove a point. I asked him what point he wished to establish. Of course, he never took the bait. He retreated, only to return in a few weeks or months with another destructive tactic. He also played the same discrediting strategy with other men who were brown, whom he considered intelligent, or who challenged him in any way. This insecure white supremacist saw brown men with any voice as a threat to his way of life.

Meanwhile, the productivity of the organization suffered. From the perspective of the brown people in the office, he preoccupied himself with trying to racially transform the labor force and diminish the power of the brown professionals while empowering the white staff into the leadership level of the company. He needed to find ways to get rid of brown workers and break their spirits in the process.

The organization withered because the brown staff was frustrated and demoralized. Many left the organization or were forced out. Some stayed and spent time gathering evidence to protect themselves from his racial assaults instead of focusing on work one hundred percent. Others who were shining stars contributing to the organization realized that while he was there, they would not be allowed to prosper. They just did the minimum to stay out of his way. Wherever this exists, and I dare say it does in most American establishments, the organization itself becomes toxic and never reaches its potential.

As with modern-day racism that kills an organization's progress, so too does the blight of towns like Wilmington, North Carolina, or Tulsa, Oklahoma, where white supremacists massacred citizens in these two prosperous and predominantly brown towns (Safier 2019). These genocides were the ultimate result of economic racism—white jealousy for their success that they believed could lead to them losing some of their white power. There is no evidence to suggest that brown townspeople in these places ever refused to do business with white people, but that's not the point. The point of economic racism is also about power and control. Without that power, white racists would likely be overwhelmed with fear.

There is only one way to fight this idiocy. Brown and non-racist white people must defy minstrelsy the world over. This is already being done. Some screen productions now portray brown people as heroes and heroines, intelligent people, bosses, leaders, and complex professionals. Even some music showcases the exhaustion and shame some white people feel towards the never-ending racial struggle. I feel some glimmer of hope when as far back as 1966, I hear a white singer say in his lyrics, "Hey, you know something, people? I'm not *black*. But there's a whole lot of times I wish I could say I'm not white (Zappa 1966)." More white people must be actively anti-racist if they genuinely want a peaceful world.

Recognize the role of marketing, the media, social media, and propaganda as the first tools of racism. Transform it to be used for good, to tell the truth, and to educate people. We need more anti-racist media productions and consumption. These will be part of building awareness. Many will resist and fight to maintain the status quo of racism. However, enlightenment would come to others, including brown people, who are exposed to the truth. Today, because of the many murders and injustices, many people abused by racism are speaking out through academic research, books like this one, film production, and social media. The traditional television and radio networks need to be openly anti-racist.

Even today, police officers that kill brown men claim they thought the guy was armed or posed a threat to justify the reason for killing the person. Most police shootings are often ruled as justified or misrepresented in the reports to cover up negative details. They know what they are doing. You often hear of white police killing an "unarmed *black* man," but rarely of an unarmed white man being killed. Plus, the phrase assumes whether the black man deserves to be murdered or not is measured by whether he was armed. Ahmaud Arbery of Brunswick, Georgia, went jogging on February 23, 2020. Three white guys hunted him and shot him dead. Whether he was armed or not, should he have been attacked and murdered?

For 400 years, the police and similar institutions protected the affluent white population, such as the plantation owners. They were armed to catch runaway enslaved people and like duties. However, today, people expect police civil servants to be neutral regarding race. They are paid to protect everyone regardless of race, class, gender, and income level (Philimon 2020). Reform, retraining, and ensuring that recruitment is community-based are the first steps in changing the police force. A police officer should know most of the families in the areas she or he is patrolling. Just as companies have a corporate social responsibility, so do the police, but even more so in all communities. The institution of the police and the communities they serve suffer from a crisis of trust. Every police abuse and wrongful murder, basically any act of incompetence, erodes trust. Can the safety and health of a community be achieved with a reimagined version of the police?

For these situations to change, brown people must help to craft the rules and make decisions about their implementation from the inside. Brown people must take charge of their image. We must take control of propaganda about us and depict brown people in a positive light.

Brown people should not succumb to the stereotypes white people set. We need to show them who we are. Ladies and gentlemen, don't be afraid to have natural hair if you so desire to avoid chemical straighteners and all the other expensive and traumatizing procedures like the hot comb. Don't be ashamed of your language, culture, or your dress style. Rock it. Be proud of who you are and know you can become anything you set your heart and mind to.

Brown people are not jailbirds or ghetto bums. I know many have been economically and socially crushed. Surrender just means more massacres in our future beyond just police killings and mass incarcerations. For brown men and boys: when you present yourself in a new positive light, get educated, dress well, keep well-groomed, and develop specialized skill sets. Life may get more complicated at the beginning, as white racists will go after you to destroy you. They are acting out of their fear and insecurity. They are regurgitating their parental upbringing and societal brainwashing. Hold your head high and hold them accountable. Ask them to say what their agenda is. Make them face their racist ways.

Don't accuse but ask them to look carefully at their behaviors and explain why they would want to return to such a dark period of this country's history. How would it benefit them and their children? Some will say they want to leave a legacy. But brown people have just as much right to a positive legacy.

Where is the balance? Brown people begin their lives with the handicap of being at the wrong end of the colonialist stick. We need more rights to counterbalance how racist whites deprive future success. Our legacy has to be greater because how else will we get the country, set backward by many years of believing in a false premise and acting upon it, on track and existing in harmony? Either that, we will continue to ruin and weaken our nation through this internal national cancer. Nobody wins from racial carnage. White racists must stop the violence and hatred over the imaginary things learned from minstrelsy.

White people must stop teaching their kids that the Confederacy was a glorious time. They should stop doing reenactments with their children of the Civil War as if it was a war of heroes. They should not block brown people from being promoted and getting pay raises when they deserve it.

Stop the micro-aggressions. Stop being surprised when a brown person defies your minstrelsy teachings. When I first worked in Florida, white people there would tell me the same thing they would say when I was a tour guide in the Caribbean. At the end of each tour, they would feel the need to declare, "You speak very good English. Did you go to school on the island?"

I would say, "Yes, we all speak like that here. Your English is not too bad either; your prepositions are sometimes off, but that's normal for you, I guess." They would take a second shocked glance at me, wondering how I had the nerve to question their proficiency in English. They openly questioned mine, but I could not question theirs because in the box of their minstrel mind, anyone brown, especially from outside America, should not be able to speak standard English. Worse, we could switch between a fancy British-sounding English, at least fancy in their ears, and a local dialect. We spoke two languages. "Is it true you can speak another language?" A white woman on a work trip with me posed this question to me. I was the only brown person in the group and seemingly the only one that spoke multiple languages. They could not believe it but also could not test me. When I was accosted by this absurdity in Florida, I always commend their English–to be mischievous. I love the shock people get when you treat them how they treat you. Yet they never stop to consider their behavior.

Some of us brown people don't want to only talk about racism and *black* or civil rights issues. We are interested in being world-renowned physicists, microbiologists, botanists, industrial engineers, marine biologists, archeologists, artists, presidents, sommeliers, movie directors, owners of publishing companies, congressmen, senators, surgeons, scientists, property moguls, heads of international organizations, and leaders in every field. We don't all aspire to be plumbers, maids, gardeners, handymen, nurses, teachers, janitors, department store clerks, guards, and low-level government workers, as necessary as those professions are. We want to be judged based only on our merit, rewarded regardless of skin color, for our children to have aspirations just like white children, and to leave a legacy for our children just like white children.

We have created a world in which there are contracts, laws, boundaries, race, religion, fairies, ghosts, and goblins. Some are fiction, and others should be destroyed when they add no value to society. Imaginations of the monarchy, a governing system having ultimate and eternal power over lesser people because of something as fictional as royal blood, are similar. Equality recognizes that some of the fights for profits and power are that many people emulate to live like royalty. The global carnage racism has caused and how it has affected economic deprivation are immeasurable.

For an economy with white people who create the minstrelsy box and the brown people who succumb to being imprisoned in that box, the only things that container serves are to destroy, create economic loss, and endorse psychological destruction on both sides. I know white racist people think racism only affects the people to whom the behavior is directed. They are wrong. Racism harms all sides. Ever wonder why it's been so hard to subjugate brown people? Some of them won't stay down, like the boxer who won't quit despite fifteen rounds of pounding. It's just not natural.

Look at the societies and towns that have embraced all races. Look at multiracial societies and at the relative harmony and economic success they achieve. All the lost potential of racism causes society to suffer, not just brown people. Most of all, it's not sustainable. It's not long-lasting. History shows that people subjugated never stay subjugated forever. It is no more natural for white people to dominate brown than for brown people to dominate white. The imagination fights with reality, and reality will win every time.

Brown people's finances are typically a mess. Since they are often deprived of free first-class education, they are burdened with lifetime student loans, culturally biased SAT, MCAT, and other exams, and job growth retardation due to an economic and social system that is fundamentally biased at all angles. Brown graduates generally have more student loans to repay, are more likely to default, and tend to own more than borrowed (Scott-Clayton and Li 2016). They may need professional advice on how to improve their net worth. How easy is it to find a certified financial planner (CFP) to advise brown people about spending and investing their money? Well, ordinarily, brown people's income is smaller than white people's. They do not earn enough to pay a good CFP.

I searched for a brown CFP. It was like the proverbial needle in a haystack challenge. According to Forbes Magazine, less than 3.5 percent of America's 80,000 CFPs are *black* or Latino. Companies with CFPs have a remuneration system to help them make money from medium to high-net-worth people. Most brown and Latino people earn less than what would be considered worth the time for a financial advisor. Those with cash and the opportunity to earn more money get advice on how to invest and make even more while learning how to make it grow (Eisenberg 2018).

A white financial adviser will assume a brown person earns like a white person. They presume their white privilege is not an advantage and that everyone must be the same regardless of skin color. They are less likely to comprehend, even a non-racist white person, that trust, opportunity, interest, pay, and circumstances are not the same for brown people. Studies show that black and Latino mortgage borrowers generally are charged higher interest—almost 0.08 percent on average—and more refinance fees than white borrowers. As we aim to end racism, research on anything that requires use in society must be revised to be representational. The way to be inclusive and remove bias creeping into artificial intelligence, algorithms, and machine learning is to hire more qualified brown people. This means providing a viable means for brown people to become university graduates who can qualify to become coders, programmers, designers, architects, and all the professions required to enter the technology supply chain to eliminate bias.

The same is true in the financial technology or fintech sector, where unintentional bias hidden in code learned from society can disadvantage brown men and women (White & Case 2017). Regulatory technology, or regtech for short, is a branch of fintech dedicated to improving the compliance structures of financial services companies. If I apply to a loan officer or an AI for credit, I should not pay a higher interest rate. These systems must be constantly monitored to determine if they are actively moving away from racism and bias.

We already know that, on average, brown people are paid less in every sector at every educational level (Wilson 2016). Even in the entertainment industry, brown actors get paid less after receiving similar accolades for their work (T. Ahmed 2016).

For example, in September 2016, actor Antony Anderson got $100,000 an episode for the sitcom black-ish, while his co-star, Tracee Ellis Ross, earned $80,000. Both got Emmy Award nominations for Best Comedy Actor and Actress. That month, their film critics' rating was 2.0 on September 21. In comparison, the core Modern Family cast, The Middle's Patricia Heaton and Last Man Standing's Tim Allen, each earned $250,000 an episode. Last Man Standing's rating was 1.1 on that same date (T. Ahmed 2016).

Brown people, because of the same system of pay disparity, have more significant challenges in financing and distributing stories from their perspective. They may say they can't find brown people to work with, but mostly they don't trust people they do not understand. As such, the few brown people have to hustle and moonlight with other jobs as insurance in case the white people pull the jobs from them due to their white solidarity.

In the film industry, brown stories need to be told from the perspective of brown people. Not everyone on the crew needs to be brown. Still, when a story is authentically brown, it should have people who understand the culture making the decisions on imagery and the storyline. Brown heroes need to be allowed to shine on the screen. Brown productions should be recognized for their quality products and have brown judges on the panel for the selection of awards, and not just as a token contributors. Speaking of tokenism, white people need to stop that token brown hire. Hire many capable brown people at all levels if you want to be part of the solution against racism.

A white friend criticized a brown movie because the heroes were brown, and the villain was white. It was one of the most popular black movies recently—yes, Black Panther. He was critical of the entire storyline, the acting, sets, costumes, and everything. It did not fit in his mental minstrelsy box. Evidently, brown people are hungry for movies like this. The box office earnings of $1.3 billion put it in the ten top-grossing title movies of all time (McClintock 2019).

We need more fantasy movies where brown people can be encouraged to be heroes and show they can save the world. White heroes should be presented as those who shun racism and embrace all people as equals. This should be the direction of Hollywood and other white productions that aim to improve the world. White people should not be afraid and uncomfortable writing stories and producing films that show the truth about colonialism.

White people should stop worrying about feeling "uncomfortable." I always hear that talking about racial issues makes white people uncomfortable (Chappet 2020). They may get offended if they are called racists, and "it's not fair to make them uncomfortable" because "it's not nice to offend people." It is a complex topic for white people to discuss, especially among brown people (R. DiAngelo 2015).

I have seen many a white person, a white reporter, a white president, a white talk show host, or a white friend get angry and defensive when there is even a mild suggestion that they may be behaving racist. It's the ultimate discomfort for them (AlterNet 2015). They feel it's unfair because the enslavement of brown people by white people was so long ago, and they had no part in it personally.

They have brown friends, marry brown spouses, and let brown people work for them, albeit in less powerful positions than them. I recall seeing a talk show host become hostile to a brown woman on his show, basically attempting to shut her down, "Are you accusing me of being racist? Are you?" Most of his fans defended him on Twitter. This was after his verbal attacks on the Duke and Duchess of Sussex, Prince Harry, and Meghan Markle's decision to live their own lives away from the regular duties of the monarchy. The U.K. media not only buckled down on their racist talk without much introspection, but they also attempted to destroy the guest's credibility (Worstall 2020).

Brown people have been uncomfortable for a long time. Having your life force mauled, physically or economically, can lead to death. That's what happened to George Floyd when a police officer kneeled on his neck for over nine minutes—the ultimate discomfort that led to death. The discomfort of white people and brown people is not equal.

When a brown person does not get the boss's job because he is brown, that's uncomfortable. Mainly if he is completely qualified for the job or even more qualified and experienced than his boss. As a brown person, you feel wronged and see the world around you as corrupt and white people as villains, interested only in maintaining a system that hurts society and benefits them.

White discomfort comes from a belief that says, "I should be ruling the world and have all the power." Brown discomfort comes from, "I don't want the police or a white supremacist to kill me, my sister, my woman, or my children, and I want to get the jobs I keep training my white boss to do." Brown people suffer from power being denied or taken from them regularly. Some brown people are given power, do not understand it, and try to hold on by helping some white people take power from other brown people. I have experienced that with some of my brown bosses. They do not understand the game they are in. They feel that while they have the power, they are somehow being recognized as equal to the white power structure, when often, they are being used to deny another brown person's strength.

I saw clashes between brown women all vying for power and recognition from a white boss in my office. Instead of remembering their history and how it's intertwined with white supremacy and working together to gain power, they fought. The old "divide and conquer" strategy will work if you let it. Make an offer of pretend power, or not even power but just a bit of position, and a brown person will betray the people that previously suffered with them for the piece of that pie. These brown women were looking at their immediate future, not the long term, the past, or the future. There was more than enough work and recognition available for all of them, but they believed it was a zero-sum game they were in, and they had to help the white guy eradicate the others to keep their position.

A friend saw this behavior among the brown women in the office and came to warn me about being betrayed for some potential or perceived reward they expect from the white guy. I knew it would come because the white boss had already exhibited racist tendencies towards a couple of other brown men in the building and me. He did not see this as an opportunity to correct the world of white supremacy but as an opportunity to perpetuate it.

These racist behaviors hurt society. Some are very well-qualified and experienced *black* men who worked in the firm and many other organizations where I worked. They contributed to the success of the company. Yet their contributions were not recognized. When a problem needed to be solved, they would be called upon but not rewarded. They were regularly either ignored until they were again required.

My frustrations are not unique to me. A Harvard Business Review study shows the results of a questionnaire of seventy-five out of 300 respondents.

Their vexations were because their white bosses were: "supportive in words only (50 percent), lacks positive direction (41 percent), has a policy of tokenism (33 percent), reluctant to accept *blacks* (33 percent), and indifferent (33 percent). The favorable descriptions that received the most mentions were encouraging (17 percent) and positive (15 percent)." I was not surprised to read several stories like mine in this HBR report (Jones 1986).

One white boss once told me my work and contribution to the organization were useless. He said my many achievements were a fluke. I had the temerity to counter him because I knew he was trying to take away the power he saw and feared in me. It was his white mediocrity and history of believing in minstrelsy that guided his disrespect to me then and after that.

My white boss' people came from a feudal class structure where there were royal families. He and his ancestry were likely loyal subjects who worked the fields and fed the royal family because they were thought to have a special noble bloodline or some ordainment from their invented deity. Of the approximately 2.6 million Europeans who immigrated to the Americas between 1492 and 1820, "no less than 25 percent were servants, convicts, and prisoners (Encyclopedia.com 2020)."

He knew he could efficiently perform economic racism. He already had the symbolic rope and noose. My salary and that of all the brown people were below the market rate. He had upgraded all the white people's salaries and given them power positions within three months of being in office. He just had to tighten the noose or pull it up high to show me who the boss was. He shouted at me, "I am the boss," in one of his attempts to break me. Eventually, if I stayed, he would show me who the boss was. Several other brown men had resigned or taken early retirement in frustration, and two brown women he fired.

Despite knowing all this, I confronted him, albeit respectfully and professionally. So often, many brown people feel they don't have the power to stand up for themselves. They fear losing their jobs. They fear economic murder. Why? Because it happened in the past. This type of vicious attack on brown people, whether you call it lynching or not, still happens today both in a physical and economic form. The result is a nation that spends time fighting citizens instead of preparing for a future where all the strengths and ingenuity of all contribute to our future. Studies have shown that this behavior leads to fewer brown people in the corporate world.

In an HBR report in 2018, there was an assessment of employment data by race, gender, and job classification used to assess management diversity with a matrix called the executive parity index (EPI). The index helped us to appreciate "how well each race and gender is being promoted up the management pipeline and, in effect, whether the corporate ecosystem has been successful in creating a more diverse workforce." The results were not too surprising. In the U.S., white men were 61.3 percent of executives nationally and eighty-one percent above parity compared to their 33.8 percent representation among non-executive professionals. "*Black* men and women still represent a meager percentage of the professional white-collar workforce (less than eight percent), given their overall representation in the population" (Gee, Why Aren't Black Employees Getting More White-Collar Jobs? 2018).

Imagine how many brown scientists, engineers, mathematicians, physicists, chemists, strategists, and leaders were denied participation in and contribution to economic and social growth. This is true for the United States and many other countries. They were murdered, beaten into submission, arrested, and thrown in jail, often without any proper form of justice one would give to someone white. How many dreams have been destroyed? When brown adults are incarcerated, their dreams and their children and community are also imprisoned. As a line in the HBR article entitled, *Black Managers*: The Dream Deferred, noted, "they cannot fulfill their dreams because all hope has been ripped from their hearts" (Jones 1986).

My white boss had not realized he was not in a zero-sum world, and his belief that all the brown men around him should be mentally and physically prostrate to him was fiction. He wasted good ideas that could have developed the company, further benefiting him. The cost of not promoting white people and brown people equally according to merit was the loss of potential success, and profit, for the organization. Racist white people at the micro-level were throwing money out the window, and at the macro level, they were ruining their nation for their children now and in the future.

My message to white people courageous enough to read this is to pause and look at what you are doing to the world you live in. Putting your head in the sand and pretending this is a brown person's problem cannot work anymore. White people should be among the group leader to help solve a problem created by their ancestry. America is what it is today, both the good and the bad, because of the contribution that everyone made to it, including people previously enslaved or indentured.

Stop racism in its tracks. Sometimes that means peacefully confronting other white people you see being racist or saying racist things. Tell them they need to be stewards to make the planet better than they found it. Refuse to watch racist shows on television or participate in businesses that are not all-inclusive, including at the leadership level. Vote for politicians, no matter the party, that are anti-racist not just in their rhetoric but also in actions, laws they support and pass, and their personal lives. Help make the world you live in better for our future generations. It's your duty too.

Ditto for brown people. Shine and grow and expect and demand to be treated with dignity and respect. Demand equal pay and treat your people as kings and queens who deserve your praise. Do not believe in the falsehood of minstrelsy. Love yourself because you deserve to inherit this planet like anyone else.

Don't create battles in your household. Use your home to fortify yourself and your loved ones so you are rejuvenated sufficiently to help eradicate racism. I know this cannot happen overnight, but we all must work together to help those who suffer from their form of racism. Change must come and come soon for a better world for all of us.

In the next chapter, I will get religious, but not in the way you may think. Religion has a role to play in ending racism.

Chapter 4

RELIGIOUS DOGMA AND RACISM

"When the missionaries came to Africa, they had the Bible, and we had the land. They said, 'Let us pray.' We closed our eyes. When we opened them, we had the Bible, and they had the land."

~ DESMOND TUTU, South African Anglican cleric, and theologian.

I had an inkling of colonialism's inhumanity when I studied economics and history in college. In my Caribbean history class in college, my teacher gave us an essay to discuss the extent to which economics or human rights factors influenced the abolition of enslavement. I wrote an extended essay on the influence of the Christian church, focusing on the moral arguments against slavery. In my report, I noted the Bible's indoctrination message: "Slaves, obey your earthly masters with respect and fear, and with sincerity of heart, just as you would obey Christ." (Ephesians 6:5 New International Version).

My conclusion? While there was a Quakers Movement agitating and exogenous factors such as the enslaved people rebelling in some territories, the main reason some stakeholders advocated for slavery to end was rational business decisions. Sugar from tropically grown cane was losing out to its competitor, beet sugar, which could be grown in temperate climates. It had a much cheaper cultivation cost than the complex supply chain of chattel production using enslaved people of African descent. I argued that with the reduced profit margins and stiff competition coupled with changing social views on production, it became more feasible to free the enslaved people and let them fend for themselves in some cases.

Admittedly, my classmates and I studied West Indian or Caribbean history as if we were outsiders. As students, we avoided the human side and explored the economics of it. We never paid much attention to the role of religion, in particular Christianity, both in perpetuating the enslavement of the so-called "lost souls" and the influence of some white people who lobby for the freedom of these people based on the same Christian doctrine. We, too, were indoctrinated by Christianity, so it was reasonable that we saw our adopted religion as the hero of our enslaved ancestors. We never realized then that Christianity was an economic tool to keep workers subjugated and accepting of their stations in life. As students, we were being prepared to enter the workforce similarly made docile by religion.

Throughout our education, religion, namely Christianity, tainted our view of the world. All schools had prayers and religious ceremonies for most celebrations. Even today, many of my fellow alumni and family believe that anything positive that happens to them results from a Christian god providing grace. Despite this indoctrination, I paid more in-depth attention to the economic structure I was experiencing after graduating from college. I saw the religious connection much later in life. In particular, I saw how a system designed for the enrichment of white people was so pervasive in our lives some 180-plus years after emancipation.

That leads me to a resulting revelation that may shock many people. Nevertheless, here goes. I used to believe in God. I prayed and went to worship regularly as a youth in the Methodist church in the Caribbean. When I was ten years of age, I surprised my grandmother by rising from beside her usual seated spot in church and heading to the pulpit to read the scriptures as part of the service.

We used to read the Bible together a lot. She had weak eyes so I would read to her. But we also took turns. It helped me get accustomed to the old English of the King James Version of the Bible. I soon got involved in church, picked up the offerings, became youth fellowship president, joined the adult and young people choir and men's fellowship, and became the church's treasurer. I was in church practically every day at one point, at one event, practice, or the other. I molded many of my leadership skills in church and school. One local pastor even asked if I wanted to become a preacher. I preached one Sunday and flopped so much that I did not do it again. In retrospect, my heart was not in it, and I did not know how to fake it. I was not as excited as I wanted and probably did not want to be excited because I did not want people to push me in this direction.

My involvement in the church allowed me to see behind the sacred veil of holiness. Perhaps I had too high an expectation. In many cases, the visage of piety was a façade. While I did not feel worthy, many, especially the men who had taken the mantle of God's servants, were probably no more deserving than me. As a teenager with uncontrolled hormones, dreams often distracted me, including daydreams of pretty girls. Indeed, in my mind, those thoughts had to be sinful to be a preacher. I believed preachers were closer to God. They were right-hand-of-God people. Plus, I did not have "the calling" in which I imagined there would be a Moses with a burning bush scene where God would tell me, "Hey, go preach my word and stop pussyfooting around."

I did not have that "calling" anyway. During the 1980s and early 1990s, in my Free-Mandela-and-end-apartheid-in-South-Africa days, I thought about becoming a politician and cleaning up the mess everyone complained about on my island home. Of course, it was a paradise for those with money and connections. Later, I worked with politicians as a civil servant and learned how to be a good politician. I might have to forsake things my morally upright grandmother taught me. I shelved that ambition. Preachers, priests, and the church have their place. People need the church for social support and often economic connections. The church has always been an institution of convenience for the powerful and wealthy. History shows it has heavy implications for racial discrimination.

For example, in 1449, in Toledo, Spain, Christians concerned that the Jewish community was gaining economic and social power passed statutes requiring anyone who wanted any form of upward mobility, whether Jewish or Muslim, to convert to Christianity (Sicroff and Assis, 2020). To distinguish between the new and old Christians, they passed other statutes requiring blood purity, defined as four generations of non-white interbreeding of their family's bloodline. This "Limpieza de Sangre" was the discrimination of "pure-blooded" Christians over everyone else. Ironically, the Roman Catholic church under Pope Alexander VI approved this statute. That triggered universities, government offices, and other institutions to discriminate on race (Chami 2000).

During my youth, I had no idea the church was complicit in such mischief. My time as a Methodist youth fellowship president impacted me. I would plan various activities to attract young people to church and keep them interested. These included not just prayer and Bible study nights but evenings out at a restaurant for pizza and fun conversation, exercise nights, game nights, and speakers who discussed contemporary topics like HIV/AIDS, teenage dating, health issues, writing a resume, or something similar.

I witnessed the decline of my church as more and more young people either left to attend somewhere with loud, exciting music, dancing, and a fire and brimstone preacher, left altogether for Rastafarianism, or just for no church at all. As the old people died, I tried to save the church by attracting more young people. When I became treasurer, I saw the collection dwindle as working young people stopped coming to church or came only during the festive season. I lost some youth group members because the Methodist church could not fulfill their needs. By this time, the evangelical churches prospered more than the older traditional churches. Pew Research Center on the decline of religion, and in this case, Christianity, also revealed similar trends like my church across multiple demographic groups (Smith et al. 2019). Surveys showed that in 2018 and 2019, 65 percent of American adults labeled themselves as Christians, a decline of 12 percent from a decade before. Unlike my time, both Protestants and Catholics are waning. Forty-three percent of U.S. adults categorized themselves as Protestants in 2019, down from 51 percent in 2009. Catholics were 20 percent, down from 23 percent in 2009.

Young people turned to evangelical churches to escape the cure-for-insomnia Methodist church for the dancing, music, and more forceful preaching of charismatic speakers. Even though some of these evangelical pastors were infamous for immigrating to America overnight upon draining the congregation's tithes from the church's bank account, along with all the building funds, these were monies made at revival services in aid of the new church.

One of my good friends and former teachers is a priest. He always dreamed of being a priest, complete with the dressing gown and all the paraphernalia of the profession. He studied in a regional seminary but fell out with some priests connected to the bishop close to graduation. The bishop wanted him to be humble and practically worship him. My proud friend refused. Not only did they not ordain him, but the church sued him for all the school tuition money, knowing he could not afford to pay them back. Because of the clergy's power and ecclesiastical connections, he could not get a job in any church as a priest. No lawyer would muddy their relationship with their clerics and the bishop by taking his case. He ended up teaching in a small private school where I met him.

To fight his case, he became a lawyer, represented himself, appealed, and won his court case against the church. A new bishop ordained him, but he was already so tainted among other priests and so disillusioned that he lost as much faith in the church as they did in him.

I visited him in the seminary college, where I met another student priest locked away in his room with orders to repent, pray, and fast because he openly protested when his professor attempted to rub his thighs near his crotch. I also learned that these priests often left the seminary as atheists. Still, they went along with it and pretended to believe in God because they had completed their studies, recognized it as a respected profession, and knew they would have a good life. It was just a job.

With my exposure to many church tribulations, I learned that the people we put on pedestals as religious leaders were as human as anyone else, complete with their frailties and faults. I used to think, like most Christians, that once you had the calling, there was some spiritual blanket of protection that kept you from doing ordinary sinful things like sleeping around with women in the church.

My then-wife and I used to alternate between the Methodist and Anglican church each week. She was Anglican and loved the incense in the church, probably more than she enjoyed the sermon. Besides, the church was the place to be seen and to meet respectable people who could help propel one's career. After one Sunday at the Methodist church, I left feeling very angry. The preacher told the congregation how horrible and sinful we were and that we had no hope but to wallow in eternal fire and hell if we did not repent.

The hymns also did not help. To this day, one that remains rooted in my head is, "Trust and obey, cause there is no other way to be happy in Jesus but to trust and obey" (Sammis and Towner 1887). I felt so much suffering in a particular group while others prospered. Enslavement, colonialism, and today's racial injustices were at the forefront of my mind. Yet, this hymn whimsically choired in verse two that I do not have to fear, in verse three, that "toil He doth richly repay," and all the tremendous "favor He shows" and "joys He bestows are for them who will trust and obey."

I listened to the hymn, to precisely what the words we were saying, and became incensed that I had spent so much of my life learning these words. I felt that I was brainwashed into an acceptance of a mirage of an all-loving God that would let someone suffer while they trusted and obeyed that life or death would be happier. In states like California, where the hymn's author eventually died, eighty percent of Native Americans were slain in twenty years by white settlers (Blakemore, California's Little-Known Genocide 2020). There was no "fellowship sweet," as the hymn suggested in its final stanza. Free brown people were not welcomed in California around the time this hymn was written. To me, hymns of this type served to defy reality and assist in subjugating an already oppressed people.

At the Anglican church, I saw all the effigies: the crucifix with a carving of a suffering, long-haired Jesus with piercings on his hands and feet, the stations of the cross, the stained-glass images of archangels and cherubim. Everything was based on white culture and people with Caucasian faces on an island with ninety-five percent of people of African descent. Even the lamb was white as snow, just like the one Mary had. The hymns described servitude, and subjugation and, like my church, reminded us of how awful we were in the sight of this white God. The pulpit and the area where the priest stood and had holy communion were not accessible to the congregation in the church without the express permission of the priest.

I then went to a church called the Living Room. The congregation worshiped in one another's houses, rotating every week, and it was more like a meeting of ordinary people to worship and talk through problems. My family was invited to one of these services held in the conference room of a rum distillery. The preacher that day was a visitor from Pennsylvania. He was not trained in theology but was a self-taught motivational speaker. He was white, and seventy percent of the congregation was white.

We sang fewer we-are-super-sinner hymns and livelier, optimistic songs. The guy talked about how God wanted us to be successful here on earth while we were alive. What a novel concept! He said God wanted us to try our business idea and not worry about failure. His God wanted us to be financially successful. My church, the Sunday before, told me I was worthless, but for the blood of a white man savior who was nailed to a cross. Typically, I leave my church thinking it's okay to be destitute now because when you die, you will get rewards in heaven if you trust and obey. My church told me it was easier for a camel to go through the eye of a needle than for a rich man to enter heaven (Matthew 19:24 New International Version). In contrast, this church wanted us to be financially successful here on earth.

I realized then that even though slavery had ended, Christianity was still being used to enslave people, even preaching different versions to brown and white people. "Slaves, obey your earthly masters with respect and fear, and with sincerity of heart, just as you would obey Christ" (Ephesians 6:5 New International Version). We paid our church to teach us these ancient rules in society and history that persistently reminds brown people that they are the slaves and the white man is the master.

After careful thought and my experience in life, I see heaven and hell intermingled here on earth. The impecunious, diseased with no hope for cures, war-torn regions, areas of famine and hunger, people who suffer oppression with little prospect of reprieve, the modern-day enslaved who must endure human trafficking, and those who are suffering without absolution are all in hell. Conversely, heaven is more likely a space of security, acceptance, and safety to love and care for the people around you without worrying about being murdered. 'Heaven' is knowing you have an equal opportunity to prosper. Admittedly, heaven is not always synonymous with wealth. Many wealthy people are miserable in their version of hell.

I am indoctrinated. I spent much of my younger years praying. I prayed for peace on earth, freeing Nelson Mandela from prison, eradicating racism and world hunger, the knowledge to pass my university exams, and a happy, collaborative relationship with everyone. Some prayers for Mandela and my exams worked out, but others did not. My then-pastor said, "Your prayers were not answered because you do not have faith." If I begged to differ and said I had lots of faith, I was told, "Well, you did not have enough faith." I would try again with more prayer. It was circular logic.

A couple of other things made me question the church as an institution. First, I did not like the way the church treated its people. My church suspended and punished a grown woman because she got pregnant out of wedlock. She was in a leadership role in the church and continued believing in and serving the church in another country.

Remember my friend who was studying to become a priest at his seminary? During my visit, I met his classmate, who was sequestered in his room for penitence. He was the one being touched in intimate places he did not welcome. He retaliated with profanity, exclaiming that he did not like the priest's physical advances.

The fathers of the seminary punished the student instead of the priest because the practice at the time was to protect the peers from allegations of misconduct. We now know this to be a regular practice of not just the seminaries but the churches themselves, as they simply moved priests from church to church after each incident of sexual predation, including on children (Schnell and Ruland 2019). We are also aware of the mental damage this caused to people even years later as they attempted to live an everyday life after this abuse of power by people they trusted (PBS Frontline 2011). I have a friend who wrestles with that because he was abused as an eleven-year-old.

My premarital counselling was woefully inadequate. I expected more from the priest, but I understand that many priest and few church leaders receive any basic training program to prepare couples for marriage or, even better, to test whether they should be married.

I studied more about Christianity when I went to college. Religion can be used to prove anything (Cline 2018). I learned how, perhaps conveniently, missionaries would be the first white people Africans would encounter before the capitalists arrived to rule them while extracting resources. Religious Studies was taught in my school, and I memorized many Bible verses. This was all part of the indoctrination.

What my religious studies never taught me was the objective history of religion and, in particular, Christianity. By this, I mean I was taught that the purpose of the insertion of Jesus Christ into the timeline of enmity between Jews and Gentiles was to reconcile a peace bringing all of God's people together again in one social harmony (Ephesians 2:11-22 New International Version).

As the religion became more Europeanized, the question remained of who should be included in this social group because inclusion bolstered power as it became an imperial religion. Anyone who was not European or non-white "became signs of failure to belong to the universal Christian community of God." Brown and Indigenous people with no hope of assimilating, whether by bloodline or appearance, were justifiably consigned to enslavement and subjugation. This state was the best they could get as part of the community (Yadav 2018).

Only later in life, when I questioned my equity in that community, did I understand that even in my family, the Christians among them often accepted belonging in the "body of Christ" in a subjugated way, as there was no natural way for them to reach whiteness.

When I recall my experience with the Living Room, I see the differentiation in the messaging. Their white philosophy of financial and societal success differed from the *black* message of the "meek inheriting the earth. My Methodist pastor taught the brown congregation about damnation as sinners because of the inherent status that European Christendom placed on non-whites.

Come Sunday is a movie depicting the true story of Carlton Pearson, an American Christian Minister. In summary, the main character proclaims that with all the suffering in the world, no righteous and just God would condemn hapless people to die in sin to eternal fire and damnation if they have never had an opportunity to experience Him. As such, Pearson concluded there was no hell (Hinchey 2018). From my perspective, taking away the option of hell runs the risk of eroding church-prescribed morality. Furthermore, it removes the incentive to allow a church and its agents to control one's will. It also eliminates the separation of Jews and Gentiles that Christianity advocates. If everyone is saved, whether Christians or not, they don't have to settle for a station of life established by a European-run imperial religion.

A lack of belief does not take away morality from people. I did not change once I stopped believing. I did not suddenly feel free to commit immoral acts like murder or be unkind to people. However, I became mentally freer and could appreciate people as they are—good, nuanced, and evil. I understood racism better, the use of religion, and the fiction people believe to justify economic racist behavior against others. I am not telling readers not to have beliefs. Religion has been around for so long. While there are sides to it that are harmful, Christianity has helped others cope with life's trials and tribulations.

It is good practice to question what you believe and determine if it helps you move in the direction you want. Question everything! Who started your religion? What did they gain? Does it truly help the people it claims to love? Why is there so much suffering, even among people who have never heard of God, Jesus or whatever deity, saint, or leader one follows? Make sure the religion truly benefits you now on earth. Be skeptical of those who tell you to seek heavenly benefits and not earthly gains, especially while they have material gains. What car are they driving, and what kind of house do they live in? How comfortable is their life compared to yours?

One of my friends who passed away used to give money to a rich pastor. He had private planes, chauffeur-driven cars, and various lived-in mansions. He paid no taxes and lived like royalty. She said she paid him for his charismatic motivational speeches every Sunday for the therapy it brought her. That's her decision, and while I don't condemn her for it, I would not make such a choice. Our brains are well developed as humans, so we want to believe we have a higher purpose. Some research suggests most of us may be predisposed to believe in a higher being (BBC 2003).

It may seem like other religions also support the enslavement of people considered different or subordinate. The Muslim faith also enslaved people from Europe and North Africa, again much in the name of religion. With the expansion of the Ottoman Empire in the 15th century, the Barbary corsairs solidified their slave trade. When Thomas Jefferson, the US ambassador to France, and John Adams, ambassador to England, visited the ambassador from Tripoli to Britain, Sidi Haji Abdul Rahman Adja, to question why they should enslave European people, he replied: "that it was founded on the Laws of their Prophet, that it was written in their Koran, that all nations who should not have acknowledged their authority were sinners, that it was their right and duty to make war upon them wherever they could be found and to make slaves of all they could take as Prisoners, and that every Musselman who should be slain in battle was sure to go to Paradise" (American Commissioners 1786).

Christianity has a similar justification for the enslavement of people. The primary go-to scripture is Genesis 9: 18-27 King James Version, about the popularized story of "The Curse of Ham," supposedly spurred by the anger of his father, Noah, after Ham witnessed him drunk and naked. The dubious story proclaims an old man cursing his grandchild for his last son being a servant. Pro-slavers added, even more, reaching out to claim Ham was from Africa, despite them all being of the same family and exact location (Rae 2018).

Some white people believe the complaints by brown people about the enslavement of Africans are unfair because they, too, were enslaved and brutally treated in the Barbary slave trade. They often refer to Thomas Sowell's *YouTube* interview, where he mentioned that statistically, many more white Europeans were traded in Africa than Africans in America (Hoover Institution 2018). Books like Giles Milton's *White Gold* tell the story of a Cornish boy spending twenty-three years in captivity by Barbary corsairs. The boy, Thomas Pellow, wrote of his time in Morocco as an enslaved person by the sultan. He wrote letters to the emissaries and royal family back home, imploring them to seek his freedom (Milton 2004).

I am still on life's journey to learn about the world's history. Admittedly, instead of high school history, I learned about the Barbary slave trade only through my research as an adult when I found *White Gold* in the bookstore at Heathrow Airport. However, I am yet to find an analysis of Africans in the Americas writing their governments and tribes back home in Africa or even being allowed to do such, to request they send government intervention to free them. I will update this book in a newer edition with such details if there are any. The other issue is that the Barbary slave trade has not left such a sticky social and economic impact of race on white people as occurred with Africans' enslavement. Economic racism exists today, and its foundation comes from Europeans and colonialism's enslavement of Africans in the West.

Growing up thinking Christianity was open to all in a harmonious community, I had no idea in my earlier life that there was this sticky social impact. I recall, in 1996, walking into a United Methodist Church in Fort Lauderdale on Sunday, happy to be in a church whose hymns were rooted in songwriters such as John and Charles Wesley. As I said before, these hymns had been imprinted in my mind since I was a child going to church with my grandmother and mother. As I walked in, the pastor gasped. He stared at me while I entered the back of the church. Some more curious members followed his gaze to see why he stopped preaching. I heard them audibly gasp too. The church service collectively paused. When they realized I was staying and had asked for a hymn book and bible, the pastor continued his homily.

After the benediction, like in my home church, Methodists like to socialize. I was curious about this strange behavior of subtle exclusion because it was all new to me. I hung around and talked with a few of the church members. One lady I was talking to said, "We have coffee and cookies after church downstairs if you are not in a hurry to leave." It sounded like a non-invitation. I stayed and had coffee and cookies and talked some more with them. "Your English is so good—where did you go to school?" someone asked. I was polite and explained where I was from, my dedication to Methodism, and why my English was so good. Then I left without an invitation to return the following Sunday. While the church had the same name as mine back home, I felt like, specifically for me, it did not have the same welcoming warmth.

Consequently, I am incredibly disappointed with how religion has been used to do the opposite of what it's said to be for, to bring people together in love. Instead, religion is used as fuel for hate. Devout Christians fear brown or *black* people entering their church. *Black* people now fear white people entering and praying with them, especially after the Charleston massacre in 2015 in the Emanuel African Methodist Episcopal Church (History.com 2020).

A CNN article revealed that "only about 5 percent of the nation's churches are racially integrated, and half of them are in the process of becoming all-*black* or all-white" (Blake 2008). It's similar to my example of the mainly *black* Methodist church versus the white Living Room church. In all instances, the all-embracing God is molded into the convenience of the believers.

I marveled at freed slaves in the Caribbean that chose the church as their first place to visit upon hearing of their emancipation (E. Williams

1970). Yet it seems like brown people have embraced the idea of God more than white people. A Pew Center survey in 2014 found that more "African-Americans believe in God—83 percent—than whites and Latinos—61 percent and 59 percent, respectively." This is true even in prosperity churches where they preach giving to receive, often with the church leaders receiving from poorer congregation members. People stay in churches like these, even if they get no empowerment growth because they need a community away from a society that at least trusts and accepts their skin color and culture. As with my experience in the United Methodist Church in Fort Lauderdale, due to a God molded into the convenience of the believer, segregated churches in America do not allow such comfort (D. Love 2018).

Politicians know the value of the church to maintain its power. They go to church, funerals, weddings, and any event. People seeing them there believe they are holy and anointed by God, so they are worth the vote. We now see the political and racial divide deepening by using Christianity as a crutch to explain belief. This is dangerous in any nation. The United States is a secular nation, but politicians have used Christianity to illustrate divides analogous to the historical divides between Jews and Gentiles (Schweitzer 2015).

White churches, like the Southern Baptist Convention, founded to uphold enslavement, did not support the Civil Rights movement that occurred in the 1960s. Today, they preach against racism, but only temporarily after an act of police violence ends in the death of another brown person. The same white evangelicals will ignore racial discrimination in the workplace, police violence, electoral disenfranchisement, a skewed prison, and justice system, and biased college enrollments since these do not gather the publicity they need for their ministry to prosper. Since few white pastors have a relationship with any black person on an equally respectable basis, they often depend on another black peer to help them prepare their sermons during the subsequent murder by a police officer (Green 2020).

Here is my recommendation to Christian churches that claim God loves everyone: prove it. When I see churches and their related neighborhoods are integrated, and there is a high degree of interracial marriages, schools, neighborhoods, and workplaces, then I can believe the church is doing a good job and is eradicating racism in its community. For now, white churches that even passively promote segregation and only come out to preach against racial violence during an uprising are failing the Jesus that aimed to bring societal harmony despite people's differences. They must stop being numb to racism.

I contend that Christianity was used and, to some extent, is still used to subjugate. However, today, using a god and religion accepted by brown

people to subjugate
them weakens its credibility as a harmonizing force. With the push to free brown people and stop the slave trade, America needed a new religion to protect its economic interests—enslaved people. That new religion is not any form of Christianity. Some experts and scholars see Race as a religion. For some people, it is more valid for their daily freedom than Christianity (A. Savage 2019). It also explains the great conflict between Christianity and Race. Despite all the love the Christian God is supposed to give, churches are still mostly segregated, just like their communities.

The definition of religion, according to Dictionary.com, is "a set of beliefs concerning the cause, nature, and purpose of the universe, especially when considered as the creation of a superhuman agency or agencies, usually involving devotional and ritual observances, and often containing a moral code governing the conduct of human affairs." Christianity is a religion with a belief in God or a god or gods, humans who have superhuman or, in other words, superior agency, a moral code in the written word like the ten commandments, or sociological norms like prayer, collective worship, church and overall guidance on how to behave in society. The grand belief is that Jesus died for the sins of all mankind, who accept the faith, so that everyone, Jews and Gentiles, brown and white, regardless of origin, can come together under one umbrella. The reward for that coming together is eternal spiritual salvation.

I agree with Professor Savage that the concept of race is also a religion. Like Christianity, Race requires belief for it to prosper. Like religion, Race, the concept, and Racism, the belief system, are like Christ and Christianity, respectively. The invention of Race is codified in our laws, the U.S. constitution, norms, unwritten rules, behaviors, rituals, institutions, clubs, and structures. Once someone believes in a race, we talk about it as a tangible entity, just like we talk about God. We have unwritten rules and norms saying that brown and white people should not live together, marry, or own businesses jointly. That leaves us with the rotten concept based on white supremacy, that white people should always be on top.

To reinforce the belief, clubs like all-white churches, all-white branches of government, all-white companies, and all-white boards facilitate the belief and, in their work, ensure that they preserve the superhuman or superior status of whiteness. These clubs may even believe that they are not acting on their Race as a religion by allowing a few token-brown people into the club while never allowing them to reach real power or authority. When a brown person is turned down for a job or not selected for a board seat that they are qualified for, these rituals are rooted in a race belief system. Rituals are repeated and known from being taught as a youth from your belief system's family. Just as practicing Christians recite the Lord's Prayer or the Benediction at the end of a service to reinforce our belief in the "holy Catholic and Apostolic Church," so too are the ritual words of "you are not qualified for this job," "you are overqualified," "you are not the right fit," and "maybe you should go get some more training, and you would probably be ready for a lower position in time," are all ritual. Behavioral words are repeated no matter what part of America they are and which white person they meet.

Other phrases like, "you speak very good English—where did you go to school?" suggest that you speak the language like a white person, but you are not white because of your complexion and hair texture. Their mind has an incongruency because what they are witnessing does not match their beliefs. The lack of care shown by white people for brown suffering is because, at the core, they believe in Race. Race, as religion, says they are superior to everyone else. In America, as Professor Savage pointed out, it is codified in the Constitution, just as Christianity is codified in the books of the Bible (A. Savage 2019).

The Race bible, the Constitution, its resulting laws, and its courts, all the way to the Supreme Court, help uphold and protect these beliefs. While we think of America as a secular nation, it is not really because on every document, application for a job, medical form, census, whatever, there is an age-old question of which race or ethnic group you belong to. Just as you can choose to tick the box whether you are a Christian, Protestant, Muslim, or Hindu, you can tick a box of whether you are White, *Black*, Hispanic, Asian, Mixed, or other. We are told that it matters to ensure that race is protected and not discriminated against. A human is "a member of the primate genus Homo, especially a member of the Homo sapiens, distinguished from other apes by a large brain and the capacity for speech" (The Free Dictionary n.d.). Since we humans are the only ones capable of completing these forms, those other fantasy selections of Race should not be there. They serve to only reinforce the belief in our heads.

I recall filling out my medical form for travel vaccinations, and it asked me about my Race. I omitted it, and the clerk, a brown lady, enshrined in the religion of Race, made a selection on my behalf. I argued with her for a while but realized she believed in Race more than God. To reinforce her beliefs, she could see one and not the other. Today, with a global pandemic, medical news shows that brown people are likely to get COVID-19 easier, not because of their allocated Race, but because of where the belief system has placed them (Golden, Coronavirus in African Americans and Other People of Color 2020). They mostly have physical jobs and environments in spaces where underlying health conditions weaken their morphology to fight the virus. These conditions are because of what Race has done to them and generations of their family for 400 years, not because of their skin color (Gupta 2020).

I started by saying that I don't believe in God or any of the proposed religions fed to us over time. Similarly, I also don't believe in the religion of Race. Yet, I live in a culture where these two are still firmly held onto. I also do not want to dictate that the solution is not to believe in anything, or at least not in these two things, since no matter what, we all believe in something, even if that's in money, a fancy car, or power or family. What, then, is the solution?

Let's start with religion, and I will stay with the one I am most familiar with, Christianity. There are many good instructions from the books of the Bible, especially when treating everyone who wants to be under the tent the same. For illustration, I believe Christians should stay out of foreign people's business who decide they don't want to be part of that religion. There should never be a church with its symbolic crucifix in the jungles of a Mayan village. Missionaries should not seek out other countries to install Christendom and eradicate their local religions. These cultures have their faith and are not imposing theirs on Western society. Leave them alone and respect their wishes. Christianity has many faults and has caused many problems, so stop thinking it is the solution to everything. Work on the crucial issues, like how Christianity can be better than and conquer the religion of Racism.

Churches need to be multi-ethnic. For that to happen, communities must be multiethnic, and for that to happen, pay balance, opportunity balance, and the entire belief system of Race must be quelled. Brown and white people must live together and be able to go to the same church. If that United Methodist Church in Fort Lauderdale were accustomed to seeing brown people in their church, neighborhood, schools, and jobs, they would not have audibly gasped when I entered the church. Brown people would not fear that a lone white man coming into their church would massacre them because they could help such a deviant before he became a radicalized terrorist. Besides, if society decided it would not worship whiteness as superior anymore, and forsake the religion of Race, then it becomes like the Broken Windows theory.

Broken Windows Theory says that "visible signs of disorder and misbehavior in an environment encourage further disorder and misbehavior, leading to serious crimes" (Psychology Today 1982). The Theory's implementation required "zero tolerance" policing policies, especially in minority communities to crime. That meant cleaning up and fixing the environment like removing graffiti and broken windows and making the community look clean like it did not tolerate people who wanted to destroy or commit a crime. Unfortunately, it also led to divisive practices such as "stop and frisk" and an escalation of police violence against brown people. This method of crime-fighting was touted as the hero in New York City in the 1980s (Fox 2019).

If people want to get rid of racism, and Race as a religion, treat it like a crime. Treat it like a broken window, because that's what it is. It's a fantasy that has fractured our society and created more turmoil and economic loss for both brown and white people as opinions from studies now show (Rinderle 2017). That means the crime of racism must be recognized and constantly pointed out by all. Apply the Broken Window Theory to Race. Where Race breaks a window to society, misallocates resources, or causes a rupture in the real togetherness of Christianity, fix it. Make Racism "zero tolerance" policing policy for all churches, businesses, workplaces, government procedures, banks, or wherever the crime raises its head. Stop policies that reinforce it. This means eradicating it from all questionnaires, forms, and applications where it is irrelevant, and enforcing measures to determine and investigate where it is suspected of causing harm to anyone. Christianity can truly only become relevant and improve if it does what it promised, bringing all the people who so desire of their free will, together under God.

Remember, Christianity is fighting a dirty history of oppression where white Christians use religion to justify their theft of land, the genocide of indigenous peoples, and the enslavement of millions of Africans to build their wealth and Christian countries. Regarding and making the religion of Race an unwelcomed alien in a civilized society will not be easy. Many white people think the costs of the broken windows to society benefits them, just as a crime mob boss thinks a crime-ridden area of town benefits their profits.

Both brown and white people must treat Race as cancer that eats away at the harmony that whatever god you worship promised you. The enemy is not your human race that looks different today because of geographical evolution.

For Christianity to stay relevant, it must evolve and truly have a Jesus that died for brown and white people, Jews and Gentiles, males, females, or nonbinary, regardless of sexual orientation or origins. Everyone needs to inherit the earth. All Christians, all persons of any religious or non-religious faith, must be proactive by being effective anti-racists.

In the next chapter, I delve into workplace racism, a phenomenon we are often afraid to discuss. It has a tangible impact on brown people's livelihood and economic growth. I will, of course, go much deeper into the damage it is causing.

Chapter 5

THE RACIST WORKPLACE

*"I look at an ant and I see myself: a native South
African, endowed by nature with a strength much
greater than my size so I might cope with the
weight of racism that crushes my spirit."*

~ MIRIAM MAKEBA, South African singer, songwriter,
actress, United Nations goodwill ambassador, and civil
rights activist.

Congratulations if you are white and were fearless enough to read this far!
You are doing what so many black people always say you should do if you
want to learn about racism. Research it yourself. Please read on because this
chapter is vital in solving workplace racism and its impact on income
inequality.

Workplace racism, although rooted in seeking gains from capitalism,
erodes those benefits from it. Racist behavior does not create sustainability
from domination. In fact, racial discrimination molded by a xenophobic
culture only leads to political and social instability. As Hales (2009) wrote,
"Oppression breeds resistance." Capitalism is maintained through violence
and exploitation. It forces us, regardless of the fictional notion of race, to
fight to be part of the ruling class where we hoard profits and use the
surplus gains to secure more wealth, influence, and exploit more labor.

In this discourse about workplace racism, we are focused on the one
exploited resource that wants to move up the pyramid of Maslow's
hierarchy of needs—humans as labor. As humans, we want to fulfill our
basic needs like food, shelter, and safety, and move up to the higher order
of wants like family, self-esteem, and self-actualization. To understand how
we as humans fit into Economic Racism, we must briefly explore the
subject of Economics. Don't worry. I won't turn this into an Economics or

Sociology course. However, it's important to understand how a racist workplace misallocates resources and wastes wealth in a way that is not sustainable.

Economics deals with producing, distributing, and consuming goods and services using scarce resources. Because the resources are often insufficient and not readily available without a cost, rational human beings—those who want to fulfill their needs and wants—are supposed to allocate resources optimally to maximize their utility or benefit from the help (Investopedia Staff 2020).

The resources allocated to produce goods and services we consume are labor, capital, and natural resources. These resources are knitted together as inputs by technology and entrepreneurship to produce an output. Think of technology like the gearbox of a car, without which the engine (imputed resources like gas, oil, and driver skills) would not efficiently transport the driver or entrepreneur along the highway, changing gears according to the road conditions (output consumption being transportation). All resources are vital in the race discussion because all are exploited in pursuing Maslow's needs and wants. However, I focus on labor (University of Minnesota Libraries Publishing 2016).

Labor, in this case, is anyone with skills, training, and experience, all of which can contribute to work in collaboration with other factors and create an output of good, intellectual property, or service. Since an economy is circular, someone selling the labor coupled with their ingenuity is also a consumer. Starve off the majority of rewards—pay, benefits, equity, humane treatment, also known as utility, gained for supplying that labor—and they cannot consume much as they remain on the periphery of survival in an economy. They may be unable to provide the first basic needs, also known as living paycheck-to-paycheck. In the U.S., the federal minimum wage is $7.25 an hour, sufficient for the cost of living in the 1960s. While many states have higher minimum wages, people still struggle in poverty (Bloomenthal 2020).

Equivalent pay and benefits for the same work are unrealistic for many brown people. According to PayScale, a compensation research firm, "When we control for education, years of experience, occupation and other compensable factors, most men and women of color still earn less than white men" (PayScale 2020). The Bureau of Labor Statistics reported that the median pay for white men was $1,025, and for white women, $910 per week in current 2020 dollars. For *black* men, it was $869, and for *black* women $768. Hispanic men were at $757 and women at $661. Similar disparity patterns exist regardless of the type of job (U.S. Department of Labor, 2020). Mind you, these statistics are the median or "middle" of a list of ranked wages, which does not account for higher levels of salaries in management. To exasperate this inequality gap further, white male professionals are in the highest rates of being in leadership roles (PayScale 2020).

Brown people expect equal opportunity, but the white males in leadership tend to hire more people that look and act like them. That practice misallocates the labor force and ideas. It jeopardizes the profits and productivity of an organization because just hiring white people due to a belief in whiteness omits the skills offered by non-whites. How do you recognize racist behavior in the workplace, and what are the solutions for dealing with this wastage and loss to a company and the economy?

I try to understand how a short-sighted perspective of capitalism rooted in beliefs, ideology, and practices reinforced by religion, as seen in the last chapter, can be removed. I entered the corporate world in America with confidence in my abilities and a record of accomplishments. When I first started comprehending micro-attacks and what I have learned are called micro-aggressive behavior, I resisted and believed the attacks were founded on ignorance. "Oppression breeds resistance." In retrospect, I was uninformed because I did not understand the history behind racism.

Micro-aggressions are statements, incidents, or actions directed against a targeted group. The attack is subtle, indirect, and may initially seem negligible or unexplainable. I always evaluate my assumptions about micro-aggressions by asking myself or people around me: has this incident, action, or assault ever happened or is likely to occur between two white persons in the organizations with no earlier trigger? Just as a white manager mistrusts my effort, would he or she also question their white colleagues with equal fervent hostility? Is that behavior as persistent against everyone as it is with non-white colleagues? I also tried to figure out what triggered the behavior.

Earlier, I mentioned a colleague that told me about her first racial experience during the first week of kindergarten. In trying to understand my own experiences, her story came to mind. To recap, she lost her new best friend, a white girl, when her mother told her not to associate herself with a brown girl. That colleague became angry with me when I told her about my visit to Selma, Alabama, with a group of friends. I had organized trips like these to various places of American historical significance where the brown populace was disaffected by white societies misguided by racist ideology. I told my colleague it appalled me that Selma was relegated to being a near-ghost town because white citizens did not want *black* citizens to vote. She thought I had no right to be outraged about the 1965 incidents in Selma (C. Klein 2015). I had not faced the intensity of racism and requisite emotional wounds she experienced, yet I had the audacity of intolerance.

I felt saddened by her pain as she relayed a story typical of many brown people here in America. First, one of her classmates in Atlanta spat on her. She was called all kinds of racial slurs by white children. The teachers never protected her but instead actively or passively encouraged the abuse she faced. The cruelty shattered her self-confidence. Stress, low self-esteem, mental health, anxiety, and poor performance in school and at work are all results of the incessant reminders by teachers, bosses, colleagues, the media, government leaders, law enforcement, the justice system, entertainment, and society that white people were somehow superior to everyone else (Graham-LoPresti et al. 2017). But for my colleague's mother's constant reminder that her daughter was praiseworthy, she would have likely struggled with anxiety which could have impacted her abilities to perform at work and function successfully in life.

Curious, I probed about the spitting incident in school because, as someone from the Caribbean, we are culturally germophobic and particularly anxious about any physical interaction with other people's unwelcomed bodily fluids. Spitting at someone signifies loathing and is meant to intentionally, or at least symbolically, contaminate and humiliate the recipient. Besides the social taboo, Caribbean people, and I believe brown Americans too, associate such a contamination attempt with annihilating about fifty-five million indigenous people, ninety percent of the Americas, between 1492 and 1600s. With the arrival of Europeans, indigenous people contracted novel diseases previously unacquainted to their immune systems, such as smallpox, measles, mumps, and rubella, or were killed (Woodward 2019). You spit at someone only if you want to kill them with your disease.

In a germaphobe society like the Caribbean, spitting at anyone for any reason, whether due to hatred or a mishap, would likely erupt into a brawl. The teachers would not have only reprimanded the assailants but punished or even expelled them. Their parents would have been summoned and, together with the guilty child, chastised by the principal, mostly to reiterate the shame brought to their family name by the behavior. We associate that behavior with poor upbringing, low class, and ignorance of the diseases that could spread.

In my colleague's case, she told the teachers, but the felonious child denied it. The teacher dismissed her story. It's not unreasonable to believe that the white teacher considered it part of the ordinary course of treating brown children with revulsion. As the award-winning anti-racism activist and educator Jane Elliott proved through her experiment, prejudice can be taught. Elliott split her class into two groups based on the color of their eyes. Those with blue eyes were discriminated against.

Meanwhile, the people with brown eyes were treated with high esteem. Elliott first conducted this exercise in her third-grade class in 1968, one day after the assassination of Dr. Martin Luther King Jr (Own 2020). She has carried out that exercise in many schools and corporations since then.

My colleague's teacher was imparting knowledge of what was socially acceptable in relationships between brown and white people. She taught the white children that they were allowed to be cruel to another human being once they were not white. She also taught the brown child that they were inferior and to expect more of this behavior. Research shows that the assaults, whether in school or the workplace, lead to the perception that you have no control over the outcome of your life. Brown people whose self-esteem has been destroyed by such trauma also internalize their abuse, believing it's their fault. The resulting anxiety leads to avoidance and often depression that is hard to shake with the cumulative racial reinforcements of aggression (Graham-LoPresti et al. 2017). Unsurprisingly, the spitting incident repeated until the girl's father visited the school to personally reprimand the main offending tormenter.

Just as the teacher allowed the maltreatment of this child, I also experienced similar white unity behavior in the corporate world in America. When a white coworker was negligent on a project, they got protection—the predominantly white bosses ignored their offenses. I referred to this in chapter 1 as "white solidarity." Here are a few examples of white solidarity.

In 2020, a brown birdwatcher asked a white woman in Central Park, New York, to put her dog on a leash, which is the rule in that area. The woman summoned her hidden acting skills of the damsel in distress. With faux hysteria, augmented by tears, she called the police and told them, "There's an African-American man threatening my life" (Shropshire 2020). It's common knowledge that police or white civilian men entering the scene of a white woman in distress in the presence of a brown man could often lead to violent or fatal consequences for the brown man. This tactic has caused many slayings in America, some as brutal as the 1955 violent killing of Emmett Till (History.com 2020). As a result of white solidarity, a white mob murdered the fourteen-year-old in Mississippi for allegedly "flirting" with a white woman. Today, such white middle-class women have acquired a nickname in popular culture. They are called a "Karen"—a white female who protects their white privilege, often with the consequence of harm to non-white people (Nagesh 2020).

In all my various careers outside the United States, companies hired me for my knowledge, experience, and skill set. Yes, they were societies where there was some racial bias, but merit was more important and, in most cases, there was a social disgrace for public racist behavior. In some countries in Europe, a white person could be ostracized for speaking racist slurs at someone in public.

In Geneva, Switzerland, while at a café in a shopping mall, a homeless guy approached me and made some racists comment in French. The barista, a white lady, expressed shock and demanded that he leave the area. She profusely apologized to me and then called her manager—also white—who also apologized and called security to find the man and eject him from the mall. Security searched for the guy, who by then had escaped knowing that his behavior was not tolerated in their civilized society. He knew he was an outcast and would remain that way as long as he distresses people with his ideologies. This is where American society needs to get to, where people who prefer to live with racist ideologies become outcasts—just as the broken window theory aims to eradicate crime, let's also eradicate racism.

I arrived in the American workplace with these experiences, where white and brown people consider themselves modern and civilized and do not tolerate racist behavior. I assumed that I would be judged on my output and professionalism. Consequently, I approached the work as a high achiever. My first boss was also a brown man, progressive and self-confident, with a wealth of experience. Many of my colleagues were also brown, and the white ones were friendly and professional, at least most of them.

In retrospect, there were many micro-aggressive behaviors. One of my brown colleagues referred to me as a "white man with *black* skin." When I probed, I was told it was because I did not behave like a *black* American. I was perplexed because I knew that people, no matter the origin, come with various skills, accents, and backgrounds, all of which cumulate to form someone valuable to the business. I learned that the concept of race was so omnipresent in every facet of life in America that it even governed expectations of what both brown and white people considered appropriate behavior for each other.

As an example of expectations, coworkers warned me not to venture out in the forests alone—I hiked for exercise, often alone. Naïvely, I asked why only to be told that I could get beaten up or even tied to a tree and left to die. I thought they must be joking. Indeed, that violent behavior was a thing of the distant past. Quickly, the news items of vicious attacks on brown people by white people, and my incidents at work, proved me wrong.

Before researching racism in America, I felt safe and confident. I believed that I would rise to the top of my organization's corporate ladder or be headhunted away by a competing company because of my accomplishments. Admittedly, I reduced the number of hikes alone after one rainy trek when I was approached by two white men going the opposite direction, who offered to give me a ride in their car. This was a ride I had not solicited. I was in the middle of an isolated, forested road in the mountains of Georgia. With thoughts of my colleagues' admonitions, my senses suggested I might have been in danger of being kidnapped or worse. Both brown and white people had internalized and accepted the society such that they questioned and warned anyone who did not behave accordingly.

My company hired a white boss a few years later—an external hire, someone less experienced and qualified than many already in the company.

Here I wondered if there was such a thing as "white-supported affirmative action." In 1961, President John F. Kennedy required entities that received a federal subsidy to take meaningful steps "to ensure that applicants are employed and that employees are treated during employment, without regard to their race, creed, color, or national origin."

Later in 1967, Lyndon Johnson added gender to the list. Today, many white people, especially white women, oppose affirmative action, citing that it's racist because, from their perspective, it helps brown people more than them. The aim was to correct some of the ills of certain sections of society due to the New Deal and its spurred Jim Crow laws. Yet, the facts are that "white men are 61.3 percent of executives nationally and 81 percent above parity when compared with their 33.8 percent representation in non-management professionals" (Gee, Why Aren't Black Employees Getting More White-Collar Jobs? 2018). At first, I assumed he must have had all the right experience for the job since, like I said, others, including me, had surpassed him. It was disappointing but unsurprising that my new boss, like many white men, was hired in a job because whiteness *is* affirmative action.

I noticed that, soon after his arrival, he promoted the few white people in the organization to leadership positions. There was no evident company strategy to guide these staff movements. I thought it looked like white solidarity, but that's the thing about racism. In a professional environment, no one says to you, "Today, I will do some racist behavior to enhance white power and suffocate *black* growth." It's there, but you can't quite put your finger on it and worry that you may become too paranoid and alienate potential allies. For many, it's hard to put into words. It's sometimes blatant, like spitting on a classmate. Still, most often, racism is subtle, like not hiring anyone of color, never appointing a brown person to a board of directors, or relegating the brown staff to non-strategic duties like explaining why all the brown people sit together in the lunchroom (Keith and Livers 2002). I recall going to conferences with thousands of people. I would be the only brown man in the room. I had a female colleague who was often the only brown woman in the room. Yet, we had to function as professionals who had a right to be there despite the white gawk and remarks suggesting we were playing actors to them.

As part of my research, I decided to test the new manager. I applied for a position I knew I was more than qualified for. To reassure myself that I was not overconfident, I confirmed with the human resources manager and other brown managers before gauging whether they thought I was qualified. I applied and told the white boss I was entering the competition for the position.

After hearing nothing for a few weeks, I asked him again whether the interviews had started. He deflected from the question, saying he understood I had applied but that he knew nothing about my background.

This is the point at which a well-meaning boss would say, "I wish you all the best, I think you would be a good candidate." Alternatively, he could have said, "You may not be the best for that position," and then explained why. I had expected encouragement because that was what happened to me in the past in similar situations, albeit outside America.

I presumed he learned enough about me in one year to allow fair competition for the job. He had promoted five white colleagues in three months without competition, so why not me? We were connected on LinkedIn social media. He heard my work program, which I presented to the leadership team, my budget, and my organizational chart. He was inauthentic. He knew enough about me to judge whether I would be a candidate to compete with others. Again, the subtleties make it easy for someone who has experienced racism to understand, but it's not proof enough for someone else without that experience, especially someone white. A white person can always use their privilege of whiteness to deny racism (Borresen 2020).

My boss micro-assaulted me. I use "micro-assaulted" him because he did not physically punch me, fire me, or kick me down the stairs. He asked, "You have a degree or something, right?" His body language and tone did not hide that he did not care whether I had tertiary education. His ideological beliefs in race told him I would never be worthwhile for that job. Again, some white people would say, "He was just asking a simple question." I maintain that if the person is there present and functioning, you should assume they deserve and are qualified to be there unless proven otherwise. I told him, "I have a bachelor's degree in management and philosophy and a master's degree in economics." Despite starting post-graduate studies in international affairs, I never completed my Ph.D. because family life and their needs took over when I needed to complete my dissertation. Later that day, I sent him a copy of my resume. I got no response.

I later heard a rumor he was trying to hire, without an interview, a retired white guy who had worked for a major client of this company—an apparent conflict of interest. I was never interviewed for the position. I felt overlooked, despite working hard and achieving much for the company. His rejection took a toll on my well-being at first. But I fought the feeling of internalizing his rebuff. That sensation of loss of control can ruin your self-confidence.

In an earlier encounter, he told me in a meeting that he was convinced I was not doing any work and that all my achievements before his arrival were happenstance. He demanded copies of all my emails for the past twelve months to scrutinize them so he could prove his conviction. Undoubtedly, this behavior shocked me like a lightning bolt. At this point, it was not a micro-assault but a full-blown open declaration of war on my professionalism. He was shouting, being dismissive, and now verbally abusive. I realized that if I had grown up totally in America, where these confrontations occur daily—symbolically spat on and reminded of alleged worthlessness according to your teacher, preacher, bosses, and even family who internalize racism—I would believe it when the new white boss said my accomplishments were meaningless. To avoid getting incensed from such insolence, I reminded myself that my boss was only doing what he had been misguided to believe was his duty to keep the order of the society of whites at the top, earning more, achieving greatness, and brown at the bottom earning less and achieving very little of significance.

Nevertheless, I told him the error of his ways and explained that I understood why he was self-misguided because he was exhibiting his lack of understanding of my industry segment. I told him that if he was trying to establish a chain of events to terminate my employment for whatever he imagined his motives were, he should bypass all the shenanigans and tell me he did not want me working in the company. I told him that other colleagues and I were well aware of my accomplishments and contributions to the organization. He, too, was not unaware, as I had briefed him many times. Therefore, his ambush on my effectiveness must be for another reason. Besides, his accusations of me not accomplishing past work before his arrival were an affront to the entire organization since the company worked as a team to realize its objectives and me. He did not speak to me directly for three months after that conversation.

Consequently, I had already established that my second application when he re-advertised the position was going to trigger some noteworthy behaviors—unlikely to lead to success. I prepared for the potential interview, even more, the second time around. I quizzed all the managers who would have immediately reported to me. I learned about their workplace tribulations and pledged that if I got the promotion, I would work with them to make their workplace more productive and functional. I believe they genuinely hoped I would become their boss. For whatever it's worth, they all wished me success—the white and brown managers.

I wanted to see how far he would take his behavior and whether he would again exclude me from an interview. In a website called Psychology Today, they described the practice of excluding minority groups from promotions and pay increases as "out grouping." It's manifested in subtle ways, like exactly what my white boss was doing—promoting the white professionals with pay increases, expanding new leadership positions and filling them with white workers while overlooking the brown professionals, and even verbally assaulting them (Bailey 2020).

Fortunately, it was a blessing in disguise because working as his immediate subordinate would have been tormenting. His incompetence, layered with his caustic behavior, convinced me that I needed to leave the organization. I would do so in my own time rather than be pushed out. He never filled the position and left the company before I did. However, before he left, he gave a third-order job to a brown lady, not because she was the most qualified or capable, but because she was the most connected with his boss. I wondered if she would have a nervous breakdown reporting to him as she yelled expletives in a staff meeting one day after her appointment. The pressure she was under did not seem parallel to that of the other white bosses.

He did not exclude me the second time in the interview. He used forty-five minutes of the one-hour interview to badger me on questions he did not expect me to answer. He asked questions unrelated to the position. Before I could respond, he would conclude that I did not know the answer and try to move on to the next one. Routinely, there were written questions, approved by the human resources department, related to the position in which all candidates were asked to demonstrate objectivity. He never consulted the written questions. I believed he was trying to humiliate me for rebutting his earlier attacks. Appallingly, he jumped up and down in his chair with excitement when he thought I would not answer and held his head in annoyance when I did.

Notwithstanding, when I answered, in between his interruptions, I did so calmly. I noticed he wrote notes whenever I replied with new ideas he thought the company use. Needless to say, the interview was horrendously adversarial. The other two panelists, representing the department for the position and human resources, used their scripted questions and remained professional throughout the carnage.

Afterward, I evaluated the interview with one of his deputies. The deputy confirmed he was impressed that I answered the questions adequately and, more outstandingly, remained dignified and calm during the spectacle of intolerance. The deputy was confident that giving me the job would have been wise under normal circumstances. He then said that as long as the white boss remained in charge of the company, I had reached my glass ceiling at my present position.

The human resources department required internal staff to explain why they were unsuccessful in their applications to improve for the next round. The white boss told me I did not have enough experience. The fact is, I had more experience in the field than he did at the time. He did not even try to be credible and laughed when I suggested he could mentor me to prepare for the job. He suggested I could get the job if I applied for it again in about seven to eight years. The other two panelists kept quiet. They were brown people. It reminded me of the torture an enslaved person would get on a plantation while others just looked on and remained silent, or worse, carried on working as if nothing was happening, in fear of the white perpetrator.

Perhaps his behavior was just him being unprofessional. Even as a child, his community taught him to act the way he did. Colleagues told me he disliked intelligent brown people. Like the white children spitting on brown children in kindergarten under the passive consent of their teachers, he has always been allowed to treat people he felt threatened by, as unworthy of anything positive. Even without intent, this behavior of treating people as unfit is based on a belief supported by fairytales passed on from one generation to the next. For example, brown people deal with myths of being more biologically predisposed to liking chicken wings and watermelons than white people. I learned this fable when I moved to Southeast America.

Some believe that educated white people are rational and not prone to such conduct. However, while in college, my daughter explained that her white American colleagues could not believe she did not like watermelons. Since she defied their expectations, they insisted she must have been faking to appear upper class. Education, as it stands currently, cannot enlighten sufficiently to eradicate racial viewpoints. I explain my views on how education needs to be modified to be more useful against racism in Chapter 8. "If we assume racism can be remedied through education, then we are assuming a privileged status for those who are educated as if those with education are more virtuous or have a greater capacity to be good" (Helsel 2018).

Even when the boss was brown, there is fear of being seen as offensive to white subordinates (Time 2001). One of my former bosses, a very competent brown woman, had to fire a white colleague for openly disobeying her instructions, putting the company in danger, and regularly undermining her authority. He was capable but could not bring himself to be subordinate to a brown woman. The next white staff she had, also a white man, had no problems with her authority but proved to be woefully incompetent. She hesitated to terminate him for fear of being branded as a "racist" by white people who like to turn guilt around—what they call 'reverse racism.' She worried about retribution from her white superiors.

Brown people also internalize some of the myths. The brown colleague who told me I behaved like a white man was perceiving an incongruency in her mind. It was her version—code switch—of saying I was "articulate" or an "uppity nigga." In other words, I did not know my place in society. To be fair to her, I don't think she meant any harm. Her comment came from the socialized lens of racism she was raised to see everything in life through. What's worse, it never occurred to her she was paddling in the same bigotry ocean she experienced as a woman. She mentioned that in school white teachers said she was violent and aggressive. Like her, white teachers and professors told my daughter she was sassy, meaning feisty, while her white classmates were "lovely young ladies."

All these are codes for intelligent brown girls acting outside their place in society. Initially, my daughter internalized these micro-aggressions as if they were corrupt traits caused by her high self-esteem. She was not immediately sure what sassy meant in this case, but the message was that one should not be *sassy*. The white girls were not described as "sassy." These micro-aggressions are code language for "you did not seem to behave as I [the white person] expected." Brown people know when we hear these coded phrases (Griffin 2015).

Even non-racist white people have the advantage of always being seen in a light that is much more positive than any brown person. The demeaning myths do not apply to them. That positivity translates into the best jobs, investment opportunities, promotions, raises, and selection for positions of political and economic power—the highest levels of trust that never question their professionalism and typically ignore their incompetence. The result is economic racism, the impact of which robs future income and prosperity from generations of brown families.

One of the key elements that create the chasm between brown and white people is trust. Trust is the "assured reliance on the character, ability, strength, or truth of someone or something" (Merriam-Webster n.d.). It's the confidence, calm and peaceful comfort one places on another person or group of people heavily influenced by past behaviors, opinions, and family upbringing. When trust is absent, it is often replaced by fear which is a strong element of distrust.

Fear stimulates anxiety, stress, and perceptions of uncontrollable or dangerous outcomes that affect one's life. The mistrust and fear complex goes deep into the psyche of brown and white people. In general, the mistrust of brown people is because of the vestiges of enslavement, racial apartheid, and present-day racial discrimination. These manifest in all the elements I have been talking about—bigotry in the workplace, education, housing, politics, and anything that drives economics. The mistrust of brown people among white people comes from their beliefs, guided by mythologies that serve to re-enforce these beliefs. These beliefs are manifested in engagement and minor behaviors of power play of whites over browns in the workplace (Wingfield 2015).

Take the topic of eye contact. At a physical level, especially in Western countries, looking at the eyes is a great way to know whether you are in the company of trustworthy people. It is often said, "the eyes are the windows to the soul." Psychologists have noted that the eyes reveal many truths about what we think of a particular situation (Ludden 2015). A colleague told me how her tall, strong brown uncle from South Carolina always bowed his head in docile humbleness when talking to a white person. He was a different person at home with his family—bubbly, with laughter and self-confidence. As a kid from New Jersey visiting her extended family in the south in the 1970s, she could not understand why he pretended to be submissive while in the presence of white people. The Southern states still had remnant behavior of enslavement or the Jim Crow era. Instinctively, her uncle knew that when he was in the presence of people who are known to commit violent public acts of torture and murder of brown people, often supported or tolerated by the local state and federal governments, his only defense was to be as unthreatening as he could be with submissiveness.

Strangely, in the Caribbean, in the old days, looking into your parents' or anyone of authority's eyes while talking to them, especially if arguing, was considered a sign of defiance and disrespect. Deviant kids learned that looking into their parents' eyes during a reprimand, even without saying a word, could make them angry and fearful of your intentions. It's the same with authoritative white figures, whether they were a plantation owner in the 18th century, a police officer in the 1960s, a white teacher in 1970, or your white boss today. Looking into their eyes causes them to be guilt-ridden (Hongbo Yu 2017).

That discomfort is felt when we confront our moral behavior towards someone else. We can also transfer guilt to others to satisfy ourselves, thus taking away our guilt, albeit under some false pretext. White people taught to be racist will defend themselves from the guilt of their violent behavior used to protect white supremacy and do their best to transfer it to the people under their subjugation. Deflecting culpability, no matter how transparent the violence, is a strategy we, as humans, even as children, are adept at to avoid vulnerability. Vulnerability opens us up to being accused. It stamps guilt for violent and inhumane behavior and depicts untrustworthiness, making a human feel rejected and unlovable (Seltzer 2013). No wonder saviorism and guilt deflecting are used to mask these vulnerabilities.

In America, the many white bosses at the top of the corporate world, some seventy-five percent of them, according to various studies, like my boss, are taught racist behavior by their teachers—the society and media in general—just like my colleague's classmate (Gino 2017).

That makes it a Sisyphean task to experience real career progression. It's simple things too. For example, I was invited to a meeting with the same white boss and his deputy. The meeting was requested within an hour without a topic or agenda forwarded in the calendar invite before that hour. My boss was white, and his deputy, in this case, was brown. The deputy was known to be submissive, like my colleague's uncle, and non-committal because his boss regularly overruled him. He had fitted the definition of a token brown hire to keep the brown staff in check. Despite him being far more intelligent and more capable than his boss, he knew, both from his boss's behavior of casting aside any important insights he had, that he was just symbolic of giving the impression of a place where browns can prosper in leadership too. When the white boss refused to speak to me for three months after I confronted his behavior, this brown deputy was used as the proxy for subjugation.

Since I was not told what the mysterious meeting was about, I assumed it was on the last topic I was working on and brought my notes and presentations related to that subject. In essence, I had no time to prepare. When someone in a professional organization invites you to a meeting without an agenda, topic, or any forewarning of what the meeting will be about, be prepared for it to either be a meeting totally about them bolstering their ego or, worse and more likely, an ambush on you.

As I sat down, he slammed a stack of papers on the conference table and started a tirade of accusations about business travel I had gone on a few months before. I had not received my reimbursement, so I was not in the mood for his racial spectacle. It amounted to thousands of dollars, which was on a personal credit card since we were not allowed to have a company card—only he was, another form of suppression where brown people are expected to be super-efficient without the tools for their work. I was astonished by the realization that this was not a professional meeting to discuss my projects but rather an interrogation as if I was an accused criminal and he was the police interrogator. He was trying to get me to incriminate myself in a crime that was not real, to tarnish my reputation and discredit my professionalism. It was an exercise of guilt switch to protect his culpability for his actions. His deputy was there as the poppet witness. The result he was aiming for was an ethics violation, where, if proven true, would have consequences ranging from spreading staff rumors of my alleged impropriety to termination with the requisite reputational ruin recorded permanently in the press and among industry colleagues, analogous to a good old-fashion street drag of a brown body tied on a rope behind a horse or truck for all to see the punishment for being a defiant brown person (Parker 2019).

I opted to defend myself because I was unwilling to walk into his gallows to help him feel less vulnerable in his guilt. I answered badgering interrogation-style questions, him standing and pacing at the head of the table and me at the other end with the deputy sitting at the side. His tone was accusatory. I responded to questions about why I took a particular route of travel versus another, why I stayed in one hotel versus another, and why I stayed the days, I did rather than another timeframe he thought I should have stayed. I answered all the questions, each time pushing through his interruptions and attempts at intimidation and yelling. I remained calm because I understood this was an attempted economic lynching.

Since he had no evidence, he needed my help to implicate me to deflect from his conduct. The stack of paper was evidence to the contrary of his accusations. However, he used it as a theatrical prop to prove his version of the story, never referring to the stack. He repeated the line of questions, changing words at least six times. Throughout the questioning, he kept picking up and slamming the stack of paper in front of him to indicate that he already had irrefutable evidence that I had committed wrongdoing dramatically. He reminded me he was the financial steward and the organization's boss. I reminded him that he was also the steward of the staff who made up the organization, and he had a duty to serve them without harm. I did not know there was a stage above going nuclear.

I watched his performance as if watching a scene from a violent movie. The brown deputy simply bowed his head and kept quiet. He would not go to the gallows with me if he could help. I nudged the deputy with a question to see if it would help him speak up in my defense. I implored him to certify what I was saying as a matter of appropriate and customary procedures for the company. The deputy mumbled something inaudible under his breath, not too strong to get him in trouble. I realized I was on my own.

When the white boss started his seventh go-round of the same questions in his attempt to get me to incriminate myself, I told him bluntly, "I have answered the same question repeatedly now, at least six times. Since I was clear, you now grasp the process, I believe you comprehend my explanation satisfactorily. Since that is true, and you persist with the line of questions, this meeting is about something else you are not revealing, and we need to spotlight this now. Are you accusing me of stealing money from my job through travel?" At this point, he paused and became visibly uncomfortable, becoming less animated.

I continued, "Since we have determined that I have not stolen any money from my workplace, then what is this meeting really about?" He got angry, stood abruptly, and headed for the door. I said to him, "Why are you leaving your meeting? I am merely trying to help you figure out what you are after here, so please stay and let's talk this through." I reminded him that I had not received my reimbursement for several months and that such a malfunctioning system is one he should have worked on fixing rather than have accusatory meetings with his professional staff. When I pointed out how previous organizations I had worked for had more efficient systems and offered my expertise if he needed help on improving it—noting I had already made recommendations to the finance staff of software used by others to help them work better—he shouted at me, "You are being condescending." I should point out that he blocked my reimbursement and another colleague who had traveled with me.

"Furthermore, you called me to the conference room with no prior information on what the meeting was about, accused me of stealing without evidence, except my back-to-office-report with the attachments from the travel officer in finance, which you purport to be a confirmation of the guilt you imagined for me. You have not shared that same evidence with me or any heads-up on whether you thought anything in my travels was questionable prior to this encounter." I asked him to consider that in my career, I have been traveling for over twenty years for work and with no accusation from anyone, least of all the head of the organization about financial impropriety. "Why do you think this is happening now?" His deputy looked at me with golf ball eyes in disbelief. I told him he needed to fix the broken travel system in the company, so it was more efficient. I also requested he provided whatever evidence he was using to accuse me so I too could have a copy for my records. Finally, I expressed I would appreciate a topic and agenda plus reasonable time before any meeting he called in the future as a matter of courtesy so I too can prepare and be able to contribute effectively.

I stood my ground because my integrity was more important than the job. An ambush meeting of any kind is designed to discredit or belittle the professionalism of the invitees. That's because you have no time to prepare or even gather your thoughts when you have no idea what the meeting topic is about. If he wanted to disgrace me for being a brown professional in defiance of his race beliefs, I wanted him to face that demon that befalls him head-on. I wanted him to say that he was making false accusations because his upbringing told him I was inferior, and for some reason, I was not acting the part. I was neither humble nor docile. He would have to publicly drag me to the gallows, accepting his culpability along the way.

I should point out another dynamic for brown people in workplace hostility. I mentioned the brown deputy manager who felt the need to stay quiet and play the role of poppet less he gets lynched himself. I also mentioned my other brown colleagues who would privately support me regardless of whether or not they would later stab me behind my back. There is another behavior exhibited by brown people in such a hostile environment. The before-mentioned travel officer in the finance department was a brown woman with a poor customer service attitude. She would do whatever she could to hold up our travel reimbursements, despite numerous complaints to her bosses about her performance and behavior. The problem was that the white boss of the company would have one-on-one meetings with her, bypassing three levels of subordination. In these meetings, he empowered her to report everything related to travel—thus the pile of paper on his desk during our ambush meeting—on people he had targeted. The boss used her. Yet, she never realized it. Maybe it was ignorance of her and racial America's history. I think she was aiming for white acceptance. Part of her interpreted the attentiveness from the white boss as special treatment to her. The other part, which I believe matters more, is that she wanted to gain favor with the boss by doing his bidding, even when it was against innocent people. However, with all the complaints from other staff about her attitude bolstered by her empowerment, they later fired her.

In the case of the travel officer, her quest for white acceptance was opportunistic. A passive approach towards seeking white approval is when a non-white person straightens their hair or dyes it blond or any other non-black color, whitens their skin, rejects their cultural foods around white people, and even code switch their dress, language, and antics to make white people feel less threatened around them and therefore be less hostile to them. Sometimes, white acceptance occurs just out of trepidation from being attacked by white people (A. Gray 2019).

A friend of mine, a Muslim lady, wore a hijab to work just as Americans wear modest clothes to church, a crucifix, or any clothes they feel like. One day a few months after September 11, 2001, attacks by foreign terrorists on the World Trade Center in New York, a white male confronted her, expressing his view that she was being disrespectful by wearing a "headscarf" in public.

Like many privileged white people, the man associated her unfamiliar clothing with a political statement of defiance. We have already understood that non-white defiance against white culture is always considered a threat and attacked with some form of violence. Meanwhile, white defiance is praised as fighting for inalienable Rights provided by men or sometimes even God.

He told her to take it off, and when she tried to back away from her assailant, he grabbed her and ripped the hijab from her head along with some locks of hair in the grasp. Her colleagues watched. Only when he threw the woman on the floor and stood over her attempting to throttle her, did the colleagues intervene. She was so traumatized by the encounter that she never wore a hijab again. For white acceptance and her family's safety, she begged her daughters not to wear the hijab for fear of being attacked by xenophobic Americans. "Hijab" means "curtain" or "partition," not "headscarf." That man violated her First Amendment Right to exercise any religion she chooses (Ahmed and Quraishi-Landes 2019).

Furthermore, the hijab is an Islamic concept of modesty and privacy. The idea is similar in Judaism and Christianity. For example, monks and friars wear a hood, and Christian nuns a veil (National Geographic n.d.).

I relayed the entire incident of the workplace interrogation to my mentor. He concluded that my boss felt he had to prove to himself and the world around him that I could not be the intelligent, well-spoken, educated, globally minded, and honest black man I appeared to be. There had to be a fault in the bedrock of my character. If he could not find one, he would invent lies of a fracture in my integrity to allow him to lynch me economically. By now, I had experienced several encounters with this boss where I'd felt like I had to armor my emotions to deal with every character assassination attempt. He commented on my dress code and expressed aloud he had not seen me wear a particular jacket. He said once, "I want to talk like you," which suggested he wanted to speak *for* me in my place to showcase his proficiency. He censored my webinars and speaking engagements at conferences where I was called upon as an expert. He stopped all training of all brown staff. It was exhausting to be distrusted and attacked by him. I worried about burnout. I wanted to do my work and enjoy the accomplishments of my labor without having to combat an enemy in a conflict. I was concerned about racial battle fatigue, which can lead to physical and mental health degradation if left unchecked (Goodwin 2018).

The encounters in the workplace seemed never-ending and popped up sometimes unexpectedly. My work projects were belittled, unsupported, and often blocked. There was never praise or a show of nonverbal support for any successes. Other brown colleagues who got recognition from outside the organization for their work in the presence of the boss would worry because they realized he did not like the commendations they received. They were concerned he would take punitive action against them in something unrelated, like when it was time for a raise. When I received an accolade from others for a successful project, he reservedly said, "great news."

While I remained cool at later aggressions, I did not always remain as calm. When my white boss first tried to belittle any successes before he arrived at the company, I stood up and told him he was wrong. To be honest, I was then so racially naïve that I thought most of his behavior was just him being a jerk. At first, his seeming ignorance made me furious because I could not understand why he behaved this way. My encounters with other white bosses and colleagues at the professional levels had always been primarily congenial and respectful such that many remained friends years later.

Other colleagues, friends, and family also shared their encounters with white, predominantly male bosses. Talking about it, at first, it seemed like we were mostly having a pity party, but I learned that it helps to rationalize with someone the hurt and attacks, if for no other reason—as statecrafts for the next battle. I was able to compare racially motivating experiences from white workmates and both give and receive encouragement to others feeling abused. Racism is emotionally draining, especially when your livelihood and career may be in jeopardy. Plus, in searching for solidarity and support, there is always the risk that the person you confide in may use what you say to report back to the offending boss in the hope of getting some favor—brown betrayal for white acceptance. That could lead to even more attacks. I did not want to be a staff focused on race and a poor-performing boss.

Part of sharing suspected or known racial encounters is to fortify yourself and fight the attacks. Ideally, the matter should be taken to the local Equal Employment Opportunity Commission (EEOC) court. The EEOC is a federal institution mandated by the U.S. Congress to enforce laws prohibiting workplace discrimination under Title VII of the Civil Rights and Age Discrimination in Employment Act. If the EEOC were a student, its grade of success would be a drop-out-of-school failing 3.2 percent. That's how many of the 1.9 million cases filed by discrimination victims over a twenty-one-year period were considered worthwhile for filing a lawsuit. Such a failing student's parents would have felt obliged to intervene to help their child. There are many reasons why the EEOC has been seen to protect discriminatory employers rather than its intended market (Barnes 2019).

The entire process of using anti-discrimination laws and institutions like the EEOC to seek remedy is designed in a racially discriminatory way. When I was denied the job I had applied for, I wondered what recourse I had. I read my human resources material about reporting a case. I realized I would have to expose myself to a department that saw its role as protector of the people with power, and the company from litigation, over the interests of employees. Remember basic economics—we were just replaceable labor supply. Taking the case to an EEOC office also meant uncovering my actions against the same white boss, which would lead to even more retribution. I would need to gather evidence—recordings that the racial boss consented to where he may have outwardly said something racist or written a racist letter. Staff would have to risk economic lynching themselves to testify about his tomfooleries. As the brown deputy boss proved, help from the team, even those under the racial whip, was not likely to happen. There is no physical evidence of micro-aggressions or the fact that I did not get the position—anything that would hold up in court.

I spoke to one of my mentors who felt I needed to talk to a lawyer, if for no other reason than to learn what I needed to do to prepare myself for a future case. I met with a white male lawyer recommended as a successful wrongful dismissal attorney. He listened attentively, was friendly, and asked a few questions about whether anyone heard him say the word "nigga," or if he openly said he hated *black* people or fired many *black* staff and hired white people to replace them. During his probing, it dawned on me that not only were the anti-discrimination laws woefully inadequate, but the total equity and anti-discrimination systems also were not functional. He informed me of the mammoth task I would have if I pursued a case. I would be "swimming upstream," he said, because in the society he lived in, racism was the accepted flow of the river. His albeit excellent rejection triggered even more trauma because he told me that the justice system not only permitted but enhanced racism and victimization.

There were a few other practical things that occurred to me. I went to a lawyer because I did not trust the company's human resources department, nor did I want to jeopardize my job since it was my only source of income. I was being underpaid, given my qualifications and experience, and racially victimized. However, I still needed to be able to financially care for myself, even at a level below what I deserved. This white lawyer costs $300 an hour. I made about $42 an hour from my corporate suit-wearing job. With my low salary at about ten percent of what my white equivalent in qualifications would earn, it's tough to afford to pay a lawyer of any integrity who would be willing to listen in a consultation. I would have to borrow the money on a credit card or forego some other need, like feeding my family, all in search of justice and fairness. It's also challenging to find a lawyer sufficiently independent to care and who is unconnected with the adversary. No good lawyer would work for you for free on a case they would unlikely win. A lawyer you can't pay won't fight for you.

Meanwhile, your white adversary has a bottomless pit of legal money as the custodian of the company with access to the company's coffers. Additionally, even if he was sued privately, he could afford to buy the service of more fervent and dedicated white-confident lawyers with his comparatively higher salary. He could defend himself while dragging me figuratively through the streets, disgraced and likely unemployed for daring to suggest that he was racist. It could become a public humiliation for the sport of white people—dealing a death knell to a brown person's career and life.

I saw my former colleagues, who used to rally with me when I shared my experiences of racial discrimination, shrink away, and stop associating with me after I confronted the boss about his behavior. They, too, were afraid for their jobs and livelihood. I can't blame them. Systemic racialization produces not only racial ideologies and inequities but also people, institutions, and laws that fail to address the real issues out of fear of revenge and a lack of humanity by lawmakers. If you are not secure and do not have a sound support system in your friends and family, you accept the micro-attacks as justified and lose self-esteem, which further impedes your future work and mental health.

On another occasion, sharing my workplace woes with another brown professional, he advised me to seek a lawyer, but a brown female one this time. I thought this should be more promising than the white male lawyer because she suffered from intersectional discrimination. I learned that she was in the corporate world and faced unfair pay, racial comments, being passed over for promotions, racial incidents like white colleagues touching her hair and skin without permission, and outright retaliation against her professionalism that was so bad that she left to establish her law firm.

My lady lawyer charged me $250 an hour for the consultation. I paid her more than my white male lawyer because she spent more time with me, listening to my attempt to turn racial dust into gold. I told her about my unfair treatment, the micro-aggression, and watching white colleagues receive automatic promotions in the company while I, despite my efforts, stood still like Fred Flintstone trying to move a car carved out of rocks with his legs.

I wondered irrationally if she had colluded with my white male lawyer. She concluded that the trouble I would have, the likelihood that I would be "*black*listed"—they should call it more accurately "*white*listed"—the effort that would be involved in gathering evidence, while the white boss would be on his guard, while working 300 percent more effort than before to keep him from firing me for some real or imagined infraction, would have destroyed my life and career. While working more, I would suffer even more onslaughts as he tried to get me to leave without gathering attention to his racism. I would have had to prepare for a case with a collection of my files, writing a daily journal, collecting any physical evidence of racial abuse such as messages and pictures, the contact information of witnesses, and statements of those willing to jeopardize their life for a racial justice they rarely see in society, company policies, and my health records to show how my health deteriorated. I wondered whether the stress was worth any money I was never guaranteed to receive. Even if I surpassed all odds and won a lawsuit, it was unlikely to be an amount for lifetime support, so I would still have to work after. Who would hire me upon hearing I have a reputation for exposing organizational racism? Plus, a gag order or a non-disclosure agreement, typical of these settlements, would prohibit me from warning other employees (Safdar 2020).

The workplace discrimination caused me mental anguish and emotional distress. I suffered many symptoms—exhibited by a feeling of humiliation even though I was not in the wrong, experienced insomnia, and chipped a tooth one night from teeth-grinding doctors accredited to stress. I had feelings of dark depression, anxiety, and high blood pressure from waves of anger—resulting from the trauma. Others in a similar situation have become self-destructive and negatively impacted their families (Peeler 2019).

The lawyer said I could only sue if there were physical harm from the abuse. I pointed to my lost income and welfare to my family and community for not being hired for a job I was qualified for, a misallocation of a valuable resource. Then I found myself thinking that in an American community, my push that I am a "valuable resource" and a brown man must sound arrogant. I was a factor of production—labor. I was again attempting to swim upstream in the river of racism.

What if I sunk my small savings and income into the lawyer's contingency fee, accepted losing the trust of colleagues, be ridiculed by many who would likely have suggested I should have let it go because "it is what it is?" Even with all the stress, let's say I take it to its conclusion, and by some miracle, I was to have won an impossible discrimination case. Like Sauntore Thomas, a brown Detroit Air Force veteran in 2020, I may have to sue the bank for refusing to cash or deposit my check from my court winnings—repeating the whole trauma (J. R. Miller 2020). In the veteran's case, the bank's staff called the police when he tried to cash his settlement check from former employees for racial discrimination. Despite calls from the bank by the man to his employment law attorney to help him explain to bank employees that the check was authentic, the police conducted a fraud investigation.

My colleagues' opinion about my white boss summed it up like this: I made a grave mistake as a brown man by refusing to accept my place in society. I was expected to pretend I was unaware of his racial behavior and act docile. He expected, like many other brown men he had confronted before, that his white privilege would protect him from any consequence.

The white bosses—remember the original white boss kept hiring only white men to be his deputies—accepted that I was knowledgeable in my work, but while they wanted output, they also wanted me to accept the status quo they created for me. In their minds, my job was to feed them ideas they pretended were theirs and sit in the shadows without expecting progress or recognition.

One white manager said, "You are overqualified for this job, so why do you stay here?" I wondered if I was white, would the question be, "How can I help you to move up to a level to match your skills?" That would have been the proper non-racist approach. The anti-racist would have gone further: "You are super-qualified and have achieved many successes that were not recognized because we live in a white supremacist nation. However, I will not tolerate restricting the company's success because of a fabricated ideology. I will make sure in a short time that you are in a position where you can make the best contribution to the growth of this company and be fairly rewarded for it." Then he would follow up for me and all who deserve it.

In all the bouts of abuse, I stood my ground, professionally and respectfully, and made it clear I expected the same from the white boss. I also wrote down everything that happened to him, even the most mundane affairs. I hoped he would be more professional, even out of fear of me bringing a lawsuit. Partly, that was wishful thinking because I also believed his privilege did not allow him to care.

This experience of disrespect and bigotry is far different from what I have come to expect of people growing up in the Caribbean. I also noticed that whether I visited Asia, Africa, South America, or even Europe, I got the same treatment as an ordinary person. The peoples I engage with in these regions are usually confident, caring, and knowledgeable about the world, with few insecurities about their sense of personal value. When I spoke of my struggles with American racism with my old classmates and family, they reminded me that I am of proud and fierce origins. Despite having to sell wood coal for cooking and barbeque, and potted plants to help pay my school fees and buy textbooks when I was a youth in school, I remained proud of whom I had become and my heritage. The love and adoration of people from my part of the world reminded me that I should not let an insecure person with white supremacist ideas or behaviors dominate my destiny.

My mother always told me to "be the best you can be at whatever you do." I found my cousin repeating this to me one day when I was relaying my boss' assaults. She said, "Even if you are a sanitation worker, be the best 'chief waste disposal officer' you can be and change the world with your efforts." I became a specialist in my field through dedication to being the best in a complex area—economics. I had a successful career and continued to be promoted until I ventured into corporate America, where my real racial journey began.

One morning, while I was having a work-related conversation with a colleague, the same white boss strolled into my office and proceeded to expound on his disappointment about us—the city we then called home— not celebrating one of his favorite holidays, Columbus Day. His community has commemorated this federal holiday where he grew up since 1937 (History.com 2020). Street parades and a holiday in Columbus' honor for his "discovery" of the New World were the features of that day. He raved about how Columbus was a great Italian hero since they did not have much to be proud of with the likes of Mussolini. Benito Mussolini was an Italian Prime Minister from 1922 to 1943 and is infamous for being Europe's first 20th Century fascist dictator (Foot and Hibbert 2020).

I marveled at the historical and cultural insensitivity of my white boss. Since 1991, many states have abandoned the notion of Columbus as a hero and replaced that day with Indigenous Peoples Day. The implications of Columbus' arrival in the Americas were well known. He enslaved native people who at first welcomed him to their land. He inadvertently brought diseases and plundered their society (A. Lee 2020). Celebrating Columbus Day with the accompanying memorials and symbols decontaminates the results of his arrival. It was asinine that he could "discover" a place inhabited by people for some 20,000 years since the Ice Age connected Asia to North America (History.com 2018). Imagine if the Chinese, Indians, or Africans invaded England today and claimed that they had discovered new land and started staking their flags everywhere while subjugating the British people, murdering those who chose to oppose this "discovery."

I said to my boss regarding his gleeful statement, "That's great for you, but what about the annihilation of an entire civilization of Native Americans that soon followed that arrival? Furthermore, what about the African people who were abducted from their homeland and brought to a strange place to be enslaved? Do these genocides inspire the celebration of your hero?"

These are part of the history of this nation. It's a past we all pretend never happened or does not matter. I told my boss, "Slavery transpired for profit, and the remnants of it still impact all of us today." He laughed it off and said they still celebrated Christopher Columbus Day, and he loved it. Then he said, "It was not so good for you guys—huh!" His cultural ineptitude outraged my colleague. I was disheartened but not furious by his response because I thought he was genuine. He was grateful for what life had given him—white supremacy—a caste system where he was automatically on the uppermost status because of the skin he was born in. Columbus opened the door to discrimination for profit and control, which continues to this day. Consequently, white people like my boss are now at the top of this food chain, and he was, understandably, delighted about it. We were powerless to go beyond being disenchanted by his comments–a result of that privilege.

I conveyed to my colleague that his pedestal may have come from a history of ancestral suffering. I reminded her that for the early settlers and immigrants, America was a means to re-create themselves, change their names, and shed the ancient, impecunious ways—of a Europe that often sent them to America as a prison sentence. Upon arrival, many were treated as lower-class people. Rich people of Europe in the 16th century saw America "as a giant workhouse where the "fry [young children] of wandering beggars that grow up idly and hurtfully and burdenous to the Realm, might be unladen and better bred up" (Alec MacGillis 2016). These people did not fit into the country's image of egalitarianism and inclusivism.

Furthermore, America has always had a tradition of ill-treating the most recent immigrant group, with brown people always at the bottom, sometimes just above Native Americans. Between 1890 and 1920, about fifty Italians were lynched for various crimes, including allegedly murdering a police officer and a disagreement over a goat (Woolf 2015). With an ancestry of people that suffered, even after the arrival of Columbus, my boss and people like him got the chance to have privileges unrecognized by brown people.

As I worked more and more to be recognized and rewarded fairly for my expertise and output in a blatantly biased workplace environment, I often thought of the myths that my boss held on to support his beliefs in this fabricated conviction of race and the negative economic impact it had on people like me. His combined presence, authority, and philosophies depressed my present and future net wealth. My entrepreneurship, education, ideas, and inventiveness were subdued since he would never tolerate me leading or even allow me to prosper from my expertise.

I had to spend more of my expenditures hedging on credit. This included expenses for work-related travel since, as seen earlier, he would delay reimbursements to other brown staff and me for months. Since we were forced to use our credit cards for upfront business expenses and seek reimbursement later, our credit usage ratio was high, which reduced our credit rating. Whenever I sought a loan to purchase a car or mortgage, I ended up paying what amounts to a racial tax. I attracted a higher payback interest rate due to my use of credit cards for work and the typical *black*-risk interest rate people get charged (K. J. Brooks 2019).

I remember innocently and angrily telling my boss, "We seem to have an issue of trust." I had naively stumbled upon it without even understanding its full implications. I shared my experience with other brown colleagues—those I trusted—to hear their stories of struggles against racism. I also shared the impact of delayed travel reimbursements on my credit status with the white deputies. Face-to-face, they patronized me with superficial sympathy. They already got promotions with salary raises within a short time of this boss's arrival. Their only deserving quality that one could observe at such short notice was their shared pigmentation level. He transferred white privilege to them through higher net wealth opportunities and societal power, including giving them their work-related travel reimbursements immediately upon return to the office.

The white boss questioned the work and blocked anyone he did not trust, which after a few months, appeared to be most of the brown staff in the company. The result was that he second-guessed the whole management level in spaces he had no expertise. I proposed many new projects and solutions to problems. I offered my experience in economics, especially given that I had over twenty-plus years of working on issues related to the company. He always rejected my input. He never sat through an entire meeting I led—and if he had to, he never bothered to listen as he scrolled through his mobile phone. It became customary for him to exit within ten minutes of my presentations, leaving the remaining staff to flounder decision-less, a tactic to ensure none of my recommendations got implemented.

He also had an inordinate amount of time to micromanage. His incompetence made the work of professionals much harder. The organization became paralyzed at the management level, unable to be conclusive in a way that moved the company forward. The white boss offered no vision, mission, a clear objective, staff motivation, or problem-solving skills.

The organization ceased preparing for significant transformation, regardless of how its environment changed. While he micromanaged, the other white staff enjoyed their newfound privileges—despite their side denunciations of the boss's lack of proficiency—and the brown team was frustrated with little or no promotions, raises, or allowance to feel pleasure from work accomplishments.

In some ways, the assault of the white boss against the professional credibility and wealth gains of his brown staff was akin to lynching—only in an economic and emotional sense, more so than the violent form that befell America following enslavement. When white Americans are violent, the calmer and more rational people like to say, "this is not who we are" (Dowling 2015). Yet America has a legacy of violence arced with the enslavement of millions of brown people, decades of terrorism, and racial intimidation brutally expressed through lynching. The birth of the civil rights movement during the 1950s and 1960s was a reaction to the continued physical attacks and violence on America's social and economic structure. South African post-apartheid truth and reconciliation commission at least attempted to harmonize society. Conversely, no such genuine attempt at harmony ever transpired in the USA.

Consequently, this legacy of racial inequality has persisted, leaving brown people vulnerable to a range of problems that continue to reveal racial disparities and injustice. In the workplace, racism manifests in a hostile working environment, often resulting in the victims losing their jobs at the hands of their assailants. The custom of people in power is to victim-blame the frustrated brown person, especially if they challenge racist behaviors. The blatant racists are bad for society. But the white bosses in suits at the office, in the boardrooms, or heading white and blue-collar jobs are just as dangerous as they deny the future of many brown people (Taiwo 2020).

White supremacy in the workplace is a microcosm of wealth and power accumulation within the capitalist system. Violence is applied to preserve power and wealth, and future rewards are reaped from that violence. My white boss was perpetuating his unspoken role within a structure where he and people like him, first white males, then white females, all reap the benefits of subjugating working-class brown people. Mine and other educated and articulate brown people threaten the circular logic in the saviorism of white supremacy—a philosophy that tells them they are the heroes to save the world and all darker-skinned peoples from the suffering caused by white people's violent domination.

It's well known that when brown dispossessions become trending in the popular media, maybe due to a newly exposed murder of a brown man, woman, or child, the corporate world would use the opportunity to market how much they are in solidarity with anti-racists. In 2020, after the video of the murder by police of an unarmed brown man, George Floyd, flooded social media and sparked global protests against racial discrimination, companies bought billboards showcasing how much they cared for brown people. Commercials in print and electronic media suddenly had brown people highlighted in stark contrast to three months before, when they were primarily white.

However, while these companies gave the outward image of being anti-racist, their staff suffered discrimination, just like my lawyer. These companies' public relations departments are concerned with their company's brand to maximize sales and protect their public reputation. They want to earn money from all customers regardless of race and gender. However, internally, they cared little about race or gender as they victimized their brown employees. Typically, the cycle is when they are exposed for internal racism, a leader may resign or be fired, a statement is made about racial sensitivity training, and once the dust settles, the company returns to its previously prejudicial ways (Starling 2020).

Ending workplace racism will require collaboration and hard work. It will require an acceptance of history that white violence is real—the violence benefits even non-violent, non-racist white people in the past, present, and future. Being defensive when confronted with these facts does not move us forward. Transferring guilt from the victim to the perpetrator requires a desire among white people to want a better society that does not put them on a pedestal of saviorism—a non-sacrifice, as nothing would be taken from white culture. White people need to stop thinking the world is a zero-sum game; for brown people to progress, they must give up their privilege.

We live in a complex interdependent, globally connected network where the factors of production are spread across diverse skills and ingenuity from all over the world, covering various cultures, languages, and ethnic groups. Prosperity emerges healthier with collective civilizations that accept group participation in group benefits. A less racially segregated company or nation benefits from complete information and knowledge, more diverse viewpoints, higher quality decisions, and wide acceptance of solutions by the group (Lumen n.d.). To truly make a difference, every engagement in society must contribute to anti-racism to reap all the benefits of collaboration. If white and brown people cast away their beliefs in racial stereotypes and believe that all humans have resources to offer, then we will grow and stay a more united and strong nation.

White people should not offer jobs to just white people nor engage in token hire. No one, least of all brown people, believes an organization is diverse with a few token hires, especially where they mistreat these people. An illuminating test I give to organizations or entire sectors—if you look around and all you see is white people, maybe with a few browns or females, I conclude that the organization is steeped in a false premise of racism. It needs an overhaul to bring it into conformity with reality. Likely, its leaders subscribe to a fantasy of superiority, which they must face and decide to end.

A recruiting agency repeatedly told me after I was rejected for several job applications, "You met all the qualifications and have all the right experience, but I don't know why you did not get the job." That statement should trigger an investigation for discrimination and either a court case or hire to rectify that mistake. The recruitment agency should be required to report the hiring companies when they notice a practice of them only hiring white applicants. The agency should have a balanced pool of applicants and workers in its own office.

In America, you will hear boilerplate phrases when a brown person is denied a job. These include statements like, "you don't have any experience for the job," "you are overqualified," "you are not the right fit," "you don't have enough experience," or "try to gain experience from different departments before trying this one." All these statements should trigger an investigation because they are regularly used to discriminate against and excuse xenophobia.

A friend of mine noted how she was constantly verbally attacked by her white female boss for months. One day, she rebuffed the boss's approach to some aspects of the work. The boss made a big show—like a "Karen"—that she felt threatened by the big brown woman to justify firing her and immediately hiring a white, less qualified friend. The white boss pulled from the code switch template of phrases similar to the ones above, customarily used to reverse guilt or victim-blame the abused— "she was fired because she created *a hostile work environment.*" That, too, should require the human resources department to protect the company by investigating the actual creator of a hostile working environment, terminating that person, and offering to rehire the one who was being abused.

We should never pretend these are pleasant white people being noble for the good of anything. When a white boss in a predominantly white organization fires a brown person because they do not conform to white culture, it is an attack meant to harm that brown person, intimidate any remaining brown staff, and hurt their company and society. Once proven to be unwarranted, that action should have immediate repercussions for the company and that perpetrating staff. They should be reported immediately and exposed for racist hiring and operation practices.

I will explain to whom the central reporting should go and the consequences. Like every individual and company have a credit rating, all organizations should have "integration ratings." I prefer integration as opposed to diversity. Diversity is used today to avoid efforts at integration. Diversity brings a few brown people into a room of white people as if to pretend they are working together, so there is little to no racism. Integration purposefully brings together cultures, languages, and ethnic groups. It puts them together in schools, churches, work, government, legal systems, and politics in positions of power to strive together and recognize each component's value (The Oak Park Regional Housing Center 2013). Diversity is useless unless it goes to achieve ethnic and cultural integration.

Poor ratings garnered from repeated offenses should increase their risk for credit, thus, higher interest rates since they are hurting their company's resources for future profits and success by suppressing their most valuable resource—labor. Higher diversity performance ratings should therefore help reduce their risk level, as they show due care for their society. Poor ratings should also attract higher tax rates, so close coordination with the IRS would be vital. Public exposure in the press and penalty for other businesses who continue to do business with poorly rated companies would be another cause for penalties. This would be for the private sector.

There are past attempts to measure diversity and inclusion (Refinitiv 2020). Unfortunately, many of these measures shy away from race and reward gaps and do not measure diversity or integration gaps. The federal government, since they have been instrumental in promoting racist policies in the past, should be the lead on a diversity or integration index or rating. There is a clear need for a federal agency to reconcile, monitor, and implement diversity and integration ratings for all public and private organizations. It should be imbued with power equal to the Internal Revenue Service (IRS). This new federal agency should have dominance over all organizations, whether public or private, state, local or federal, for-profit or not-for-profit, and whether they have foreign offices, subsidiaries, or branches.

This agency should work closely with the IRS to penalize violators via a revised tax regime that includes integration ratings in the corporate tax structure. It should also have regional offices to investigate all violators as outlined above and seek remedies in conformity with new enforceable rules outlawing racial discrimination. The point is that since racism misallocates and wastes resources to the detriment of the capitalist system, the capitalist system itself must be incentivized to solve racism to save itself. It should have a clear objective to equate the remuneration of people with similar qualifications regardless of their skin color or ethnicity. A Secretary of Integration and Diversity should report to the President of the United States. Just as there are tax, immigration, economic, foreign affairs, and trade debates, discussions on race equity should be a regular part of political discourse. While the agency should be budgeted like any other, it should also be allowed to collect a racial discrimination tax or penalties from companies that refuse to conform. Racism should be deemed inhumane and un-American, with the requisite disgrace ascribed to perpetrators.

Companies with white top-heavy leadership and boards should automatically get dinged in their ratings. Companies that sponsor non-profit think tanks and hate groups that are known to promote white supremacy should be penalized and made public so that others can avoid doing business with them for fear of themselves losing points in their integration rating. On the contrary, companies that are openly and anti-racist in their operations, who make valid efforts to come into conformity, should gain from tax breaks and a positive image they can market to gain profits. Similarly, for independent contractors and contracts, any violators should be reported and required to conform in a short time and face time-based penalties.

I was in a reception at the British High Commission's house when another white guy told me a story I had heard before of how white folks get jobs they are not qualified for but get to learn on the job. Fifteen years ago, his wife left him at home one day while she was out preparing for a job in a small wealth management bank on the Cayman Islands. His wife's new boss called them to see how her packing was coming on. Then the conversation meandered to what he, the husband, would do when he got to the Cayman Islands. He had no clue. He could be a beach bum, househusband, or look after the kids when the nanny was off.

The boss offered him a management job at the same bank—he'd create a department. The guy said he knew nothing about banking or wealth management. The boss replied, "The local team is very efficient, and they could teach you." He got a previously non-existent job he was not qualified for without an interview, making an upper-six-figure salary plus benefits and housing, all based on the trust that exists between white people of a particular class. Between him and his wife, they netted over $1 million annually plus benefits like an international private school for the kids, and housing with a pool, maids, and a nanny for the children, all while living in paradise. The funny thing is his good fortune did not surprise him. For him, this was the norm in white culture. He may well be a fantastic employee. But I very rarely hear this happening for brown people. Brown folks almost always have to be overqualified with years of experience to even make it in the room for an interview. An anti-racist society would allow the same chances to occur for brown and black professionals. A diversity agency would penalize any U.S. company from doing business with that company in Cayman.

The Foreign Corrupt Practices Act of 1977 was enacted with anti-bribery provisions to prevent corrupt business practices. We have laws against business with countries that openly practice human rights violations and environmental degradation. We must show strong American values by adding violators of equity laws but be the first to enforce them at home.

Because of their relatively small salary, a brown person often must work two or three jobs to make the same as a white guy. That leaves no time for reflection and expansion of the way of thinking with new ideas because they always have survival on their mind. I have met many people in America who have never traveled, do not own a passport, or maybe traveled overseas just once. They cannot even afford to see a different perspective of how the world works outside of what they are taught about American exceptionalism. Even professionals feel they must moonlight on another job or have a side hustle as an insurance policy in case a white person jeopardizes their day job. They see Economic Racism daily and know what happens if you depend on the one job controlled by racist people. The proposed diversity and integration agency should study these phenomena to ensure equity and job security.

Instead of penalizing brown people with prison sentences and giving white people rehabilitation for drug addiction, both should be treated equally, with due care and support, so that they can recover. Criminalizing and incarcerating mostly brown people should be seen as a flaw in the system and fixed. The agency, to be credible, must also have race and gender diversity at all levels.

In the medium term, white supremacy will fight against any agency that seeks to penalize them, so this proposal will not happen overnight. Solutions are needed to at least continue to survive in the flawed system that exists. When faced with workplace racism, you must exhibit strength and integrity against the tide of cruelty. Here are some tips for dealing with daily racism in a workspace or just in your daily lives:

Talk to your parent, partner, or spouse about the experience.

Share with genuine friends and family that love you no matter who is against you.

Talking about racial experiences helps get the facts straight into your head. This is important for your sanity, so you don't internalize the abuse. It also enables you to strategize for future assaults. Don't allow yourself to be alone in the abuse.

Be comfortable in your appearance and attire while remaining professional and groomed to promote your positive self-image. Keep in mind that you may be attacked for your appearance because, in the mind of a believer of whiteness, you should not look good.

Cultivate self-regimes of physical exercise, including with people who are genuine and actively anti-racist.

Read and write restorative material to keep your body and mind fit. Use the assaults as an opportunity to learn about your history, pre-1400s. Learn about African history, all history, in detail, including about authentic white history beyond what you were taught in school today. Your improved knowledge helps you to educate yourself, build your self-esteem, and help promote anti-racist behavior among people around you.

Sometimes the trauma and depression make us want to avoid public spaces due to the shame shelled out by our aggressor. The attacks are not your fault, so don't internalize them. We are not infallible, so talking to others helps you determine your culpability. However, you don't deserve cruelty. Don't hide in shame for a racist history you never created. Remain in public spaces. I continued to accept speaking engagements and offered my opinions on work-related issues on social media to show others my expertise. I did this despite being criticized for having that knowledge.

Don't rest on your laurels. Racist people actively believe they will lose something if they stop being racist. Plant seeds of skepticism with anyone who will listen to the knowledge you gain from your research. Spread the news of your successes and achievements. Remember, your adversarial boss may be on a crusade to discredit you. The predominant message will prevail if you sit still and accept the negative image they portray of you.

Very rarely can you appeal to their humanity? Don't try. Stand firm in your belief in yourself and know their belief and engagement are based on a false premise. But don't pity them either. Remember, they aim to dominate or destroy.

Once you understand white racists will do anything to keep power, even murder brown people on video cameras in daylight, with witnesses, it is not far-fetched to believe they will use their cronies to get to you. The white boss coming after you could set you up, plant contraband in your desk or locker, and monitor your desk phone and assigned cell phone, emails, and web browsing when these are the company's equipment. Some will even surveil your devices, especially in countries with inadequate privacy laws. One of my former brown supervisors used to tell me he checked his office daily for listening devices and cameras. In most countries, they have a right to monitor their equipment usage. Keep this in mind.

The racist boss may micromanage the workplace because he does not trust his brown staff. If you are the boss, pay attention to white employees who may seek to undermine your success even if it hurts them too. Remember, do not try to apply rationality to an irrational belief system.

Based on the above, they will always want to see you in your space. This is called presenteeism. The practice erodes staff productivity because the culture changes to rewards for being present rather than actual output. It, therefore, kills creativity. Stay current and observe how you are being watched. I had a boss that would either walk the halls checking who was in their offices or send around the deputy or other people loyal to him. So, be punctual at work and leave when you should. You must also mind your Ps and Qs as they are looking for a fracture they could use to attack.

Remember that organizations may hire people who are duds or spongers either because of standard hiring errors or via deliberate nepotism. These people are not qualified for their jobs, got the job through political or family relationships, sexual favors, may be cruising to retirement, or racial ties of trust. You may or may not fit into any of those categories. You may be a great worker but be frustrated with the unfair reward structure. The best you can do is tolerate it until you can escape for good. Complaining too much will alienate some of these people. Remember, a bigger dysfunctional national system is not their fault, which made their corrupt hire possible.

Beware of colleagues who come suddenly as if they care and act like friends with you, seeking your comment about the boss or other colleagues. Typically, they are baiting you for negative feedback, which they will relay to the boss or someone affiliated with the boss to boost their value. They aim to entrap you while seeking white acceptance.

In the case of using your white colleagues against you, cultures vary. In Continental Europe, because of their experience with Nazism, successful white people do not tolerate racism. They are more likely to speak out against that behavior to the boss. In the USA, the opposite usually happens. Non-racist white people prefer to be complicit than speak out against it. That is changing, as many white people protest during racial unrest. The change is happening slowly, though, as white supremacy is still ingrained in U.S. society.

The company could even cyber-bug your home Wi-Fi network in countries with antiquated privacy laws. One company I worked for that provided a work laptop and phone installed a hidden program on their devices so they could spy on all your private computer files.

To avoid snooping from your white supremacist boss, keep your private phone, computer, and other digital equipment for personal use, and don't mix it with work equipment. The boss may surveil your communication equipment legally or otherwise. They will double down on surveillance to protect themselves if they are doing illegal or unethical activities.

I once worked for a company for a short time where my peer manager proudly told me he had hired an exceptionally slim, pretty, young secretary because he wanted her as his sex toy. He hired her, and she became his mistress soon to keep her job. There were better-qualified candidates, but they were less vulnerable. Sexual misconduct was the toxic culture of this organization. When you are in a company that is mismatched with your values, you must leave or plan to go as soon as possible.

You must be patient with remarks that suggest surprise at your intelligence. This will happen in interviews, on the job, and on daily engagements where there are racist believers in your space. Don't succumb to them or get angry. Your newfound enlightenment has put you in a place they may not be able to reach unless they shun the false religion of race.

You may end up being a token hire. This could mean that you may never be called on for strategy, promoted, or respected despite your qualifications. Like the white senior executives wearing BLM lapel pins, or the occasional brown student on the college brochure, you are there to give the image of inclusiveness. You will have no choice but to take advantage of being there and work for the respect you deserve.

Write about your experiences. If you suspect you may be victimized for your thoughts, do so with a pseudonym and be careful not to write anything defaming or exposing to your company or colleagues. A friend of mine had been overlooked for promotion, despite her MBA qualifications. She became frustrated with constantly having to train her new white bosses. Her experience encouraged her to study racism and sexism in corporate culture. Her Ph.D. research will help us understand how to alleviate the damage caused by such behavior. More studies, writings, and research must reveal both the struggles and the progress that the public and private sector makes toward racial justice. Leaders who focus on social equity should be given their deserving kudos.

Don't hesitate to accept training where it will help you get promoted or even increase your knowledge base.

Remember that you must be prepared to challenge observable racism and risk losing your job. Like another friend, when you challenge them, be prepared for the boilerplate statement, "we are having cutbacks and have to let you go." Always find out if they hired someone else to replace you and that person's background. Then write them to let them know you know what they did. Some won't care, but others may at least consider it before conducting the next racial staff-switching exercise. Who knows, you may have a valid discrimination case.

When you hear comments such as "*black* people are lazy," probe for an explanation. To me, "lazy" is an emotional and subjective word that seeks to justify one's biases. That means checking how you talk about brown people too. Don't tell your brown colleague that they behave like a white person or your Latin colleague that you love Taco Bell or 15 de Mayo is your favorite holiday. It's better to listen to and learn about cultures you don't understand rather than judge, primarily using words you heard from white racists.

Beware of any white person that declares that they are not racists and don't understand such people. They are generally in denial with such grand declarations. No white person escaped the colonial impact on society. They may later opt to improve their mindset, which is commendable, but just saying, "I am not a racist," does not mean they are anti-racist. If they are focused on saviorism, for example, when associated with a church helping poor people abroad, not in their own country, and living in a white suburb, it's all an act, even if they believe their delusion. Would they allow their daughter or son to date or marry a brown person? If not, then you know.

If you or a former brown boss developed sound systems that help the company, the white staff might try to dismantle or remodel them. There is always a fear of leaving a legacy that will encourage future brown employees, or worse, to disprove the validity of white supremacy to other white people.

If you are doing well, the white boss may cut your staff and resources to force you to fail. You must find ways to improvise and continue to do well. The beauty of life is that constraints are the birthplace of innovation. It's frustrating but more frustrating for the white boss when you thrive despite attempts to ruin.

Always remember that you are a leader in your community. Inspire others to reach where you are and surpass you. As more brown-qualified people make it up the corporate ladder, it will benefit others below, but only if we aspire to inspire others. Leaders encourage people around them to bring out their best and challenge them to overcome significant obstacles. Be ready to teach and mentor others. It will help you to be stronger as well.

Stay away from the narcissistic boss or colleagues. Mentally, they do not live in the same world as you do. They will destroy you and manipulate you to the point where you doubt your sanity in engaging with them. Do not expect rational, humane, or ethical behavior. By definition, they cannot offer such.

Along with narcissism, maybe a deep sense of insecurity and low self-esteem originates from as far back as their childhood. They generate self-esteem from putting down others. This is regardless of race. A clue is if they often repeat their resume to anyone who will listen. Meanwhile, they quickly find faults with others and try—in vain—to hide their weaknesses. Just be aware of them and avoid confrontation as much as possible.

Encourage your team and work with them with care. Don't take out your anger on your boss on them. Show you are a better leader than your boss by inspiring and mentoring them, including on how to deal with bosses like yours.

Leadership makes or breaks the organization. I firmly believe in an adage British entrepreneur Richard Branson once said: "train your staff well enough that they are qualified to leave your company and treat them well enough that they will stay." Former United States Secretary of State Colin Powell said in his book, "Take care of your troops, and the rest will take care of itself" (Powell and Koltz 2012).

I had lunch one day with an unassuming Indian billionaire whom people in his company adored. After introducing him to my then-white boss, I asked him about his management style. He said, "I mentor my team, treat them like family, give them the tools they need, reward them, so they never have to worry about money, and get out of their way." The company is very successful, and he has reaped the rewards of his leadership style.

I could not understand why my manager would see all these great examples of success around him and tell their best employees to leave the organization for a promotion and to better their careers. He got angry at me when I pointed out the ignorance of that approach to leadership.

As a company, there is no sense in employing the best people, training them to be better, then treating them with such disdain and low value that they leave to improve your competitors or another industry. I conclude that an organization that does not work to keep its rising stars will burn out and fail. Inevitably, the rising stars will leave and should because that organization will die unless it's a government-run organization where it will linger on forever with no hope of ever being transformational.

Once, a deputy manager got mad at me—with his face trembling, a deputy manager got mad at me and said, "You will never make CEO of this company because you're *black* and not connected politically. They will always surpass you and give it to some less qualified person." He expressed that in each job he'd had, he'd had to leave the company to get promoted. I had probably pushed the boundaries and struck a nerve. He was neither in the political circle nor white. He had reached his glass ceiling, and he accepted it. He suffered so much that he gave up. He was a bundle of misery.

My message to those who work with people like that is to be observant and pick them out of a crowd. They will not genuinely risk themselves for anybody. They are eternally selfish. Don't completely trust them. They will lie or deceive you at any opportunity to get some of those breadcrumbs as a reward. They may or may not recognize that their selfishness has made them miss out on life and beautiful people they could have known. They don't want to know too many beautiful people because they cannot feel proud of anyone, not even themselves.

At heads of department meetings, one of the department managers who ran a department with many blue-collar workers illustrated her management style during the coffee break. We asked her how she managed the technical workers, who were often badly treated and disgruntled. She said she matched their behavior and showed she was just as challenging. She was not afraid to confront staff physically to show them she was a particular type of inner-city hoodlum from the Chicago West Side. Her expressive face showed she felt she was succeeding. Yikes! My first thought was that she was probably succeeding at letting them think she was a poor leader and likely got her job through nefarious means in a dysfunctional system. Not surprisingly, morale was low and turnover high. She blamed the dysfunction of her department on her staff.

One of my colleagues reminded me how one of our former CEOs used to help build the morale of that same department, not with immediate pay increases nor with hoodlum behavior. He simply visited the staff from time to time, ate lunch or dinner with them, talked to them about their work, lives, and families, listened to their concerns, and explained what he was doing, however small, to help them. They were super loyal and went the extra mile to make the company successful.

Another of my colleagues managed in the hospitality industry, a place with lots of blue-collar workers. He would do the same and go to the space where they worked, not to spy on or intimidate them, but to talk to them, see their work and understand their challenges so he knew how to plug holes and improve efficiencies.

Acts of kindness are encouraging. With all the practical approaches above, use compassion to let them go when your staff needs time off because a child is home ill or needs to go home to deal with an urgent matter like a pipe leak. Build trust by trusting them. Remind them to complete their work with the priority you have delegated to each task.

My experience is that you get the staff that will stay late into the night or arrives early to get what they need to do because you gave them the time, and they will give you back even more of theirs. They are eager to come to work because their boss is interested in their welfare. They ask them about their children, that event they planned on attending last weekend, or an ill mother.

Bad bosses think these things are private and have no place in the workplace, and sure, you don't spend all day talking about this. But you get a feel for their mental and physical condition once you know what's happening outside the office.

Don't overdo the talk about stuff outside the office to the detriment of the company work. I have also met colleagues who want to talk about their life, especially their private life, to anyone who will listen, often to gain sympathy or seek attention.

I remember working in a bank research department where I was supposed to pull checks involved in financial fraud cases. While I drew hundreds of checks from micro-fiche per day, often doing overtime, my boss would come in late, walk around the office when she arrived, and talk to everyone about frivolous matters most of the day, such that her output was negligible. Her supervisor started to notice. One day she came in and said her dog had shit on her bed, so that's why she was late. Her colleagues had had it. They protested to her supervisor about her disturbance to their work. The supervisor also noticed I was producing perhaps one hundred percent more work than she was. She was fired.

Workplace racism can be solved nationally in a big way with real, effective federal intervention. The agency I proposed earlier would provide much further benefits than debating reparations for decades and never really doing anything. It puts the Congressional apologies for enslavement into meaningful action. When we had mass protests in mid-2020 due to police killing and abuse of brown people, that was my main expectation for an outcome. The solution should focus on equity reconstruction with incentives and an integrative approach that measures results in a constant feedback loop.

I wanted companies to hire brown and more female leaders. I expected a federal stance on race to make it uncomfortable to continue. Workplace racism is a fundamental problem because it affects income, taxes, education, and many other areas. We must first start with the mind and realize that the premise of race is wrong and illogical and keeps us from achieving true sustainability as a great nation.

Sometimes I wonder if the belief in race degrades the believer's mentality. It's a power play, but is it also the hollow sound from an empty vessel? Let's see this in the next chapter.

Chapter 6

POWER PLAY

"We learn to be racist, therefore we can learn not to be racist. Racism is not genetical. It has everything to do with power."

~ JANE ELLIOTT, teacher, lecturer, diversity trainer, and recipient of the National Mental Health Association Award for Excellence in Education

In Georgia in 2005, a Latin American teenager was dating a blond, blue-eyed bombshell. He regularly experienced racist snobbery from other people who refused to accept that it was normal for him to date a white woman. One night they went on a date to a bar, and afterward, they left for him to escort her home. She was tipsy, and he had to hold her up while trying to secure her purse. Eight white guys attacked him, under the pretext that they believed he was assaulting the girl.

Despite the guy's pleas that he was not assaulting her but was her boyfriend, he was not only beaten up, but they also called the police, who, upon arrival, pointed a gun at the guy, not at the white men doing the assaulting. Then they arrested the Latin American teen for allegedly assaulting the girl and for disorderly conduct with the eight white teenagers. This was an extreme case of what often happened to this guy. Eventually, the scars taught him not to get beaten up, threatened by police, or shot. He was better off dating a Latin American woman than a white one.

There are many stories of white men, even today, who frown upon or even attack brown-skinned men who date white women, especially if these women are what society considers beautiful. It acts like an informal tool to limit mixed marriages, which is likely the intention in the back of their minds.

The same happens in the job market. Negative experiences in the white corporate world discourage brown people from trying to work in these areas. I have had negative experiences with my first white American male boss, which I outlined in the previous chapter, so I was tempted to judge all white American male bosses the same. I tend to be distrustful initially, but I allow them time to prove themselves through their character and actions. I judge whether they are more interested in the company and its work or agenda around promulgating white supremacist ideologies. I must keep in mind that I have had white bosses that are still friends today because of their camaraderie.

It's hard not to stereotype if you don't understand the history that helps form white people's opinions of brown folks. White people expect that brown people should behave according to what they were taught through minstrelsy (Clarke 2019).

I recall being on a trade mission where I was the only brown person in a group of 20. One lady in the group asked me in disbelief, "Is it true you speak two languages?!" I told her I spoke three languages poorly and chuckled so they would not feel diminished because I could speak all three. Distracted by her dumbfounded amazement, she could not tell I was being facetious.

Speaking multiple languages is not unusual in many other parts of the world, perhaps except in America. She also couldn't believe I had lived in various countries. I admit I was naïve at the time, thinking they would accept me for who I was and that my accolades mattered to them as much as theirs mattered to me. I knew their disbelief was because I was a brown person, and perhaps it was unfamiliar territory for them to meet brown people outside of their universe. At first, I thought it was because they were from the southern states of America, a region with an unjustifiable reputation for being more racist than the north (Harriot 2017). After a few years in America, visiting places like Selma, Alabama, and reading more about American history, I realized it was not as simple as their ignorance and my brownness. There was a history, societal conditioning, and a system of automatic racism I had not considered before that made these people distrust me and look on in awe as if I was a unicorn.

The question remains, how can white people be racists? Even educated ones always deny that they are racist. One white man said to me during a discussion of racism in America with some Europeans, "I am from Florida, and I was a minority there, so I don't know why they are so racist in Georgia."

Many brown parents must explain to their young children, who are starting to go out into the world, why people refer to them as *black* when "my skin is brown, and their skin is not really white." This is a complicated discussion at tender ages between three to seven because kids have an innocent sense of reason.

No logic tells them they should be called *black* and their best friend in school white and that they should not be friends because of the color of their skin. So, as parents of brown and any form of non-white kids, this complex and absurd lesson of racism is necessary.

Let's talk a bit about building communities. When I lived in the Caribbean, we had various community adhesive approaches. We had picnics, church events, revivals, and parties at friends' houses. People who cared about marine life would gather at the beach during the turtle run to protect the baby hatchling struggling through sand towards the sea. People would keep away dogs and cats that may want to have a turtle dinner. Afterward, they would meet up at the local bar for beers.

We had community exercises like the Hash House Harriers running and walking club. I coordinated pizza night as president of a Methodist Church Youth Group. In Europe, communities held a *meet and greeted* over wine and snacks in the lobbies of their apartments and condos. Neighbors met each other and built trust with people living in proximity. These community practices counter isolation, a typical indicator of people primed to commit mass shootings against a group for which they invoke hate.

One of my former CEOs used every opportunity to get his staff together to build community. He did this through recognition, praise for tasks and jobs well done, and gave staff a sense of value beyond what salaries were paid for. He built morale in the communities we were part of. I had one European boss who treated his professional staff with respect and supported their work. For his unit, we would have one-hour breaks during the day to celebrate a colleague's birthday. I adopted that approach to leadership—bringing the team together for non-work activities—in my office when I was their boss. The result was that staff would work for more time outside their regular hours and remain focused on their work and contribution to their "community." Colleagues became more professionally intimate and operated to support each other with a deep sense of job satisfaction.

Similarly, this works in family and couples' relationships. Couples that take time out to celebrate each other's achievements, build memories through experiences, and share in activities get stronger as couples. Families that take time to share experiences also remain close. I know one family whose mechanism for family togetherness is taking an annual boat cruise. It can be anything, even a picnic at a park. Experiences, where people share a common goal, help build communities, whether as a couple, a family, or as a job or neighborhood community (Curtin 2013).

The same sense of camaraderie can be built among communities made up of different cultures and races. It takes effort, trust, and openness since we have spent too many lives and so much time and resources doing the opposite. The result would be a close-knit community that protects itself, works to build like a close family, and shares in each other's new experiences regardless of assigned race. It's a richness in living that has evaded many racist people for so long. They miss the occasions to meet pleasingly new and wonderful people. Imagine a world where you are free to date and marry whomever you want without feeling you are breaking some norm rooted in fiction. I had friends who were a mixed couple living in Europe that turned down opportunities to live and work in New York because they did not like being stared at by New Yorkers because one was white and the other brown. Part of the solution is that every daily social engagement should help us discover our real history and the derived culture. Neighborhoods, churches, the private sector, and governments should be socially constructed to build relationships with people from different cultures, become allies to those victimized individuals, overcome internalized persecution, and build multicultural associations and partnerships (Axner 2020).

Part of community building is to make people feel valued and welcomed. Those who don't feel lonely and depressed adopt a variety of vices to find solutions, such as drug-taking, eating disorders, and more. Community building is a process aimed at strengthening the capacity of individuals and organizations to develop and sustain conditions that support all aspects of community life (K. Lee 2020).

The community cannot be cohesive through self-adulation of one's contribution over others. "Community cohesion describes the ability of communities to function and grow in harmony together rather than in conflict" (Browne et al. 2005). It's an understanding of cultural togetherness that requires leadership committed to such. I once saw a manager change the name of a quarterly employee collaborative meeting to let people know it was no longer about them but about him. The forum was initially designed to spotlight the work of all employees to give them recognition among their peers—thus building community cohesion.

The new manager—a white guy—changed the name to "Sessions with [his name inserted here]" and focus on just him speaking to the entire staff. Immediately, the staff realized it was no longer an organization running on a team effort. He exhibited qualities such as being unsympathetic, uncaring, and narcissistic, which withdrew the community cohesion present before. His exhibitions suggested a delusional sense of grandeur—including racial superiority, arrogance, and exploitative nature, unfortunately, especially to the brown staff. A narcissist is incapable of appreciating anyone but themselves (Exploring Your Mind 2020). Studies suggest certain reasons that may lead to Narcissistic Personality Disorder (NPD). One could be childhood abuse that leads the individual to adopt a sense of superiority—

and inflated self-image—with people around them as a defense mechanism of compensation for never being a victim of abuse. The past neglect, abuse, and loneliness are compensated by using authority to induce an audience to love them, even if it's fake admiration—as in the case of this manager (Exploring Your Mind 2018).

The exhibited narcissism also translated into prohibition or extreme jealousy of anyone else in the spotlight. I mentioned to the new manager that I typically get invited to speak on various topics as an expert. He informed me that the organization will no longer pay for my travel expenses or give me time off to speak, incidentally, even if it's a promotion of the same organization. When conference organizers specifically asked for me to speak, he established a new company policy that all invitations were to be vetted by him. He used this new censorship system to deny my participation without even an explanation.

His behavior made me wonder about the connection between people who exhibit narcissistic behavior and those with racist behavior. Narcissists have a grandiose sense of self-importance, fantasies of unlimited intelligence, power, authority, beauty, feeling of entitlement, and require constant attention and admiration. Their response to criticism is indifference, translating into a lack of empathy—the inability to appreciate how others feel. They will devalue others they consider beneath them— brown people, women, foreigners, non-Christians, and anyone who does not fit their image of the ideal. With a lack of empathy, they have no problem exploiting others to indulge their desires for self-praise, while totally disregarding how their actions make others suffer. Their whims vacillate between over-idealization and cultural erasure of anyone unlike them (Bell, Racism: A Symptom of the Narcissistic Personality 1980).

Since they both involve people acting on their ill-founded beliefs about themselves and the world, I wondered if they intersected. Like the late psychiatrist Carl C. Bell, M.D., CCHP, I questioned, "What characteristics cause an individual to accommodate to racist views which are in direct opposition to the value of a democratic free society?" (A. Moore 2020).

I never put myself into spaces where there are white supremacy extremists (FBI 2020). On the contrary, I have lived mainly in working-class communities where my circles of white people tended to be politically liberal or conservative, educated, exposed, and economically and professionally successful such that they believe and convince many others that their sophistication rises above racism. My community of white professionals did not think of themselves as white per se, nor that they benefit from unique advantages. They do not believe they feel or act superior due to their whiteness. Like a narcissist, if confronted with someone who points out their privilege, they feel attacked and become defensive because they desperately need to protect the image of being "good." At this juncture, the default is usually to counterattack, show a lack of empathy, and if they can, they may punish the person for the attempted disgrace to their "goodness" (Miller and Josephs 2013).

These white folks pull racist phrases from their template like, "So, you are pulling the race card." White people use this as their defense when acting out their beliefs. They will likely react with a simultaneous attempt to shift guilt while pummeling the victim for daring to point out their emotional frailty, never seeing the irony. Think of police officers whose traffic stops are based on racially profiling their victims—worse if the car seems expensive. Studies confirm racial profiling in police stops, something brown people have been asserting for years. Sometimes, innocuous traffic stops end violently, even fatally, for the one pulled over (Ortiz 2019).

My boss's approach to the power play of muzzling his brown professionals led me eventually to adjust my expectations of growth and success for the company and me. I had grown accustomed to his behavior and knew beforehand that he would block anything he perceives may advance my success. I laughed with another brown colleague as we discussed how we expected his rejection to approve a personal invitation I received to speak at a senate hearing as an expert. I still got invited to speak and usually had to take a vacation when asked outside my home territory.

I had stumbled on something that Bell, the late psychiatrist, pointed out in his study. He noted, "If the man behind the institution is a narcissist of the grandiose fashion (as was Hitler), then a racist institution is bound to be established." I noticed that the company was becoming like a snowcapped mountain, white and cold, with more people like my boss, all working to keep the brown professionals in their place, even to the detriment of the company (Bell, Racism: A Symptom of the Narcissistic Personality Disorder 1980).

To me, it made sense that my boss would be a narcissistic racist. His grandiose display of self-importance, lack of empathy for other cultures and their suffering, and likelihood to be defensive or attacking— "you are being condescending"—drives him towards power and control. I recalled when I felt very hurt by his rejection before I started to study racism more meticulously. Earlier rejections felt like tiny deaths. The feeling of disappointment resembles the hurt I feel when someone I love dies. It also feels like when you get wrongfully dismissed from a job you loved and were good at or when you get a divorce. In other words, you suffer. When a racist narcissist sees this suffering in others, it spurs them further.

Like so many brown parents feeling the hurt of having to explain to their children the reason for the verbal and physical abuse at school, I denied the sequences of micro-aggressions. I got sad and angry, and later, to cope, I realized I was becoming accepting. Unlike many parents who will tell their children that people discriminate because of the victim's race, I accepted that white people discriminate because they believe in a farce. It has nothing to do with my skin color. As I have pointed out, racism is a perception, a belief. I would not internalize their idea to say they hate me because I am brown. That is what I accept.

When you shift the blame to where it fits, to the aggressor, it sits where it belongs. Doing otherwise means you tear your peace of mind apart, trying to find white acceptance. White acceptance cannot exist because white superiority is a belief system not rooted in the truth.

Unfortunately, many brown people internalize the hate and think it's their fault. What does a brown person who has given up look like? They look like the brown professional who, no matter how intelligent she is, will never be the company's head because of her skin color. They look like someone who concludes they will never be on the board of a major company. They look like the guy in prison for eternity because he sold two spliffs on the street trying to get money to feed his family. He was intelligent in school, but his white teachers blocked his opportunities, and his brown parents, focusing on survival, never thought they could get him out of the ghetto. Redlining and low wages made sure they could not escape. Their low income and lack of ideas in a poor neighborhood gave him no college expectations. Besides, his parents could not afford to pay the application fees, much less the SAT exam fee.

They are the brown teenager in high school who dreams of becoming an engineer yet hides the thought. His classmates, who have already given up because they know their parents and friends have suffered many tiny deaths, would laugh and ridicule him if he expressed his dreams openly. They are jealous that he still bothers to dream because they have stopped aspiring, knowing that society, the racist system, is rigged against them. They prefer to stay in a pretend happiness depicted by frivolous laughter behind the latest electronic screen distraction, a stupor fueled by social media, drugs, and a don't-care attitude because it's less torment. As one of my brown bosses lamented, he would never be head of the corporation. He is defeated before he starts. With what seems like endless agony, he also believe in the fallacy of race.

Only the genuinely defiant among us will fight to be recognized and call out xenophobia every time it raises its head. But even then, when we do, people say we are causing trouble. Once I met the late congressman, John Lewis, who took the time to greet us in a parking lot in Atlanta. He spoke to my group for a few minutes and encouraged us to "cause trouble" to get freedom. The late Congressman Lewis was among the "Big Six" leaders of the civil rights movement in the 1960s. These were pivotal points for America's freedom. His work, protests, campaigns, and strategizing led to the passing of the Civil Rights Act in 1965. With white people fearing some version of equality, what in their minds led to white oppression, they denied brown people their right to vote in the southern states. Meanwhile, their violence against non-white people and white people that supported brown people continued.

To show the world this injustice, Lewis and his colleagues led a peaceful march from Selma to Montgomery, Alabama, on March 7, 1965. I visited Selma with some of my friends one summer, all seeking to understand the nature of American racism. It saddened me to see how even fifty years later, the town was poor, with dilapidated buildings and hardly an economy because white people had pulled out all their investments. They moved away from Selma, some forming other smaller towns just because they feared equal rights with brown people.

The 1965 violence on the Edmund Pettus Bridge illustrates the inhumanity that narcissistic racists can impart to people they don't consider human. State troopers attacked Lewis and the other marchers. Lewis was brutally beaten, resulting in a fractured skull. Since joining Congress in 1987, he has continued to use his power and influence to fight for civil rights (Biography.com 2021).

Maybe not so ironic, Edmund Pettus, a leader of the Ku Klux Klan, the terrorist hate group dedicated to white supremacy, died in 1907. Yet the bridge was dedicated to him in 1940. He was considered a civil war hero by the white people of Selma, Alabama. He felt that the South could not prosper without enslaving brown people. His "heroism" in terrorizing brown people was honored by naming the bridge after him at a time when white "hero" worship was springing up everywhere, especially in the South, as racist white people grappled with how to retain power as they saw brown people growing in economic resources. In the minds of white racists then, brown people had developed too fast economically and were so comfortable that they had achieved great success considering their grandparents and parents were enslaved less than one hundred years before (Whack 2015).

Like John Lewis, brown and white people who truly love America and yearn for peace will not allow defeatism and fear to control them. Doing so leads society to lose all the potentially great people regardless of their so-called "race." When that brown engineer can't study to become an engineer and build a giant bridge or tunnel with superior technology created with his mind that would benefit all of society, that's an opportunity lost and a lost benefit for the whole society.

Our world is deficient in many ways because we accept the abortion of our ideas. People are afraid of the emotional injury that's expected to nail into their souls from a job rejection and termination only because they bravely stood up asking why they were not promoted while then being required to teach their new white boss how to do their job, or worse, do it for them.

In government agencies that are less likely to fail and go bankrupt because of poor leadership, they may dampen all brown ambitions. The profit motive may not matter as much as their functioning to provide a public service. However, even in the private sector, skilled brown people teach unqualified white bosses to keep their jobs.

Sometimes, brown people are willing to teach white people. Why does it seem like some brown people behave so much like opposing tribes? Why does it seem like some brown people turn to crime or negative behavior while others do not?

These are questions that both brown and white people ask. I recall one candidate for U.S. President denounced what he termed "minority groups" for their crimes. The minority groups were brown people of all origins. He promoted the "stop-and-frisk" policy—a legalized harassment of minority groups (Gold and Southall 2020). Today, this approach to fighting crime is still widespread.

Consequently, the police force in the U.S. is needlessly militarized. They resemble soldiers in a war zone with all the demobilizing equipment and killing tools attached to them. Coupled with their military training and lack of regard for brown lives, they end up killing brown people (Akpan 2018).

News broadcasts, police crime television shows, and wanted-posted notices showing a brown criminal who has committed some fill-in-the-blank crime, rarely review the individual's history. Furthermore, I can't recall ever seeing a report that dives into the history of the individual in question, their parents, their environment, and the system and history that brought him or her to that point. They never look that closely because doing so truthfully will point back to the system created since white-run colonialism. Furthermore, since there are few, if any, producers and content developers who are brown, the content tells the same perpetual myth that anyone except the police is evil and violence to enforce the law is justified and heroic (Evelyn 2020).

White racists love to omit themselves with the "what about" strategy to deflect their obsession with the power play at the cost of human lives. They might ask, "What about *black*-on-*black* crime?" or "why are so many *black* people in prison?" or "you're living in your poverty, your schools are not good, you have no jobs, fifty-eight percent of your youth is unemployed, what the hell do you have to lose?" The last idiotic appeal was an attempt to garner brown votes for a U.S. Presidential election. This question suggests that brown people use their franchise to vote for someone who openly supports groups that murder and oppress them—someone who himself was a major part of the problem in America (J. Smith 2020). The multitude of scandals, the many either treasonous or adjacent to sedition, tax cuts for the rich, and the normalization of racially motivated violence through the rallying cry—"stand back and stand by" message to racial hate groups—and make the country such an international joke. The fear of further global devastation from his incompetence all showed everyone what they could have lost (Quinn 2020).

White people who believe that poor people and brown people are synonymous are showing how much they believe in their religion of race. Despite white power play, not all *black* people are poor. Not all white people are wealthy or even well-to-do. One of the pieces of misinformation peddling used to promote so-called "*black* laziness" is for white racists to point out how many brown people are on welfare. Yet, most brown people I know are not receiving welfare. If they are in low-income jobs, they are either working while going to school to improve their future income or working two or more jobs.

Anecdotally, one friend who came from abroad to study married a white man she met in school. He was a good husband until his family started visiting, reminding him of his roots. Many of them did not work. They were on welfare. My friend realized she knew nothing about American social problems until she married into it. Her husband was not just from a lower-class structure than her but was racist without even understanding he was—buying his adult wife a motorized monkey and throwing it at her to activate it while she slept. He would then call his family to share the horrid look on her face as he laughed at his humor. The fact is that in America, white people are the primary users of welfare benefits from the Supplemental Nutrition Assistance Program (SNAP). The U.S. Department of Agriculture administers the program. They reported that in 2013, 40.2 percent of SNAP recipients were white, 25.7 percent were *black*, 10.3 percent were Hispanic, 2.1 percent were Asian, and 1.2 percent were Native American. This was always the trend (Delaney and Scheller 2015).

Another false narrative used to deflect white guilt is the idea sometimes expressed as the statement that "slavery was a long time ago and brown people are still not pulling themselves up from their bootstraps." Followed by, "When are *black* people going to get their act together?" I suppose the simple answer is that white racists leave *black* people alone. When oppression ends, that would go a long way toward bringing peace. The age-old question is still asked by white racists, and some brown people unfamiliar with the history, "since slavery ended, why can't *black* people prosper?" The answer is that enslavement has not ended. It is constantly re-birthed and hidden under the laws and norms of a white supremacist society. In a timeline of white supremacy discussed by Josh Tucker, he points out that enslavement was replaced by many successor systems of labor and control that had the result, albeit more subtly, of slavery. The new systems proved more profitable for white oppressors.

The Thirteenth Amendment of the Constitution, while it banned slavery— "neither slavery nor involuntary servitude, *except* as a punishment for crime whereof the party shall have been duly convicted, shall exist within the United States." That *exception* linked directly to a particular group of people, brown people most recently "freed," opened a whole other enslavement labor system. Enslavement of brown people from the 1600s to 1865 was followed by sharecropping, vagrant laws, convict leasing, and debt peonage. "By such an accounting, slavery in America lasted from 1619 until 1945—a total of 326 years" (Tucker 2016).

Unfortunately, enslavement under other names remains with us even today as the various systems to boost whites while oppressing brown people overlapped and continue today as a power play. These include the Jim Crow's separate-but-equal laws, ending in 1965, and the establishment of discriminatory Federal Housing Administration redlining from 1934 to 1968, whose bankrolling rules specifically worked against and degraded neighborhoods comprising brown minorities. These were rulings that destroyed any "bootstrap" of brown people's parents. I have colleagues and friends whose parents migrated north to escape southern re-enslavement from the new methods to extract labor. In the early 1900s, over six million mostly educated brown people sought refuge in cities like Chicago and New York, only to be victimized by predatory housing and lending policies (Mock 2018).

Despite the victimization and the redlining into ghettos, many still made better off than they would have if they had stayed in southern states. The presence of more brown people working in the northern states, some five percent of the population, made white people think that brown people were "taking jobs that they thought [white people] should have." White racial and economic anxiety was likely a push factor to encourage many white people to move from the northern states to states like Wisconsin, Ohio, and Michigan, where they could live in mainly white-only communities (Mock 2018). Today, as I mentioned before, brown people are still living in mostly segregated communities and pay more for mortgages than white people.

In no time since the nation's brown ancestors were kidnapped and brought forcefully to the Americas, was life made easy. A form of enslavement continued in other forms such as the war on drugs and mass incarceration, which started in 1971 to the present, of mostly brown people for petty crimes many white people do not get prosecuted for, or often for no crime at all.

Many times, the American justice system run by mainly white people, seems to see itself as a means to reduce the brown population. Curtis Flowers, a brown man from Mississippi, was tried six times for the same crime, by the same prosecutor, a white man, with nothing to connect Flowers to the crime. At twenty-seven years of age, he was sentenced to death with each conviction being overturned for prosecutorial misconduct, including misrepresenting evidence and removing brown jurors—of the six trials, sixty-one of the seventy-two jurors were white. All sixty-one voted to convict. It took an investigative journalist making the affair public to get him free after twenty years in a Mississippi State Penitentiary waiting to be murdered by the system that was supposed to protect him. The prosecutor is still free as the system he works for supports his malfeasance and the corruption of the justice system. So far, none of his other cases have been investigated for similar irregularities (Alfonsi 2021). It's difficult for a brown person to have confidence in a justice system determined to murder them and their future legacy either at the court level or at the police law enforcement level.

It's not only the justice system that is rife with systemic racism. It's likely everywhere. Four hundred years of building the experiment of America provides enough time for weaving white supremacy into every fabric of society. Recently, I applied for life insurance. In my application, one question was whether I was a felon. Going to prison, I thought, even if I went to prison and served my time, does that mean I cannot even get life insurance? Like an enslaved person, I would not have the right to vote in many states and could not get a decent job or a loan, among other things. With the label of a felon, most likely derived from some spurious racially motivated attack or just societal racially divine destiny, I would not be able to even get insurance.

The stamp of "felon" on your records for life, despite already serving time in prison, likely providing free labor, now relegates the victim to either commit more crime to survive, and be re-incarcerated or to work outside the formal system getting below minimum wage.

I recall a guy I met once on the small island of Anguilla. He was in prison for murder, albeit a crime of passion. It was Christmas, and when I met him, he was with his extended family celebrating the holidays. He was a professional baker, of beautiful cakes, iced and decorated like works of art. After celebrating with his family, he returned to prison that evening—on his own without an escort. I learned that he held a job outside the prison and often visited his family on weekends. To my mind, he was rehabilitated and reintegrated. While he held remorse for his crime, he was not being persistently punished for life.

Germany's Prison Act states that "the sole aim of incarceration is to enable prisoners to lead a life of social responsibility free of crime upon release." The aim is rehabilitation and reintegration into society. The American justice system and systemic racism labels "ex-convicts"—a derogatory term—and cut off all rights as human beings, reverting them to enslavement. This does not help them or society—that society rejects people after conviction. In Germany and the Netherlands, prisoners have rights even behind bars—they can vote, receive some welfare benefits, and like the guy in Anguilla, they can spend time away from prison with their family and go home on weekends and even work outside of prison. The connection to family and friends, the ability to vote, and to get life insurance, keeps them integrated into society. The very practice is therapeutic and leads to rehabilitation. There may be some violent criminals that cannot be treated with such freedoms, but that's typically the minority (Fuchs 2014).

In America, not only can conviction lead to a life of punishment for adults, but it is also often the same for children. Trying juveniles as adults and sending them to maximum-security prison facilities where they could get life without parole is normal. If they were not sufficiently criminalized by their environment outside imprisonment, inside, the violence of prison culture would do the trick (Scott 2012).

There is still debate on how to treat human beings, but I think the argument is wrong. Voters need to insist that politicians eliminate and punish all elements that seek to corrupt the justice system based on a belief in race and every damage that that belief causes society. Prisoners, whether adult or juvenile, should first focus on rehabilitation and reintegration with permanent incarcerations or mental health facilities left only for the most violent, not the most brown or poor. For this to happen, white people would have to face their guilt, and repeatedly reinforcement of their guilt with more deflection.

We always refer to white people feeling uncomfortable talking about racism. That's not discomfort. That's guilt. Suffering is a real discomfort. We never talk about how uncomfortable it is not being able to provide sufficiently for a family so they can educate or financially uplift brown children because one cannot get ahead due to active racism. That's discomfort. I am generalizing because many successful brown people have found a path, albeit painfully so, through racial torment toward success. Unfortunately, they are more of an exception than a rule.

We, whether brown or white, must be strong enough to eradicate racism. There is a practical part to this. You might think, "That's easy for you to say because you earn money from your writing and probably have other gigs." Yes, I do. As your insurance, you must have a side gig that you enjoy, that does not take too much time if you have a full-time job, and that side gig should be scalable just in case you lose your job. I learned this the hard way. It means you have less time for leisure, but at least you can walk out of that job when the white boss says you need to train your new white supervisor that's been hired to do a job you should have.

As one of my late uncles, who worked for himself, used to say rather crudely, "People just want your pound of flesh, they don't care about you." One of my former bosses used to say, "Companies, organizations, do not have souls." Don't get me wrong. Do your work well. Be efficient, productive, and proud of your work. Enjoy it. But also get a hobby, especially one that sharpens your skills towards something you can use to make a living. Have a life outside work. Always be willing to learn something new, no matter what. You never can tell where that skill set, once transferred, will lead you. You also never know when they will kick you out.

My grandmother made me fix whatever was broken in the house. I had to be a plumber, carpenter, electrician, painter, mason, interior designer, and gardener. I never told her I did not know how to do something. I was expected to figure it out. Today, when I meet the occasional "that-can't-be-done" person, I am usually disgusted with them for refusing to even try or get help. A good attitude takes you further than fine skills.

Prepare for racist people in life. Never let a racist remark rest. Probe to let them explain their idiocy. That's the best way to rebut and call out racism where you see it. Do so gently and professionally, and keep perfectly calm and composed. Walk the high road because you are not the one who believes in a fake religion. They have a psychological problem they need to reconcile. Don't internalize their problem and pretend it's your fault. Keep your emotions level and remember you are facing someone grasping for meaning in their life defined by you. Avoid anger. If you are angry at the moment, let some time pass to allow you the space to calm down. Don't give them that power. I know how infuriating they make you and how much angrier you will get when they use their white privilege to deny their racism and end up turning it on you. As they often say in one of their template defenses, "You are a racist for calling me a racist!" The very sentence is asinine and affirms white freedom to deflect culpability.

I told a friend of mine that not all white people are racist. Remember, "white" is a belief system, much more than it is a people. Some intrinsically understand the power and want to keep it. Your white boss, who is creating a top-heavy organization of white managers with few brown workers at the bottom, is focused mostly on maintaining power based on what he believes about white supremacy, not on the productivity of the organization. Do you know what happens to a ship with lots of captains and only a few crew members?

The white people, even when they are not themselves racist, will take the benefit to progress. Should we hold them at fault? They know that if they were to speak up about the discrimination they observed, they, too, would be victimized. In the 1960s Civil Rights protests, white people were also beaten and killed for supporting brown people's movement for the right to vote for their destiny.

Brown people need to keep in mind that most white people will do anything to keep power, even when it seems innocuous. In one club I was in, they rigged the elections, where even though a brown person won the presidency, they re-voted and re-voted until they got the results they wanted. The guy in charge of the elections even tried to get everyone to declare whom they voted for, probably so he could victimize them. Imagine a political election for a state or federal representative. The stakes are much higher, so anything goes to keep power, as they feel a sense of *weltschmerz* that they are losing their country to people different from them. White anxiety comes from the knowledge in the back of their minds that they, too, came here from somewhere (Metzl 2020).

Many brown people do not understand the essence of power. Some believe the fight is for consumables, but never for real power play because we have not known it for several centuries now. The last time African kingdoms had ample power to control their destiny, the Europeans were either being attacked or some were enslaved by Moors.

Some white people, despite their privilege, want to help. They, too, may recognize that there is a bigger world out there where their fears of being subjugated are as false as the premise of white supremacy. People who want to improve themselves could follow some of the suggestions below:

Read and research, to be and teach others to be anti-racist, on your own or in your household with your children and family. There are many books like this one, and endless studies and articles about racism and how to overcome it. If you are white and never truly appreciated your privilege, you may feel guilty at first. Don't deflect the guilt and don't be overwhelmed by it. Being a little guilty will not kill you. It only makes you humane. You are not a wretched person as you were likely taught by your community to believe in a fallacy.

Brown and white people should also learn pre-colonial history. There were kingdoms before those in Europe or America. Some were ruled by brown people, and that's okay once you don't believe in white supremacy.

Brown people also need to educate themselves about racism. Many brown people encourage racism in their community via colorism and other behaviors in search of white acceptance and white choice.

When in a position to do so, white people should hire, promote, train, encourage, mentor, and lead qualified brown people. Sometimes they don't have the experience, but neither did you when you started. Yet someone gave you a chance to try, learn and provided support until you prospered. Do the same for a brown person.

Justice reform, immigration reform, prison reform, and reform of political parties, housing, and tax system, cannot happen if the people who make the decisions are not as diverse as America. Any white leader who claims they will reform a system without decision-making qualified brown people advising them, or leading the process without interference, is just paying lip service. To develop a socially just system with balance where police "protect and serve," everyone, all the time, regardless of race, and the court treats everyone equally, there must be integration. Prosecutors that have a reputation for pursuing brown people should be investigated for prejudice and for any implicit bias that may lead them innocently to abuse brown people.

Inclusivity must also include our entertainment. I have Netflix, Amazon Prime, and Hulu. Often, I cannot find anything wholesome to watch which has diversity. By wholesome, I mean one without racial tropes like the "Magical Negro," best friend, sidekick, or mammy who saves the white people without saving themselves. Worse, they may depict non-white people only in a negative light (Nittle, Persistent Racial Stereotypes in TV Shows and Movies 2020). A typical white-produced, white-written and directed show may have a brown person somewhere as a token. They self-tick the box of diversity if they have a male and a female, albeit without developed characters. When I do find a movie that comes close to being wholesomely diverse to represent the world, such as *Star Wars: The Last Jedi*, released in 2017, racist white fans criticize the movie for having too many leads that are not white and male (Nero 2018). By the way, it's fiction. It was fiction when all white people were cast, and it still is with non-white people in the lead. These people prefer to believe the fiction of race. Ending racism means showing more movies and television shows like this, with brown leads, developed and evolving characters, and positive, even non-racial outlooks on their lives.

The algorithms of these on-demand broadcasters must also be adjusted to allow white people to see wholesome, brown-produced content. I have no problems searching for brown or white content. However, I was at a white friend's house one day on his account and tried to find some of the brown content I was watching to show him one of my favorite African reality television shows. When I could not find it, I tried to search for all the other wholesome African shows I typically watch. Despite it being the same platform with one library, his account blocked most positive brown content. Research shows that the way code is written reinforces racism (Katyal 2020). That's not surprising when most coders are white and male (Collins 2017). I wondered how he could be enlightened if he only saw people that looked like him being successful. When you can, tell your white friends about positive brown television so they could see for instance, that Africa is far more developed than they realize due to the brainwashing they receive.

Speaking of racially charged implicit bias, we must accept that after hundreds of years of taught stereotypes about groups of people, everyone has an implicit bias about some "other" group. Not only should we address the intentional forms of discrimination, but we must also address biases that operate at a level below the consciousness (IHI Multimedia Team 2017). Training to reduce racial stereotyping requires genuine exposure to a variety of people with whom you have built trust. White people need to go to brown events and make friends and acquaintances with non-white people, individuals with different gender identities, and sexual orientations, and even white people who are not in your class structure. Put yourself in their shoes. Open your mind to the fact your parents and what you see in the media may be false. Be curious and probe to be able to individuate brown people and put yourself in their shoes. Empathize, show respect, and be humane while also sharing your story.

When a brown or white person is in a position of power, like hiring someone, don't "fish for a fault." By fish for a fault, I mean when you get a job candidate that does not fit a taught stereotype, don't fish for that one fault that will fulfill your stereotype of that person. I mentioned one interview I was in where the white lady on my interview panel wanted to disqualify me because I seemed to "know too much about the subject." In her mind, because she had stereotyped me as a brown American man who could not be as intelligent as I appeared in the interview, answering all the questions, she suspected I was somehow play-acting or someone had trained me for the interview. In this case, a brown, female, or other non-white person does not get the same judgment as a white male. In another interview, one-panel member hung on to one sentence he interpreted his way as negative, which negated all the brilliant responses I made. He was accustomed to hiring white men who did not have to prove themselves. He was "fishing for a fault." My point is that you should recognize your biases. Whether you are brown or white, focus on the skills you want, like in a blind audition.

As a white person, you have the privilege not only to benefit from a white supremacist country, but that same privilege gives you the most power to speak up against it. Speak up against racist encounters, whether shared with you privately or used in front of you to denigrate a brown person. Treat the behavior, not the person, as anathema to the acceptable culture.

If a brown person wins an election for anything or gets selected to lead anything, let them do it. Don't cheat the system repeatedly until you get a white-preferred outcome. Furthermore, if you add ethnic integration and diversity to any leadership position, you will likely get new outcomes and solutions beyond what white people would produce because most see the world through one lens. Brown people are forced to see the world through the prism of white people in their search for white acceptance while still doing their jobs double time to be recognized as making an effort.

In all these efforts, talk to children to help eradicate racism and any symptom early. This can be done in schools among teachers, in churches, at home, and anywhere there is a gathering of group. This is such a crisis, just as we have reminders of emergency exits and the location of toilets, we should have reminders to be open to and to cite racial bias whenever exhibited by the leader or anyone else in the group. It should be as natural to do so as starting a show by singing the national anthem.

I learned some damning words from another author who writes about racial issues. She introduced me to two terms I had not heard before: "doxing" and "swatting." Doxing is where people hostile to your message gather as much personal information on you as they can find online—social security number, telephone number, email, work and home address, photographs, and post it online to their peers. Then they proceed to destroy your life with all your personal information by sharing the information with racist groups (GH Admin 2017). "Swatting" is where the perpetrator uses "spoofing" technology pretending to be your telephone number, to call the police about a violent fake crime. The Swat team breaks your door and may even shoot you or your family if they make a sudden move. Racists are also doing this to non-racists. There need to be stricter laws against "doxing" and "swatting."

Schools at all levels and education departments should mix the ethnicities of teachers from everywhere. Mix the students as well. Mix the education departments at both local, state, and federal levels, so the curriculum can be as diverse, and as representative as the people they are supposed to serve. By 'mix,' I mean 'integrate.' Teach real history. Don't be scared. Brown people are not the monsters some mothers, fathers, or television portray. Brown people are just people who want all the same things that white people have: an opportunity to prosper economically equally, without bias, based on trust and harmony. White people can also avoid becoming monsters by being anti-racist.

Don't ask brown people what they earned in a previous job. Hire diverse races and gender of people and pay them whatever you would pay a white man of similar skills. Brown people will bring diversity and a rich culture to the output of the company, church organization, and even your family. They will provide a new way of looking at business so you can be more inclusive of non-white people in ways your white colleagues can't because they don't interact with brown culture as much or at all.

Set systems in place for brown wealth to grow and prosper over generations. Removing many of the racial biases in financial markets, immigration, politics, courts, police law enforcement, healthcare, laws, education, and even religion would all go towards improving brown wealth. Anxious white people should appreciate that there are enough resources to go around. You will not lose anything. A component of ending racism is for brown people to own resources and have access to ownership and be innovative.

Another part of ending racism involves informing brown people that their lives were more than just enslavement. The narrative based on white-controlled media is that there was a void of nothingness for brown people before the 1500s. No matter who we are, any level of common sense will reveal that life, love, civilization, language, music, food, economy, and family all existed for brown people for thousands, even millions of years, before colonization and the invention of race. This needs not only to be taught in schools, but just as the rich schools organize New York or London field trips to study theater or school missions to learn about European culture, so too must brown students go on field trips to their African homeland and learn about their ancestry. This should be a federal program that not only teaches American history but truly comprehensive history from Africa, Asia, Europe, and other regions of the world before the common era. By college, every brown child in America should have had a field trip to some part of Africa, paid for by federal taxpayers' dollars. Just as the tax dollar pays for physical infrastructure to make the country prosperous, it should pay for social infrastructure for the same reasons.

I mentioned above that one of the main reasons for racism is fear of the unknown future and lack of identity, not just of brown people, but white people also don't know where they came from. I meet many white people who will ask me where I am from but cannot reciprocate with an answer when I pose it to them. They usually reply, for example, "I am from Wisconsin, Boston, or Oregon." But many have no idea where their ancestry came from. They, too, must learn of their origins and then be open to learning to live with other cultures and see them as unthreatening. Every white person in America should know at some point, that their families came here from somewhere for a better life, just like new immigrants. I know America advertises itself as the land of promise, home of the brave and free. That's got to be true for everyone. White immigration and its linkage with European culture must be taught—all of it, the good, ugly, and the bad.

Brown people, please don't be afraid to create. We have a movement now where many white people who are not racist, or who may be racist but want to be better for their planet, are ready to help. These are just some ways to help improve the planet, or at least America. I suspect, though, that if America can be a true moral leader for the world, many, probably not all countries, but many will follow.

Since racism is ingrained, there may be many trials and failures as we adjust. As usual, opinions on the right path will vary. Some who want to maintain the status quo, or even revert to the "good old days" of Jim Crow laws, will build walls against anti-racism. Some may think brown people's progress is a threat to their advancement. To many people influenced by the insecurity of xenophobia, equality of race means oppression to them.

Despite this opposition, work with them. Ease their hearts and reiterate that they will not die from equality. Your understanding of racism helps you understand that for some, they believe their mortality is somehow in danger. But be pushy, don't give up. We must all be committed to ending racism. It will not be an easy journey. There may even be misguided brown people who seem to be fighting against the natural evolution toward equity. They are afraid of causing trouble, as the late Congressman John Lewis used to say (Labode 2020). They may be too traumatized. Still work with them. Educate them. Be patient, but still push.

By the time my children are adults, I hope to leave a world where they can move around life being less judged than I was, have better opportunities than I did, and have an existence closer to the ease of their white counterparts. Give brown people power. Let society get better. Stop the carnage. Let's all be part of the solution and not the problem.

One of the major solutions is under the theme of land ownership. In the next chapter, I will take my usual deep dive into that area.

Chapter 7

RACISM AND LAND ACQUISITION

*"People tend to think of gentrification in terms
of race because it's presented that way, and I
think it's presented that way because in poor
cities that's what's going on. Beyond that, I think
it's presented that way as a way for the people
who are pushing it to make it just a black
problem, so people don't care."*

~ MICHAEL SANTIAGO RENDER, AKA, KILLER

MIKE, rapper, songwriter, actor, and activist

What happens when people move and live with others in a multicultural society? What neighborhood would you say you live in? A brown, white, Mexican, Korean, Chinese, or Caribbean neighborhood? Are your neighbors mainly brown or white?

This chapter examines land, the other resource I mentioned in Chapter 1. The land is a source of wealth. Wealth provides the means to power. Racism is about power. Make the land productive, and you receive rent. Consequently, you see a plethora of schemes selling the idea of rent as residual income so everyone could have financial freedom.

There was a time when Native Americans roamed and controlled the lands of America. Ownership of land in the strict demarcated European sense with private, legally binding boundaries (as opposed to traditional boundaries) and the need to protect your land with war was not part of Native American culture, at least not in the European sense of title deed ownership. For a feudal society such as Europe, possession of the land was the possession of power. The more you had, with more valuable resources you could exploit, and the more powerful you were. This was all wrapped up in the need to have growth, especially in wealth and power (Jackson 2011).

Europeans considered that God ordained that they should take any unproductive land and make it productive to plant food and rent for people to live and work, and to make their wealth grow. In the 15th Century, Pope Nicholas V passed a law permitting enslaving non-Christians and taking whatever land they were found on. His Bull stated, "*We [therefore] … granted … free and ample faculty…to invade, search out, capture, vanquish, and subdue all Saracens [Muslims] and pagans whatsoever, and other enemies of Christ wheresoever placed, and the kingdoms, dukedoms, principalities, dominions, possessions, and all movable and immovable goods whatsoever held and possessed by them and to reduce their persons to perpetual slavery [of non-Christians]*" (Wise and Wheat 2016).

This is called the "Doctrine of Discovery" and remains a legal precedent, having been cited in court as recently as 2005 in the County of Oneida v. Oneida Indian Nation of N. Y (J. P. Stevens 1985). In this case, Native Americans could not sell land to private citizens, only the right to occupy the land. Without getting into the legal jargon, the court noted that because of the principles set out in the Discovery Doctrine, any sale of Native American land was void. The purchaser would have no sovereign right to the land.

Centuries of applying the Discovery Doctrine principles translate today into people of European origin owning ninety-eight percent of all lands in America, about 856 million acres, worth over a trillion dollars. Brown people own less than one percent, only eight million acres, worth about $14 billion. According to the USDA Economic Research Service, "U.S. agricultural land, Whites account for 96 percent of the owners, 97 percent of the value, and 98 percent of the acres . . . *Blacks* possess 7.8 million acres "of overall rural land" . . . For a century after the end of slavery, *Black* farmers tended to be tenants rather than owners." Brown farming fell from between sixteen and nineteen million acres in 1910 to 1.5 million in 1997 (A. Moore 2017). The land was lost due to white people's violence, often forcing brown owners to flee for their lives. "Banished – The Ethnic Cleansing of *Blacks* in America," a 2007 documentary by Marco Williams, chronicles some of the atrocities of white people stealing land from brown people (Williams and Harris 2006).

With no compensation, this impacted wealth for generations up to the present day. Today, these lands have been passed on to other white people, repeatedly sold, and increased their fortunes. During the early 1900s, towns like Forsyth, Georgia, Harrison, Arkansas, and Pierce City, Louisiana, were examples of ethnically cleansed counties to violently steal and murder, sometimes forming a line of firing squads to shoot into black communities.

One article from The Levenworth Post on December 19, 2012, headline is indicative of the carnage then. The headline said, "Drives Negros Out – North Georgia Does Not Want Them in State." I thought the sub-headline ironic. It noted, "So many forced to go that planter's wives and daughters are doing housework." Today, these towns, filled with "good Christian people," deny their legacy of racial cleansing (Phillips 2016). It's also telling that the surrounding counties' citizens and state and federal governments allowed this crime to happen. But for four out of thousands of cases, the families have never been compensated. Often, white violence is described as a result of mental health, or it's hidden or deflected with whataboutism, and the statement is made, "this is not who we are as Americans." That's because we market America as a country of "good" people. But all history, and the present day, says, *this is America.*

Today, the landgrab practice is more sophisticated. White-run farming banks and USDA loan and assistance programs spent decades conducting deceitful loan practices that discriminated against brown farmers. In 1997, farmers filed a class-action lawsuit against the federal government citing that for decades, the practices included: 'denying brown farmers' loan requests; delaying brown farmers' loan approval until the end of the planting season, thus rendering them with debt and no means to repay; and denying crop disaster payments to brown farmers.' The result is that between 1910 and 1997, Brown farmers lost around 90 percent of the land they owned (James Scott Farrin 2010). According to a USDA survey in 2021, the result is out of the 3.4 million farmers in the U.S. today, only 45,000 are brown (Shoppe Black 2021). In more recent attempts to compensate for over 100 years of white landgrab, the USDA had scheduled payouts of a $ 4 billion loan forgiveness plan included in the $ 1.9 trillion coronavirus relief bill that passed Congress in March 2021. Their efforts have been blocked as white-own farmers sue for discrimination halting the payments to brown farmers (Jordan 2021).

Those stolen lands have produced prosperity for generations of white people. With the Discovery Doctrine enshrined in this behavior, the never-ending need to grow wealth made every interaction transactional. Cultures such as the Native Americans refer to land, and nature in general, as things to be respected and to live with in harmony. Their beliefs and traditions mostly encouraged them to see themselves as a part of nature, not conquerors of it. They are not perfect, but their approach is more sustainable than the European-Discovery-Doctrine-profit incentive of exploiting as much land (and anyone found there) until it's no longer useful.

When the rules changed and land deeds, private ownership, and boundaries were introduced in America, Europeans naturally felt that non-productive lands—in the European sense—should be taken and made beneficial. This clash of cultures happened not just in America, but anywhere that was colonized. Indigenous people tended to have reverence for the land and collaborated for the most part to fulfill the needs for livelihood. The need for growth, just for the sake of accumulation and hoarding of resources, in the European-economic sense was not necessary.

Excess is unnecessary to live. The feudal system said that you needed to own the land, and cultivate it, as well as show your power and wealth with such royal sceneries as manicured lawns, orchards, and manicured gardens. The result is what we have today. Houses depict the wealth and want-to-be wealth of a European feudal class (Harari 2015).

White people made land ownership for all class structures of Europeans a reality through colonialism. By 1865, when enslaved people were given their legal freedom by the federal government, the majority were not given land but remained in tenantries as laborers—supported by vagrancy laws. White people knew that owning and controlling land meant power and resources in the European sense, so when Abraham Lincoln formed the Freedmen's Bureau in 1865, to redistribute the famous "forty acres and a mule" (actual left-over mules from the Civil War), the confederacy knew they were taking away their power. President Andrew Johnson's overturning of the progress of Lincoln, and the aforementioned violence of white people attacking brown landowners return brown people to being a landless class.

Today, the land is still a source of power. Unless you have a legal right to land, plus a martial system to protect it from thieves and squatters, and conquerors, you could lose it. There are law contracts, land certificates and deeds, and boundaries. However, without the power of the gunpowder to enforce those laws, they are a sense of false security, especially in a place where people don't respect the rule of law much, or are willing to thwart it, when it comes to hoarding wealth. As an aside, I always believe there is a positive correlation between a place that does not respect the rule of law and one where almost everyone has a gun to protect themselves.

The problem is that land is tied to money. Europeans just assumed lands, where native peoples lived, were freely theirs for the taking because the people that lived there did not occupy the land according to European culture and values. The land is valued based on its best and highest productive status. Lands occupied by people with money are worth more than lands occupied by poor people. This is, of course, unless the lands with the poor people suddenly have a natural resource, are fertile, are on higher ground, have a water source, or are close to a city center that's prospering. Then, we have gentrification.

On my 2019 trip to Selma, Alabama, we hired a tour guide, a woman who was nine years old when she experienced the attacks, riots, massacre, and murder of people. This was in 1965, ironically one hundred years after enslaved *black* and brown people were freed by federal laws that sparked a civil war. I still have plans to visit as many places as I can be impacted by racial violence of any kind to study the impact today. I was also inspired by a podcast called White Lies, which investigates the murder of Reverend James Reeb and the surrounding events (NPR 2019).

Ms. "B," our tour guide, told us how she and her eleven-year-old sister were arrested and thrown in jail by the white police officers for joining the protests to make the white people of Selma follow the federal law. The white racist people would do things like intimidate brown people, threaten them when they tried to register to vote, ask them to read a complex text they could not read, or guess how many jellybeans were in a gallon-size jar (History.com 2021).

According to our tour guide and the exhibits of the National Voting Rights Museum and Institute in Selma, President Lyndon B. Johnson sent 2,500 National guards, federalized state, and FBI agents to help maintain peace during marches and registration of brown people to vote. The gruesome murder of three activists by a Klan lynch mob, orchestrated by a former clan member, in Mississippi also brought national attention to the crimes against humanity in the South. Three victims, Andrew Goodman, Michael Schwerner, and James Chaney, journeyed to Neshoba County, Mississippi, to help brown voters registered in 1964. Goodman and Schwerner were white men, and Chaney was brown. The 1988 movie, *Mississippi Burning* is based on their work and the murders (Kaleem 2016). The number of people attacked and some killed to keep brown people from voting would take up several other volumes of books.

White people of 1965 were horrified about brown people voting because they worried that if brown people had access to the ballot, they might want to become lawmakers. Lawmakers could change the law in favor of their people, shifting land ownership and causing a shift in power with it. They knew they would lose one of the main tools used to protect white supremacy—the power of the majority vote.

In Selma, we also saw houses surrounded by beautiful gardens that were clearly from another era—homes of wealthy white people. Some of these are for sale, and they are worth buying as an investment. We saw multiple signs of a missing brown young man. I wondered if kidnapping and lynching still happened in this town but were not talked about because the people here were brown and poor. The sidewalks were not well-maintained. The façades of the buildings were like an old town deserted for over fifty years. People looked dismal, sad, and hopeless. Belief in race destroyed this place. We felt their pain.

The first thing that struck me when we drove into town was how much prime real estate on the riverfront was not only dilapidated and overgrown with shrubbery, but the doors and windows were boarded shut with rotting plywood boards.

Selma, Alabama, seemed like a small American town with no real economy. The few remaining young people roamed the streets with little aim. No parents were rushing their kids to their football, gymnastics, dance or music classes, or tennis practice, there was no place for art classes, no town theater, or amusement park. There were no major hotel chains. There was no recreational area, no bustling businesses. I don't recall seeing a Walmart, Lowes, Home Depot, or any of the typical stores on any average American landscape. There was one operational restaurant that day, but it was so crowded that we could not get in, so we left without eating. A lady was starting another restaurant on the same street where four white men beat Reverend Reeb to death.

Gentrification comes in many forms. Sometimes it's a mass massacre like in Wilmington, North Carolina, or Tulsa, Oklahoma. In Tulsa, white people massacred an entire town of brown people in 1898 with the support of the North Carolina Democratic Party. In another case, it was the 1923 Rosewood Massacre in Florida. The details of mass attacks against brown people to take the land are too much to print in one book. There are attempts to document as many of the "race riots"—the agreed-upon euphemism for white attacks on brown people (BlackPast 2021).

The list does not include individual attacks or police assaults on brown people. Many more have been hidden. White's public denial of their racism and control of the media, justice system, law enforcement, and politics means they do not get protection, justice, or any form of retribution. Much of that information was hidden. Survivors had to leave town with whatever they could carry. In the case of Wilmington, when no federal military or National Guard came to the rescue, the white Democratic Party realized they were free to commit genocide without repercussions. They massacred brown people and white people who helped them throughout the South (Everett 2015). Simpler forms of gentrification may be when a white-controlled local government suddenly raised taxes to get poor brown people out via tax liens.

Countries, cities, towns, neighborhoods, a brown family, or any community group can experience economic lynching on the micro-scale, such as a person being denied a job. At the macro level, there are brown-run countries that have done well, have or have had natural resources, a seemingly thriving society that went along its business for tens of thousands of years. These countries of native people had developed systems that worked for their climate, society, and environment. I can think of the Aborigines in Australia, pre-colonialism, as an example, the oldest living civilization on the planet (C. Klein 2018). Then colonialism arrived and changed their lives forever.

I wonder it would be equally appropriate for that community to come to

Europe and teach Europeans about African gods, and educate them about African cultures such that it displaced the European way of life. Would Europe accept the prosperity and technology that African ancient civilizations could bring to Europe, with the experience of thousands of years of progress? Who decided one culture was better than the other? I remember meeting a white woman who was proud to tell me she was going into the deep countryside of Liberia to teach the people there English and build Western-style houses for them. In her way of thinking, she was somehow bringing civilization to savages, even as she did so through a modern-day missionary Christian lens. These people lived their way of life undisturbed for thousands of years only now to be given the tools to allow them to be colonized—Western people with the indoctrination of Western languages, food, and housing—likely that they do not account for the raw materials and skills in that area—and a new religion that teaches them they are inferior to Europeanism.

The irony is that if brown people master the white culture and decide they will operate it on their own and do it well, and have power and authority over themselves, the economies are quickly destabilized by a white-run country (MacAskill 2017). Destabilization may come with a sudden assassination of a good and respected leader, an influx of weapons including ammunition to gangs in places that typically never had gangs or weapons, human trafficking, child labor, and using countries of the Global South as dumping grounds for waste. Proxy armies supported by mercenaries, mysteriously turn against their governments and accept bribes to orchestrate a *coup d'état*, sometimes in ways that never seem to make sense and often have obvious or secret outside interference from a white-dominated country (Boyle 2014).

My Caribbean friends and I always marvel at how many guns are available in our countries when there is not even one factory. Plus, there always seems to be a steady supply of ammunition. How can we take advantage of that logistical supply chain for moving the food we grow and the products we produce to the metropole? That would solve so many trade barrier issues. In America, we believe we are a law-abiding country, but why do we encourage everyone to have a gun to take the law into their own hands? Why are good leaders murdered who take care of their people and bad leaders tolerated? These leaders arrange for the murder of their people and rob their treasuries to enrich themselves with no real long-term goal except accumulating and hoarding wealth.

I recall a Liberian friend of mine noting this paradoxical foresight. She wondered if these corrupt leaders have it right. They probably know that if they stay corrupt, foreign white governments will continue to give them money, and just grumble in the background about how dishonest they are. Yet, in public, they will support them the more outrageous they are. United

States government supported figureheads, like Rafael Trujillo, a dictator in the Dominican Republic who ruled from 1930 to 1961—murdered thousands of his people, as well as 20,000 Haitians in 1937 (History.com 2020). Others in this club include Mohamed Suharto of Indonesia, who ruled from 1967 to 1998 and amassed between $15 and $35 billion. His strong anti-communist stance gained him economic and diplomatic support from the West (Mmoujeke 2018).

I don't approve of a corrupt leader that wants nothing for his country but only serves to enrich him or herself. I don't think that's progressive for any nation, no matter the ethnicity of the leader. I equally don't think it's progressive when white leaders hoard contracts while blocking brown companies. There is a narrative in the press that brown leaders cannot run their own countries without graft. That's been proven false so many times by many great brown leaders. The point is there are great brown and white leaders. There are also corrupt white and brown leaders. Since the most influential global news media companies are run by white people, the press mostly showcases corruption in brown-run countries and diminishes embezzlement by their people.

When the British news talks about land being appropriated from white farmers in Zimbabwe and given to brown incompetent people, they never explain in a balanced way how all white families without interracial marriage got hold of that much land in an all-brown country—normally through violence and subjugation through colonialism. They pretend colonialism did not happen. History is written by the most recent conquerors and replayed to make them seem altruistic and dominated, fortunate to have been saved from themselves.

White-run countries are no less unethical. Remember, appropriation of foreign lands, regardless of any Doctrine of Discovery, and murdering brown people for commercial gain and power is also corruption. It's probably the ultimate form of exploitation. Similarly, it is corruption and a human rights violation, and therefore an international crime when the federal government support redlining and police-sanctioned executions. These violations of humanity are eloquently outlined in the H.R. 40 commission for the U.S. program of Human Rights Watch, delivered by Dreisen Heath on February 17, 2021. This is a call to Study and Develop the Reparation Proposals for African Americans Act, finding a viable "pathway to explore federal reparations for the legacy of slavery" (Heath 2021).

In February 2021, the United States signaled its aim to become more engaged with global human rights by seeking a seat at the United Nations Human Rights Council. Unfortunately, the aim does not seem to indicate improvements in its human rights violations but rather to use the U.N. body to vindicate its allies and chastise its foes (Keaten 2021). The United

States should become a State party to the Rome Statute of the International Criminal Court (ICC) and ratify the treaty. The Court provides a permanent international criminal court that "investigates and, where warranted, tries individuals charged with the gravest crimes of concern to the international community: genocide, war crimes, crimes against humanity, and the crime of aggression," when national courts are unable or unwilling to do so (International Criminal Court 2021).

These principles are essential to truly helping America surpass its past and present internal conflicts with itself. According to the ICC's primary objectives, "Justice is a key prerequisite for lasting peace...stability, and equitable development in post-conflict societies, [like the United States of America]. These elements are foundational for building a future free of violence." America cannot afford to hide its head in exceptionalism, thinking it can reconcile its racism alone. Just as it proves its dominance through military power, it must prove its dominance in morality and truly make its laws and violent perpetrators of human rights, vulnerable to scrutiny by courts beyond the Supreme Court—a body that often suffers from the same racial malaise of the society it serves.

Human rights abuses are rampant in America. There is a focus on other countries' human rights violations either for internal political fuel such as that regarding Cuba, or global geopolitical power—China is often cited for its human rights violations against one million-plus Muslim Uighurs interned since 2017 in some eighty-five detention camps within Xinjiang, an autonomous region in Northwest China (Romano, Schifrin and Yu 2020). The U.S. calls the Chinese government's suppression of Uighur culture, language, and religion, "cultural genocide"—something the U.S. is familiar with in white supremacy programs that wiped out the Native American culture, suppressed women, committed genocide, enslavement, segregated societies, and now incarcerate and criminalize brown people. As if to reinforce the absurdity, violent white people whether government, law enforcement, courts, or civilians are excused and left to continue unabated—on January 6, 2021, white supremacists stormed U.S. Capitol with support from politicians and law enforcement (Devereaux 2021).

Certainly, the world has seen through the propaganda machine at least between 2016 and 2021, if they forgot the 1950s to 1960s and the many attacks by law enforcement. The expectation of a great morally upright America has been diminished. Associates of mine in 2021 say that given the state of social injustice in America, it's not an "upgrade" to move there from their homeland. America is built on the backs of immigrants and will continue to be so as brown people try their best to save the country, even with their own lives at stake. The nation can build a reputation of morality based on the reality of equality for all its people. Courts like the ICC can be utilized to ensure appropriate compensation for white landgrab for over

100 years. It can be used to provide equity where the American court system fails.

Sometimes, brown people, who are not mentally emancipated, as beseeched by Marcus Garvey and Robert Nester Marley, might also agree with the sentiment of whiteness because they are so colonized, they may think you do not know your place and that defect in your body and mind needs to be fixed, punished, or beaten out of you. Envy sometimes guides their sabotage of a brown business and investment in favor of white prosperity. The very notion of a brown person investing in a major project that could lead to their prosperity is abhorrence to them. The example of brown farmers losing most of their farming land due to white aggression can help us understand why sometimes exhaustion makes us surrender and fight each other for whatever the white people have yet to take. I call this behavior a crab-in-the-barrel syndrome, because brown people may believe in whiteness so much, that they may try to destroy each other, never realizing that cooperation would be better to overcome the false beliefs. White supremacists incorrectly believe that is their God-given domain. Breaking News: brown people deserve all those possessions and more.

Some brown people are still mentally enslaved due to all this propaganda, brown people economically lynch other brown people, often without the help of instruction from any visible white person. A common phrase used in many situations asks, "What is he playing at?" The insinuation is you are pretending to be someone you should not aspire to be because the white people have arranged societal norms and you are messing it up—" causing trouble."

These are lost brown people, who have been indoctrinated to think that only white people should prosper. They will help the white persevere because they expect some reward, normally trinkets, or some recognition for loyalty. They never stop to think they could have that great mansion or powerful job, or all that land too if they supported a different narrative. They passively accept their own lynching, or that of their children, whether via economic deprivation, or physical maiming and murder, and believe, "if I can't have it, nobody [that looks like me] can." Another explanation may be that, due to centuries of torment, some brown people suffer from a version of Stockholm Syndrome. As victims, they may come to sympathize with their oppressors due to conditioning and as a coping mechanism for the mistreatment (Healthline 2019).

So, what's the solution? Brown people are still waiting for their 40-acre-and-a-mule promised upon emancipation in 1865 to formerly enslaved people by the William T. Sherman Special Field Order No. 15, which appropriated lands previously given to Southern landowners. The land was about 400,000 acres from the coastline of Charleston, South Carolina, going south to the St. John's River in Florida. About six months later, after the assassination of President Lincoln, the new president, Andrew Johnson, overturned Sherman's directive. Almost all the land was returned to the original descendants of people who stole the lands from Native Americans and later caused the civil war to maintain enslavement (Myers 2020).

That cultural mentality of white people committing crimes against humanity without retribution persists today. Fortified with that understanding, many do not empathize or show care for brown causes or movements. Further, for some white people, the status quo is what they are familiar with, and it works for them—why change it?

While mortgage companies promote their adherence to the Fair Housing Act passed to prevent housing discrimination— "equal housing lender"—interest rates are still higher for brown people while their incomes are lower. In an analysis on realtor.com, in 2018 and 2019, brown communities typically receive mortgages with interest rates that are thirteen basis points higher than in the white population. (One basis point is 1/100 of one percent. The difference between a mortgage rate of 3.25 percent and a rate of 3.35 percent is ten basis points).

The problem is not easily solved. Interest rates are also higher because credit scores for brown people tend to be relatively low—687 compared to 727 for the average white consumer—out of a maximum of 850. Since they make lower incomes, the investment available for a deposit tends to be lower, which means any loan requires additional fees in the form of private mortgage insurance (PMI) to protect the lender in case of non-payment (Trapasso 2020). White families with generational wealth, received from lands stolen or purchased fairly, can help adult children with the first home purchase, often eliminating the PMI and ensuring they pay a minimum monthly mortgage. The reprieve allows them to invest their higher-than-brown-people earnings such that they can help their children with college and new homes when their time comes. There is a clear need to form mixed communities.

Mixed, unified, or integrated communities mean that when brown people move into a neighborhood, white people should not run away by moving to another white neighborhood. White people cannot learn or contribute to improvements in their society if they do that. Stay and learn to integrate. They will need to stay and discover something useful about another culture. Don't be alarmed when your children play together. I say they should not worry about their children hooking up in mixed-race relationships. While race is invented, biology is natural. Real science does not apply to a man-made concept of race.

I always imagine an America with a grid of fast rail connecting cities and states. It would change the real estate landscape. People could have their residences in far neighboring towns in the countryside while working in the city. Small dying towns would get revived because suddenly, they could have an influx of new people bringing in money and development. America would have so much more prosperity. But for all of that to happen, racist white people must stop demonizing brown people and be willing to open small towns, modernize and integrate.

America has so much land and resources that there is no reason for homelessness (or the unhoused, which may be a better term), or for people to live in slums. There are many examples in Scandinavian countries of how to address the homeless situation. I like the model in Finland the best. Their homelessness numbers are decreasing while everyone else's increasing even during a global pandemic. They provide a home for the homeless with support from the community, volunteers, and public health officials to help them get back on their feet (A. Gray 2018).

In the U.S., homelessness went up forty percent between 2018 and 2019 and continues to rise way past the half-million mark from then (Moiz 2020). The National Alliance to End Homelessness stated that "Seventeen out of every 10,000 people in the United States were experiencing homelessness on a single night in January 2019" (National Alliance to End Homelessness 2020).

The scary part is that many of us, regardless of race, but especially brown people, is not far removed from that statistic. While poverty is the main cause, common triggers include losing a job, rising rent, domestic violence, legal and financial problems, drug abuse and alcoholism, and mental and physical illness. A self-employed business owner without health insurance can become homeless in a few months after needing an expensive life-saving procedure. The tragic decision is to sell your assets quickly and cheaply to make medical bill payments or die.

Then, to add insult to injury, police are used to drive the homeless from one part of town to the other. People with property don't want the homeless around them to offend their sensibilities or steal out of desperation, so the police are there to protect them. Law enforcement is typically wholly unqualified to deal with homelessness or any person with mental health challenges. However, due to vagrancy laws, whose origins come from 16th century England to maintain the social hierarchy and protect property owners, police are the tools to preserve social order (Goluboff 2016). These laws proliferated around 1865 to 1890, to preserve new forms of enslavement—*Black* Codes, vagrancy laws, sharecropping arrangements, the convict lease system—today, the mass incarceration and prison industrial system (Adamson 1983). The root of these vagrancy laws remains today.

Another group that does not fit into the U.S. Department of Housing Development's (HUD) definition of "homeless," but lives in destitute situations, often with their families, are hidden people who get stuck in temporary housing, like motels or extended-stay hotels. They never make enough money to cover a deposit and rent due to the types of employment available. For HUD, the "homeless" are individuals or families who lack a "fixed nighttime residence." You must be living in a shelter or on the street. Doubling up with family on the floor, moving nomadically between motels, and couch surfing do not count (S. S. Ali 2020).

Homelessness, inequality, and skewed land and residential ownership are all linked to white hoarding of prosperity and its symptomatic white supremacy. Along with the redistribution of this prosperity, brown people need educational programs at all levels, including remedial and vocational training to be better able to manage finances, and assets and support their prosperity growth with what could be provided by a federal conciliation program. Don't leave out any class that was disadvantaged and still suffers today. Native Americans also need to be beneficiaries because the first major crime against humanity was committed against them upon the arrival and occupation of America by the Europeans.

The federal and state governments also need to regulate home and commercial mortgages to offer a compensatory advantage to brown people to finance residential and commercial projects for agriculture or commercial purposes. The precedent for such a model is enshrined in the Federal Housing Administration's National Housing Act of 1934, which at the time was geared toward building wealth for white people (Digital Chicago Lake Foerst College 2021).

The Fair Housing Act, sections of Title VIII of the Civil Rights Act of 1968 and the Equal Credit Opportunity Act (1974), and the Community Reinvestment Act (CRA) of 1977 all aimed to provide "fair" rules for housing for people regardless of race. The CRA had aimed to go even further to support reinvestment in black and brown formally disadvantaged communities. It failed. Democratic Senator Chris Coons of Delaware said in 2020, "it is unlikely to encourage investment in under-resourced and overlooked regions." Attempts to provide even weak measures of efficiency in this Act also failed. During a crisis of brown people's diminished ownership of land and property, further exasperated by a global and financial crisis, remnants of redlining practice persist.

You cannot equate a society, marred by 400-plus years of violence-induced inequity with a few short years of feeble laws branded as "Fair," "Civil Rights," and "Equal Credit." The only way to right the wrongs done by racism is to turn the entire system on its head. Today, the purpose of anti-racial regulation should be conciliation that leads to transformational changes that measurably chip away at racist structures over time. These proposals are not suggesting the main tool should be direct handouts or subventions for brown people. Grand public apologies are mostly seen as false acknowledgments that excuse the maintenance of the status quo. Apologies do not give brown people land or capital or provide a real reconstruction to support their advancement after enslavement. Anti-racist solutions must show tangible, sustainable, wealth-building, cultural protective results.

There are forty-six countries worldwide that have a structure resembling the South African Truth and Reconciliation Commission. These are all aimed at healing national division for the good of their society. Some of these commissions try to heal a society after events like a violent dictatorship that murdered unknown amounts of people to maintain power like in Argentina, civil war or genocide like in Rwanda, civil war like in El Salvador, or ethnic cleansing like in the Solomon Islands. I think the United States can form its version of a "Reconciliation Commission," but if it can't, due to internal resistance, it should seek assistance from those who have. Canada's International Center for Transitional Justice could help (Souli 2020). The United States of America's social fabric is not stable and continues to experience pockets of explosions and violent breakdowns. Rebalancing wealth accumulation opportunities to counter America's versions of apartheid holds a strong case to support a harmonious and socially stable Union.

I have made several recommendations in addition to the references made above to forming institutions to help bring this Union together. Racism is a crisis, especially in America. Denying it and pretending the nation has a clean record of crimes against humanity will not work forever. Furthermore, isolating—physically, historically, and mentally—communities based on race is a foundation of ignorance fostering even more prejudice, including implicit bias. I believe the following are some worthwhile approaches toward eradicating racism related to physical spaces of people in terms of housing, land ownership, and commercial business opportunities:

The biggest challenge I foresee is solving the problem of land distribution in America. Due to the mentality first driven by the Doctrine of Discovery that the earth's resources must be owned and wealth from it hoarded by white Christians, it's hard to unravel the damage caused by this belief that still prevails today. The solution must involve not only legislation but a variety of incentives to support the reform of agrarian and residential land ownership. The discussion will require incentives for private landowners, financiers, federal, state, and county governments, non-governmental organizations and civil society, retail and wholesale real estate stakeholders, educational institutions, and think tanks. There will likely be much resistance from groups and families that benefited from stealing land, and it's easy to muddle the resolution with questions of who deserves to be repaired. The fact is, those discussions about process, "who-gets-how-much-of-what," are designed to make the brown groups argue among themselves while the crime continues. It's the old divide-and-conquer distraction. Add violent groups who will certainly defend the real estate they or their ancestors stole, and we could have a mess. As shown, more recently, white farm owners will tie up any attempt at compensation or equity, with lawsuits claiming discrimination against them. However, since land is a major component of wealth and power, it must be part of ending racism.

Congress and the Senate, with the full support of any present or future President of the United States, should pass an act "to encourage improvements in housing standards and conditions, to provide a system of mutual mortgage insurance," by providing national housing insurance of insured guaranteed mortgages. The big caveat is that it must favor brown people to have a reparatory effect. To avoid lawsuits from rich white people, use a wealth level threshold. Make it available to all regardless of ethnicity or race that fit the requirements.

Any city council government, tax administrators of the state, city, or county governments who suddenly increases taxes such that they force out people who live in the area, should be investigated, and exposed by the federal government and be legally forced to orient the tax structure based on the net wealth of each household. Set the tax rates such that it does not have the effect of forcing brown people from their homes due to property tax increases.

Any program that wants to help brown people more than white people is often heavily debated as impossible. It's much easier to picture and implement the reverse. The idea that equity is oppression for white people is forged from beliefs in racism. Anyone who argues that there should not be a remodeling of the real estate landscape is just perpetuating the same old white supremacist culture. But for America to be sustainably prosperous and stop the present and slow crumbling of an empire, it must adapt and correct its past mistakes. Lawsuits by white people claiming discrimination should be properly reviewed and, in each case, follow through an investigation on how that farmer or landowner acquired that land going back at least 150 years. In such cases where the land was acquired illegally by any owner within 150 years, that landowner should be made to split their lands for redistribution to brown people. For example, the white landowners who recently filed a lawsuit for discrimination would automatically trigger such an investigation. The knowledge of such a redistribution of their land would incentivize white landowners to avoid obstructing brown compensation cases, lest they lose land.

Banks and any company in the supply chain of the housing business, commercial properties, and farmland, whether they are mortgage companies, title lawyers, realtors, or brokers, especially those of the big chains, should be graded both by the stock market if they are publicly traded, and by the Better Business Bureau on their business practices that encourages or discourages redlining. Those that avoid the so-called blighted areas, known to be predominantly poor white or brown, should receive a lower rating for their lack of diversity in their staffing, their clientele, and, for example, for mortgage banks, the extent to which they discriminate on their loans. Statistics should be regularly collected, and they should legally have to display their actual implementation of "equal housing lending." Interest rates and any fees they charge everyone should be made public so that borrowers can review their practices and decide whether they are a fair company to borrow from. Their success and very existence should be governed by how measurably committed they are to being anti-racist in their practices.

Incentives both at the federal and state level should be given to developers and real estate investment trusts (REITs) that focus on integration and mixed-family facilities. Those that focus on developing communities to attract diverse cultures and recreations that allow for people of different origins to mix and commune, should be incentivized via the tax structures. Lending and insurance companies that finance such projects should also benefit from tax incentives. These facilities should have common spaces such as parks, and walkable areas, reduce unneeded automobiles or vehicle-less streets, and include more efficient public transport, community centers, and Homeowners' Associations (HOAs) that are not just focused on the physical aspect of the community, but also the social health.

I visited Athens, Greece. While there I took public transport around the city, packed with people at 10:30 PM. While in the city I watch a street football match and hung out with local people in lighted parks talking and eating snacks. There were no police chasing people for vagrancy. I saw no police but never felt unsafe. Some city development and design experts refer to these as "healthy corridors" (Community Toolbox 2020). Building healthy corridors involves connecting neighborhoods with amply wide and well-lit sidewalks and green spaces where people can congregate, sit, meet in the open, or have shops like coffee, tea, ice cream, open-air street markets, and bookshops.

In the U.S., planners should be required to engage with the community to get the development or retrofitting of the present environment right. Engagement with the people who live there and with people of diverse cultural backgrounds goes without saying. What is missing from these attempts to build connected neighborhoods in the U.S., are the actual people's (from the affected community) involvement in the decision-making, design, and construction of these spaces. For example, who decides what's the right city artwork? If it's just white planners, they are less likely to truly represent everyone, even with the best of intentions. The requirement to build connected communities with all the features as described by The University of Kansas' Community Toolbox. This, and comparable approaches should be a federal mandate for property development. Just as there are environmental and building codes, community corridors should be enshrined in building code regulations. The National Institute for Standards and Technology (NIST) focuses on public safety and physical resilience in building codes, among all other standards (Gilbert, et al. 2015). It also needs to add a mandate to include social cohesion in commercial and residential construction, road, tram, and train (including changing the way tracks are laid in America—examples can be found in Europe where tracks do not interrupt flow and cross-movement), and city layout. Design for social health promotion, if done right, can translate into neighbors that trust each other, appreciate each other's cultures, food, languages, and origins, and therefore live in better harmony.

Designing for social cohesion, connected communities that are safe and inclusive, should also be a standard developed by the International Organization for Standardization (ISO), based in Geneva, Switzerland. The ISO is a non-governmental international organization with 165 national standards bodies as members. This organization brings together to share knowledge and develop voluntary, consensus-based, international standards. For example, ISO 2575:2010 standard on airbags sets the standard followed by all car manufacturers globally to ensure they have the same behavior when deployed during an accident. What do standards have to do with eradicating racism? ISO's 2030 Strategy includes reorienting the organization to meet the needs of its members. One of these major needs is to develop standards that are inclusive and robust enough to be measured and improved over time. Goal number 2, entitled "All Voices Heard," is a big objective often omitted by many international agencies. They are accustomed to a top-down approach—normally headed by white leadership, or a brown person who feels obliged to satisfy the Global North to maintain their jobs. They tell countries of the Global South what their capacity building and standards should look like. I am suggesting that more brown people need to also be in the decision-making positions of these organizations to develop global standards to aim to eradicate the ills of colonialism and its influence on domestic standards—in this case, standards for building codes of infrastructure. Diversity, integration, and inclusion must allow everyone to flourish, as suggested by ISO's brochure. They must also actively seek out diverse viewpoints and implement them (The International Organization for Standardization 2021). ISO has a package of highly sought-after standards for international recognition: ISO 9000 quality management standard, ISO 14001 environmental management system standard, ISO 50001 energy management standard, and perhaps the one that comes the closest to my recommendation, ISO 26000 providing guidelines for social responsibility. There is none no ethnic or racial equity. There should be, and companies can market this as they become more inclusive, just as they do other ISO-hallmarked standards. The idea of international organizations being more inclusive and diverse in their staffing, membership, and viewpoints, goes for any international organization and their participating national stakeholders. America, among other Global North countries with racial social upheavals, will need influence from inside and outside to help them adjust in this lifetime.

A federally established Department of Conciliation needs to also have a reparations department to return lands stolen from descendants of families and provide support through legislation and law enforcement to protect those that have been compensated for lands and resources stolen. This is not going to be easy because a white man that paid the market price for farmland today will fight to keep it despite that he may have purchased land stolen fifty to one hundred years ago. If we start with the premise that something as asinine as the Doctrine of Discovery led to all colonial lands being appropriated from their native population, then we know we started with a crime. A ninety-eight percent white ownership of rural lands in America suggests that the crime has grown unheeded. It's probably too late for all white people to give back all the lands stolen—it would probably trigger the next civil war—but ignoring the imbalance is not an option. If it means that federal governments pay for this land and give a tax credit for brown landowners for a selected timeframe, then so be it. If it means that the federal government compensates brown former landowners by providing those who so desire, capital, such that they become owners of capital required for investment in the lands, providing the means to purchase major equity in global companies, then this is a viable option for compensation.

Some white people speak the language of money so well that to brown people, it's like a foreign language. Remember, white people, trust and help each other, share the tax, stock, and investment tips, and even invite each other to participate in business ventures with much more trust than they extend to brown people. Brown people need to be educated on how to manage money and not necessarily by white people. Many savvy brown people understand and know how to grow money. However, schools should teach about credit ratings, stocks, bonds, mortgages, retirement, the need to take a regular vacation, get health checks, and exercise, all of which should start from primary school.

Link the national educational curriculum with the economy now and plans for the future. Scholastic equity in a national program tied to the requirements and vision of a harmonious economy provides a future workforce and people that would be more equipped to repress racism. In Switzerland, all schools are required to take their students on ski trips as part of their curriculum at least once a year. Parents get paid well enough to also take their children on ski trips during the school's winter break. The result is that they create their winter tourist market of people going skiing in the midwinter, providing employment and income to the country. Foreigners also come as tourists to add to the economy. U.S. public schools should have positive educational field trips that involve exercise or knowledge immersion in different historical civilizations, industrial developments, and infrastructure appreciation in diverse parts of America, on whatever type of terrain they have available: hikes and horseback riding in the mountains, swimming or marine activities in the coastal region, training on business development, land utilization and food supply on a farm in the agricultural plains, skiing in the Rocky Mountains, utilizing whatever advantage that region has to showcase activities that the children can enjoy as tourists when they become adults. Collaborate with the private sector in all aspects of finance, agriculture and food science, fintech, high-tech companies, services, and production of intellectual property to allow young people to understand the range of careers available to them.

After seeing election results of minority racist parties winning because of the flaws in the U.S. electoral college system, the brutality of law enforcement against brown people, courts that seem eager to incarcerate a brown person with little evidence while excusing a white criminal caught red-handed, politicians that support these systems, and even civilians that try their best to make create more racist and abusive systems for fear of losing some of their white power, often digging their heels in to make things even worse, I have serious doubt America can solve racism on its own. Despite many white people suddenly seeing racism mainly in 2020, there are still entrenched home-grown extremists, including anti-government militias and white supremacists (Hosenball 2021). This nation will need help from other nations. As Americans, we should show our exceptionalism not by pretending we are a great nation free of imperfections, but by displaying how imperfect we are with a great aspiration for a healthier Union. Then we can become an example for others to follow.

Often city councils and local politicians tainted by racism—whether brown or white—will increase taxes unjustifiably to promote gentrification. The typical strategy is to increase the property tax in a declining community, typically inhabited by brown people too abused in the income base to upkeep the area. Their properties are so devalued that it's easy for a developer or an intermediary before the developer purchases an area wholesale. The developer then gets a tax exemption to rebuild and resell the new construction to new higher-income people who have a richer tax base than the previous occupants. This approach helps improve housing areas and prevents blight, and property devaluation, and keeps the economy ticking over. However, it removes brown families from lands and eliminates their opportunity to build wealth for themselves and future generations.

Governments need to focus on bringing in industries and providing an environment where all can invest, rather than just raise taxes that result in pushing out poor people. Raising the welfare of the region provides more prosperity in the long run than the short to medium-term approach of gentrification.

There should be a federal and state ban that makes any racially impactful covenants illegal. Any discrimination exhibited by real estate developers should halt their financing, construction, and permit approvals upon curing their prejudiced regulations. In some instances, property covenants claim that anyone other than white people will hurt value. In 2016, a family brought a house in El Dorado Hills, California with an HOA agreement that stated, "No persons except those of the White Caucasian race shall use, occupy or reside, upon any residential lot or plot in this subdivision, except when employed as a servant or domestic in the household of a White Caucasian tenant of the owner." The federal government should make any such covenant null and void, even when they are no longer adhered to. Such written regulations, deeds, racial covenants, and HOA regulations should be relegated to museum exhibitions (News 1130 2016).

Voter intimidation still happens today. In Jonesboro, Georgia, in the 2016 general elections, two police stations were used for the sixty percent brown population in that area to vote (Niesse 2019). It's well documented that brown people are harassed by police, so putting a polling station in a police office building as one civil rights activist stated is, tantamount to "government-sponsored voter intimidation" (Levine 2019). We cannot end racism through voter suppression. To help adjust laws, brown people must be able to participate in the electoral system without restriction.

Related to the above recommendation, no political candidate, regardless of party, for any public office, whether brown or white, without a comprehensive anti-racism program as part of the campaign, should be considered viable by any voter. Once in office, slow or lack of implementation of the program, should trigger a vote of no confidence, to replace them, at the next election, if not sooner, with someone else who will function as an anti-racist in all their policies. There are many ideas from this book they could pull from, as well as other sources and people who have made similar proposals.

A country as great as America should not have the level of homelessness that it does. Start by recognizing that homeless people are not customarily or automatically criminals. They end up in the situation often for reasons having nothing to do with crime. As such, their interlocutors should not be the police. That is a waste of law enforcement resources. It should be social and health care workers. Most homeless people need their own space and support to get back on their feet. They need a private space to work out their challenges with dignity. Like the program in Finland, the government should implement a plan that incentivizes the private sector developers to have low-income homes and some subsidized homes designated for the unhoused. To relieve the crisis, the solution should start with State provision of housing for the unhoused under federal supervision.

Eradicate any remnant of vagrancy laws. Their origins are from 16th century England and were used to protect rich Europeans against poor whites, and in the case of America today, both poor whites and anyone of color. Even if they are not harming, rich white people don't want to face their conscience. Indulging in excess in front of underprivileged people offends their feelings. The police are therefore used to remove anyone who offends these sensibilities—the poor, gay, trans, deviants of any kind, soap-box preacher, political upstart, protestor, group of brown men that may seem "threatening," white people who enjoy the company of brown people, basically anyone who may seem like they will upset the status quo. Vagrancy laws give the police too much-unneeded power to abuse, brutalize and even murder brown people, again, anyone they feel will offend the property owners. Police brutality is legitimized by these laws. Vagrancy laws are not productive for a modern progressive society.

Collecting statistics on progress and race removal compliance is going to be important. Universities and colleges will have to develop courses on how to measure the impact of anti-racial policies, behaviors, and laws even when racial discrimination is unintended. Federal, state, and local governments and the private sector will need to develop measures and make this public so the community to understand their performance towards progress. While racism will not end overnight, society must show incremental improvements. We should see more and more brown people owning their own homes, and investing in commercial real estate, and large-scale farms.

As race discrimination is a global problem, America must lead toward anti-racism rules. These should also apply to its trade and investment relations with other countries. Countries that practice human rights violations against other ethnic groups not in power must be called into question and technical support provided by Americans on how to eliminate racism. All of these recommendations are designed to improve and bring us closer together in tighter, healthier relationships. Relationships are the molecule of human behavior. It ties us together to solve problems. People who don't interact because of the physical environment, beliefs, or laws, cannot have relationships, and therefore cannot together eradicate racism.

In the next chapter, I will discuss the need to enhance education to help eradicate racism.

Chapter 8

RACISM AND EDUCATION

"Education is the passport to the future, for tomorrow belongs to those who prepare for it today."

~ MALCOLM X, Muslim minister, and human rights activist.

This false narrative that says brown people are genetically not as evolved or intelligent is a great white fantasy. This belief negatively affects both white and brown cultures. A white man who loves basketball is told he will never be any good because he is white. A white person who loves a brown individual is often scorned by their family and relegated to a life of misery because they can't peacefully be with the ones they love. Similarly, a brown person who is an expert in physics may be constantly hassled about something unrelated to his work to prove to themselves that physicist before them could not be real. The ultimate religion of racism translates into people's lives.

I think of my brother who grew up in the U.S. He returned to college for a second degree he believed would help change the trajectory of his life. For many years his life was like being in the ocean caught under a net just below the surface. He could see the sky but could not break the surface to breath.

My brother went to a school where white teachers showed no expectation of his success. Often, they were more discouraging than encouraging in motivating his efforts to learn. It was like an invisible puppet string that guided their racial actions to promote white supremacy. Earlier I called this behavior, "white solidarity." Perhaps my brother had what we would now call an attention deficit disorder, like 9.4 percent of the population diagnosed in 2016, often coupled with another disorder (Centers For Disease Control and Prevention 2020). Without a professional diagnosis, with just the evidence of their belief that he must be mentally deficient, they put him in "special education classes for slow children." When he failed mathematics or some other subject, he was not given extra classes or help but left at the same level to repeat the class. In the 1980s, parent advocacy led to students with "mild disabilities" to remain in regular classrooms, often with no specialized teachings (Villegas 2017).

My brother lamented that he was often the tallest kid in class. The shorter and younger kids would poke fun at him, supportive of the teachers' assessment of his alleged mental deficiency. The teacher not only expected him to be among the least intelligent student in the class but also the worse behaved. This was in the 1980s in schools in the Bronx, New York. Today, studies done for primary school and secondary school teachers show that they are more likely to observe and punish brown children, especially brown boys for misbehavior. In one study, when the teachers were told to watch a table of children for misbehavior on a video, eye-tracking software showed that they focused on the lone brown boy in the group.

Even when a teacher means well and does not want to be racist, implicit bias comes into play due to social segregation. Teachers told of their students' poor circumstances in the above Yale study and empathized only with students of the same race. In America, brown children accounted for twenty percent of all preschool students from 2013 to 2014. However, brown students made up a stunning forty-seven percent of students suspended (Brown 2016).

I must admit that I am flabbergasted by these statistics. In my entire school life in the Caribbean, I only know of one student in my school who was expelled, and he was already sixteen years, soon to complete school. Upon being expelled, he went to work, never gracing the confines of jail. I have never seen the police in my school for any reason. We never suspended or expelled preschoolers for any reason. These were children, so what would be the point? Parents were called in for dire cases. The teachers' philosophy, including the few white ones, was that the child needed even more education if they were troublemakers. I cannot comprehend why the solution for any misbehaved child would be to give up on them and deprive them of an education. I would add the behavior of introducing children to the brutality of law enforcement to the list of inhumane racist behavior. Any educational system that uses law enforcement to discipline children is broken and in need of a crisis-justified overhaul. Police should only show up to a school for a law-breaking adult, never a child, of any race.

Like so many brown people that were also abandoned by their educational system, my brother developed low self-esteem, thinking he was unintelligent because all the people in authority told him and our mother so. The taunting reinforced it daily. By the time I tried to intervene when he was in his mid-teens, he had all the symptoms of growing up as a brown male in America. The educational system, especially at the primary, middle, and high school levels in America has failed its students.

There are endless stories of police handcuffing children and arresting them, and often treating them with brute force. These children are mostly brown. The national incarceration rate for "*black* youth placement rate was 433 per 100,000, compared to 86 per 100,000 for white youth." In six states, brown kids are ten times more likely to be arrested and placed in some form of incarceration than white kids: New Jersey, Wisconsin, Montana, Delaware, Connecticut, and Massachusetts (Equal Justice Initiative 2017). I cannot understand how any politician in any state can win their elections from either party when they never solve such national catastrophes. Kids do not belong in jail. Every effort should be made to educate them, not introduce them to the industrial prison system at an age when they have not even figured it out themselves.

The problem stems back to adult teachers believing and fearing brown kids. Sometimes it's their implicit bias guiding them to respond to a child's aggression by calling the police, but the fact that this is done mostly to brown kids signals more than just implicit bias in some cases. When a child as young as eight years old misbehaves, and an adult feels so defenseless that they must call the police, knowing the police are ill-trained and ill-equipped to deal with social problems—police in America are militarized and trained for war, not for civilian conflicts—that adult generally knows they are destroying that child (Adachi 2021). That is intentional. The police who show up and treat the child, normally a brown child like a criminal, know exactly what they are doing. They intend to traumatize that child to nudge them along the path towards the prison, towards renewed enslavement (Newman 2016).

Police brutality—and I include security or resource officers at schools that are also armed and behave like typical street police rather than a protector of the children, especially for people of color, reminds us that they are not there to protect brown people from criminals. They are there to protect white people, property, and wealth. Again, I am appalled by this system, even aiming to arm teachers—like some wild trickery of a Western movie—supposedly to protect students against an active shooter. If I was a teacher, I would promptly quit and move somewhere where greater sanity reigns (S. Johnson 2018). Here is the logic, the solution to something dangerous, is to add more of that something: add more alcohol to alcoholics, more fatty foods to obese people, more sugar to diabetics, more drugs to a drug addict, more guns to a shootout. I can only guess that this stems from a lack of care for human life and the belief that some human lives are more valuable than others.

Sometimes the racism is not as obvious as a school resource officer attacking brown children. As we see throughout the book, often it's a psychological attack. A friend told me this story which I recount verbatim. For readers who may not be familiar, I need to provide some backstory. Stone Mountain is 3,200 acres of Georgia State Park often visited by hikers and nature lovers eager to enjoy the attractions, outdoor recreational activities, and on-site lodging and camping options (Stone Mountain Park 2022). The Park opened in 1965 to the public, the same year brown people got the right to vote. Then, the Park was owned by the Venable brothers who were rock quarry owners from Dekalb County, Georgia. Venable was involved in the resurgence of the Ku Klux Klan in 1915 and the creation of the nation's largest Confederate memorial on Stone Mountain, Georgia (St-Amant 2016). The carving portrays three Confederate leaders of the Civil War on horseback: the president of the Confederacy throughout the Civil War, and two generals. Sam Venable granted the Klan an easement to the mountain in 1923 for their headquarters (Waldrop and Lynch 2021). It was from this period that the Klan, now emboldened for the next 50 years with Klan rallies energized by their anger at what they perceived as brown progress, their memorial symbolism, and government support, embarked on a violent land grab from brown people. The State bought the Park in 1958. My point is that this mountain was a memorial to maintain the old way of life where the U.S. southern white elite stayed wealthy using the labor of enslaved people. To protect this way of life, they ignited a civil war. Unless you are telling the objective truth, this is not a place for a school excursion for any child of any race.

My friend recounted, "We had [field trips] in my elementary school, but [some] were truly the most bizarre experience. One year we hiked Stone Mountain, but at the beginning of the trip our tour guide gushed about the forefathers in the carving, and as we climbed, they hammered into us how grateful we should be for their "sacrifices". The next year we were taken to a farm, but not just any farm, a cotton farm, where not too long ago, enslaved people were forced to work. They showed us the wooden structure where they were meant to sleep and the cotton mill that the owner, in modern times, purchased to help "alleviate all the work to be done after the emancipation". All was normal until they gave all of us baskets, the little brown and *black* children, and told us for the next hour we will be picking cotton to "feel what they felt". We did as we were told, some of us cutting our fingers on the thorns, and at the very end, we had to give our baskets filled with cotton to the tour guide, who was also the owner of the farm. A couple of years later, I asked my friend who went to the white elementary school if they had gone to this farm. She looked at me like I was crazy. The white students in the same school were taken to a museum."

My friend recounted this story after I told her about my own experience on field trips as a child in school. I fondly recalled going to Radio City Music Hall and playing on Broadway as well as a planetarium in New York or examining rock formations for geography on coastlines in the Caribbean. My children had field trips to plays and science museums. Her story of Stone Mountain and the cotton-picking experience shocked me. Her psychological scars from that experience remained into adulthood.

As brown parents, you must pay attention to how your child is being educated. No brown parent should allow what happened above to my friend to happen to their child. You must set expectations by being involved in school and making sure the teachers understand your standards for your child's education. Notwithstanding, please be careful of violent teachers or school police officers, because just protecting your child could be dangerous. But do it anyway.

I once visited one of my kid's schools to talk to the teacher about a bully in her class. This was a primary school. I was upset because my child came home with a swollen lip and stories of the other kid throwing his lunch in the toilet. I never experienced such behavior in my childhood and never tolerated it for my children. As parents, we took a heavy interest in our children's education to advance themselves. We knew there were always racial overtones in most places we lived, so as responsible parents, we paid attention to their time in school.

I took photos of his face and approached the teacher about the attack. She denied it at first until I showed her the pictures. Her denial angered me, and I started shouting at her. Always remember, your children are your legacy and you as parents must protect them. Eventually, the principal came. Now, the teacher was a short, five-foot-tall, slight white woman, and I am a tall, over six feet, brown man. Kids crowded and gawked at the spectacle. In the upper class, the older children told my child's sibling that their father was in another class beating a teacher. I was not. Children, like adults, exaggerate for a spectacle. The principal and I calmly had a discussion in his office about my expectations for my child's education and for the teacher to be able to handle the bully. He assured me he would deal with it, and it would not happen again.

Eventually, as parents, we decided to address the bully ourselves. I had already told the kid in front of the entire class that if he hits my son again, he will be in a lot of trouble with me. Yes, I threatened a child. But I would not arrest the child, put handcuffs on him, or abuse him like the police. I spoke to the kid to alert him to leave my son alone. I never touched him, nor did I intend to. I approached the situation with an understanding of where bullies come from. Bullies are typically scared or insecure people who were bullied themselves, normally by someone more powerful than them, like a parent. More than 60 percent of bullies are physically, mentally, or sexually abused by parents or someone else in their home (Kirkpatrick 2022). The same is true for any adult bully you work with.

We later realized that the child, a white child, was from a poor family. We have no idea of what was happening to him at home, nor did we have any influence over that aspect of his life. He regularly bullied kids in school. When my child had his next birthday party, we did something unprecedented. We invited the bully. He had never been to any of the other children's birthday parties because the parents of the kids he bullied scorned him. At the party, I treated all the children as friends of my son. The joy on this kid's face, having been invited to a birthday party and treated as equals, was blissful. He thanked us profusely for inviting him to the point that I teared up. The bully was neutralized and started making friends in school.

Do you think this experience happened in America? What do you think would be the first response of the teacher or the principal? Let's add an armed and trigger-happy school resource officer to the midst, one who grew up in a culture where guns are more treasured than a stranger's life (BBC 2022). Would I even be allowed to see the teacher unannounced like that? Perhaps if a white parent did what I did in America, they may escape without incident, but I have doubts that would work the same for me. This experience happened in Switzerland.

My point is, there are solutions for even an irate parent that does not need to involve firearms or law enforcement. I was not breaking any law, so why call the police? The concept of calling the police for every minuscule conflict—kids fighting, an eight-year-old assaulting a teacher, or an irritated parent—is a waste of resources, and in America, is dangerous, especially to brown people.

The education system, along with the ease at which law enforcement can descend upon a school and pummel students, and the absurdity of arresting children, sends a signal that the system does not want to educate brown kids. Law enforcement has lost its credibility with brown children and adults. Do they even care?

The educational system in America, because it's layered with exceptionalism and is itself motivated by racism, ruins the self-esteem of those being abused. Exceptionalism and the resulting educational system not only harm brown people but to a lesser extent, also harms white people. I have been in senior executive meetings in corporate America where regardless of the so-called "race," people did not understand that Africa is not a country, but an entire continent with vast languages, peoples, landscapes, climates, cuisine, architecture, economies, resources, and cultures.

One CEO thought Liberia was a town in a country in Africa. Another did not understand the difference between Hong Kong and Singapore. Often Sweden and Switzerland are mixed up, and Europe is thought to be more dangerous than America with gun violence. For the record, America has three times more guns than the European country with the most guns—Montenegro (Nicholls, Tidey, and Beswick 2019). Even with all the gun violence removed, America would still be the most violent country compared to its industrialized peers (Epstein 2019).

This violence bleeds into the schools' culture—teachers calling the police for preschool and primary school children to be arrested for temper tantrums, teenagers shooting their schoolmates with their parents' readily available guns because of some minor hurt in their lives, and a school system that fails in comparison to their peers in other countries.

Studies, such as the Program for International Student Assessment (PISA) which comprises fifteen-year-old students' performance in reading, mathematics, and science literacy conducted every three years, shows that the U.S. is not investing in its human capital as other developed countries. High-ranking countries that outpace the U.S. include Singapore, Hong Kong, Macao, Taiwan, and Japan. In 2018, the U.S. placed eleventh out of seventy-nine nations in science. It ranked worse in math at thirtieth. These low scores have been consistent for decades. Yet Americans believe their education system is among the best, or is the best, in the world (Amadeo 2021).

During my second visit to the top-ranking country, Singapore, in 2003, they had a program of investing in their human capital as their most valued resource. I went to an exhibition of primary school inventors. There, children as young as seven years showcased new inventions that they developed with the encouragement of the schools and supported by the private sector. By the time students graduated high school, they already owned several patents and had a mindset to invent and innovate to solve the world's problems. They never worried about student loans or structural inequality because the government believed that everyone in the population was a valuable human resource.

That structural inequality seeps into the minds of everyone in the United States. Due to American exceptionalism, white students perceive they should be on top, even if their education is not as good as in other countries. White students, once they passed childhood, learn racism, and believe their white privilege will see them through to education and the working world. Students from poor households suffer even more because their schools are worse than the schools in rich, predominantly white areas. Research shows that low-income students are more likely to be exposed to weaker content in schools. Rich students in the U.S. do better than poor students because of structural inequality (Schmidt, Henion, and Geary 2015).

While in Singapore, a primary school student is taught to believe she or he can invent something new from their ingenuity, and profit from it by owning patents, my brown brother in America is taught his human capital is not worth investing in and he should not even expect to be educated. I took him to an open day at a local college in Florida to listen to the various curriculum offerings. He too had the mindset of inequality seeped into him. He was scared to go into a room filled with white people. When we visited a college for an open-day presentation, he was terrified I would walk to the front of the meeting hall to take a seat which I did because that was the only available seat. Besides, I typically go to the front of any classroom setting to absorb as much information as I can unobstructed. He wanted to be invisible. His body language spoke of someone who was defeated before he started the battle, much less the war.

Some readers might say he would also have had brown teachers who perpetuated his low self-esteem. Since our mother passed away, he was raised by relatives. His guardians too, accepting their diminished place in society, did not see the merit in helping him achieve the highest educational attainment. They chuckled when I told them we went to a college open day, and he wanted to become an architect. They said he was not "college material" and when he applied, they refused to sign the authorization and federal funding documents for him to study. I believe part of that was fear. I believe they thought, suppose he makes it better than us. Suppose he goes beyond his expected stature in this unequal system. He could be in danger as so many other brown people in the past who 'behaved white' but had 'brown skin.'

So, yes, we as brown people sometimes keep ourselves down in our families out of fear of this unknown success. One relative told me, upon hearing I wanted to become a lawyer when I was ten years old, "a lawyer, that is so hard!" I still applied to study law just to defy him. To be fair, their acquiescence to mediocrity all stems from colonialism and the perpetuation of the myth. Colonialism and its present-day system of structural inequality and racism tell us that only white and rich people are allowed to be transformational. We are all brainwashed, both brown people and white people, in ways we may never unearth ultimately.

In the U.S., teaching is not as honorable a profession as say being a politician, lawyer, or doctor. In the Caribbean, it is. Teachers' salaries are relatively low in the Caribbean. Despite this, we esteem teachers over lawyers. Legal practitioners are considered crooks. Caribbean society believes that teachers make lives and doctors save lives, so people respect teachers sometimes more than they do a doctor. Our parents refer to teachers respectfully as Mr. and Mrs. So-and-so, or Teacher So-and-so. We revere them because education is a means of getting out of poverty and building their legacy. A teacher who contributes to that achievement is extraordinary. The mentality is that children who do well in school, because of great teachers, can get out of poverty and help take care of their poor parents. In this case, the teachers, and therefore the educational system, are a tool to reduce social and economic inequality.

Many of my teachers and I are still friends today, and I often visit them whenever I get an opportunity. My classmates do the same. We are middle-aged, but we still refer to our teachers reverently. They are proud of us when we are successful and see their efforts rewarded in us. When we found a subject challenging, they took the time to teach us, even if it meant staying back without additional pay to teach us extra lessons. Our teachers believe that when a child fails in class, the teaching has failed them. A kid repeating a course is the teacher's failure. As a teenage student, I was encouraged to argue respectfully with evidence and sound logic. There were families where children were seen and not heard, but not with me. My brother, but for the brief time spent in the Caribbean, had none of that encouragement. His experience was the same for millions of other brown Americans if we count generational legacy.

When my brother reported his excitement at getting top grades and his surprise because, in school, he rarely got good grades. This saddened me. I opined that he was always an intelligent person, and I knew this because I talked to him all the time about an assortment of topics. I believed him to be cerebral and compassionate about the world and the treatment of human beings. He was always a reasonable, insightful person, and not taken to unjustified intolerance. He was what they called an even-keel kind of guy. I was not surprised he got top grades.

When he was young in New York, the teachers declared he was too slow for regular school. I thought the regular schools had their problems, but when they put a normal kid in special needs classes, especially because he is brown, that kid is doomed. Special needs classes may help some kids, but in America, those classes make you feel unintelligent and are informally designed to take in brown kids their teachers don't want to teach.

Our mother, like many others who trade their skills and labor for money, worked hard to pay for her expenses. She had no trust fund, income from family company equity, or family inheritance money, nor her own "self-made millions" to send her kids to elite schools or bribe the schools to take her kids and treat them normally.

Rich kids very rarely, if ever, go to special education programs unless they truly have a mental deficiency, and even then, they are not put through the public system. Rich, below-average kids, especially white ones, get sent to regular schools and graduate even if they must pay for the diploma. U.S. Cases revealed that rich parents paid officials to make their children pass

SAT and other college entrance exams. The Federal Bureau of Investigation found that the wealthy bribed one man about $25 million from wealthy parents. He took his cut and spent the rest bribing the admissions systems of elite, proctors of entrance tests, and college coaches to recruit students based on fake athletic records (Glaun 2019).

Brown people knew these things were happening all along, just not the magnitude. Meanwhile, brown parents who can't afford to live in a high-performing school district can commit a felony if they falsify their address to get their child into a better school (NPR 2011). I just imagine how many student scholarships $25 million would pay for poor students. I think one of the fines for any rich person who pays bribes to a school or officials to accept their child, should be made to pay an amount at least equivalent to poor children to attend the same elite schools.

The sad truth is that rich children not only take space that could have been provided to someone more deserving of it due to social and economic inequality, they are taking the space of a poor, but an academically productive child. They know they did not get in on their merit, and they are so entitled, that they are not usually interested in even trying according to professors who teach them, because they do not have to exert any energy to be financially successful (Anonymous 2019).

Professors are reduced to remedial teachers and servants at the whims of rich students and their parents, cooking up bogus grades to preserve their careers. Upon graduation, their parents will have spaces in companies or political connections to help them get work where their lack of scholarly prowess will not even matter to their remuneration or the level of power they would likely assume. Technically, whether they do well or not in school is irrelevant. Yet, poor child, they have no choice but to do exceptionally or be considered a failure. The poor will get a student loan—from a finance company owned by the rich—and spend the rest of their lives on a diminished disposable income dedicated to servicing debt for an education meant to relieve them from poverty.

Unfortunately, when you are stuck at the bottom of inequity, it's like quicksand. The more my mother struggled to provide for her American-born son, the more she sank into her inequity at work and in society. Her circumstances did not allow her to homeschool her child. She was also a single mother. The result is that she believed this nonsense from the school and that he needed to be treated like a special-needs kid. Consequently, even today, he doubts the good grades he received after going back to college at forty years of age. When I told him the education system had betrayed him, he fell silent.

I have some Caribbean friends who, when they realized the education was subpar, homeschooled their children rather than deal with the challenges of primary schools here in the USA. They sent them to middle and high school later. By then, the children were way ahead of the other students who had done in-school education at the primary level. The home-schooled children did not have the distractions of racism and enjoyed learning in a safe, non-pressure environment. Until schools become learning institutions for all people without regard to race, class, and income levels, and the household can survive on one income, or one parent can work from home, it's worth homeschooling, if feasible. Plus, it allows the family to purchase a home in a less expensive location outside the "good" school districts.

We should all aim to be better versions of ourselves over time. No one is ever too old to learn new life skills. I encourage anyone of any age to go back to college or technical school or go if you never did before. Even if it's not college, never give up an opportunity to learn something new. Soak up all the training your organization offers, or anything you can get. Whatever knowledge you put in your head, short of killing you, no one can take that from you. I have seen moochers get angry—with themselves, with hatred—because the person next to them is smarter. Never stop learning. Besides, there are always new ideas coming up as you get older. If you don't keep up, you will become obsolete just like an old computer or a mobile phone. That's why my brother at forty decided to go back to college.

Words power intent and more often than not, affect reality. Saying positive things like "be the best in the world at whatever you decide to do," or "you are a smart and inventive child" encourages the child. During a high school career day, I spoke to a troubled teenager, named Rodrick, as part of a class I was teaching. He was in a high school where the teachers locked the schoolroom to keep the kids in, and they kicked others out of the classroom to stop them from disrupting other students. Teachers locked the bathrooms to prevent kids from taking drugs in the toilet stalls. It seemed like a fancy prison to me. The kids spent their entire day locked up physically and mentally. I would never send my children to a school where they had to lock the doors to the classrooms and bathrooms. The mere act of being in an impenetrable schoolroom cannot send a positive signal to a child. I can't see a rich parent sending their kid to any school that had this policy.

I bet this school had a solitary confinement room. This is a padded room, called a "scream room," where students, who are, according to a teacher, "out of control," are placed until they calm down. It's like a prelude to real prison solitary confinement. ProPublica, an independent, nonprofit investigative journalism outfit, reports that the restraint and isolation punishment included "pinning uncooperative children faced down on the floor, locking them in dark closets and tying them up with straps, handcuffs, bungee cords or even duct tape" (Vogell 2014).

Upon entering the class where Rodrick was one of the students, the teacher locked the door so no one else outside could get in. Rodrick was attempting an escape, strolling to the front of the class to join those in the hallways that had previously been ejected from other classes for troublemaking. The teacher had surrendered and was ready to boot him out to join his friends. He was a tall teenager and probably powerful enough to have body-slammed me had he the inclination. The thought crossed my mind when I stood in front of him to block his exit. I feigned bravery and faced him. I told him to ignore the students in the hallway and not to let them or the snickering students inside the classroom distract him. I asked him what he wanted to do when he left school. He looked at me as if sizing me up on the trust scale. I suspect that this was the first time in this kid's life that someone had been interested in what he wanted to do with his future. Finally, after I prodded him a little, he said he wanted to be an engineer. That drew a din of laughter from his classmates. He was very precise, so clearly, he had thought about it but never mentioned it for fear of being ridiculed.

I outlined the many engineering possibilities I could think of such as industrial, automotive, aeronautical, electrical, chemical, material, robotics, software, computer tech, and architectural. I could almost see his mental gears grinding as he soaked up what I was imparting. I had his attention. "Georgia Technical Institute or the Massachusetts Institute of Technology are the schools you should attend." I also said he would face many obstacles to get there from his classmates, teachers, white people, brown people, his family, girlfriend, and best friends. I noted that all these people likely would say he couldn't or should not pursue his dreams. They are unlikely to have a good reason, other than mentally, to them, such ambition is outside his perceived station in life. I gave him some of the reasons they might give him to give up on the idea: "you just should not do this" to a plethora of excuses like no money, nowhere to study, and no support— former students tell me that many brown students are weeded out of Georgia Tech after their first year — "you are not smart enough," and "you are not college material."

What they would not say outwardly, is that he should not aim too high because he is a poor brown kid from nowhere important, and his family background and history are equally unimportant, and he should know his place that has been dictated by a history of domination, slavery, and lynching. He, like every brown kid of similar means and background, should never aim to have the power of knowledge or a skill set the world needs to grow, and for him to develop his community.

He should not aim to have economic power from his education. He should not aim to have a family and leave a legacy for his children to follow and to become even better engineers. He should not put himself in a position to make great structures with his name on them. He should not build bridges, airplanes, buildings, electrical circuitry, or new information technology platforms that benefit the world, because he is brown, and doing so will encourage power in other people that look like him. He should not leave a positive legacy.

Words do have power. After career day, he made an impression on me, that is until my life challenges took over. Occasionally, I would think about Rodrick and the many like him. To be honest, I do not know if he made it to MIT or Georgia Tech. However, I had a similar discussion with another teenager. I also knew his grandmother and was better able to keep track of him. He interned with me, so I had a chance to encourage him one-on-one. He was on a football scholarship. I told him that football without academic intake will lead him to a future of painfully ruined joints, and likely chronic traumatic encephalopathy (CTE), a type of degenerative brain disorder related to repetitive head shock (Sifferlin 2017). He dropped football once he found other ways to pay for school. So far, he is doing well and headed to do great things contributing to the world.

Before publishing this book, the second young man dropped out of college. I am still working on his self-confidence to get him back in. Ideally, he needs to leave the U.S. to a place where he can see more people that look like him doing well. He is still a work in progress.

At my schools in the Caribbean, most, if not all, of my teachers were brown people. The school principals, or headmasters, as we say in former British colonies, were also brown. None of my teachers ever telling me I was stupid, not even the worse among them.

Today, we are proud prodigies and sometimes relate to our teachers as surrogate parents while our real parents toiled to keep us fed and housed. My classmates from primary, secondary, and tertiary education all strive for success knowing full well they can do anything they desire.

One of my very successful mentors who lives in the United States once said in a commencement speech for a college that growing up in his island state, he never had thoughts that limited him. Growing up, he had parents, family, and often an entire village encouraging him. This is typical of the islands. Plus, everyone in authority like the police, politicians, priests, bank managers, and CEOs all looked like us. They spoke like us and had our culture. We knew we would grow up and fill one of those roles.

In America, as with anywhere, that suppresses other ethnicities, the effect of not seeing anyone that looks like you at the top of the food chain can be demoralizing. Many brown people feel they do not deserve wealth because everything around them screams that message. Politicians call them super-predators, hooligans, and gangbangers. Pastors call them wretched sinners. Police call them criminals and lock them away. Teachers call them stupid. Neighbors prevent their kids from playing together. White classmates call them monkeys. Ignorant white people call brown people indolent, or whatever invented stereotype they have allotted to a specific ethnicity. With all that bombardment of negative energy, it is hard to have the self-confidence to climb to the top.

I know the usual refrain. Look at the so-and-so-rich brown person. They made it. Sure, they did. But let them drive alone in a luxury car without all the bodyguards, and they could be murdered just like any other brown person if they come across the wrong police officer. Besides, no matter how rich or powerful you become in America, as a brown person, you are still in danger, perhaps even more so, because your success is a threat to some white people. The result is often described as a "whitelash," where violent white people would attack brown people, and non-violent white people would change laws and systems to discriminate (Reynolds 2018).

Any other form of integration sets up the students for failure. The brown students will fail because the white system does not know how to help them and probably doesn't want to. The white students will also be at a disadvantage because they won't have teachers and a school system that can help them understand the world outside their white bubble. Eradicating educational and real estate apartheid will allow more diversity of people to be available as students, teachers, and education workers.

Note the next challenge is opening the colleges and universities while linking them with an internship or apprenticeship program to the public and private sectors. That must start by rewriting all the standardized tests to remove the racist and chauvinistic biases. It's no surprise that aptitude, intelligence, and standardized tests were developed to prevent the infiltration of brown people, and anyone whom white supremacists considered needed to be excluded from their perfect society (Rosales 2018).

On the Scholastic Aptitude Test (SAT), twenty-five percent of the questions address European history, and only ten percent African, Asian, or any other culture. The Eurocentric nature of these tests caters to some of the gaps in the results (Public Broadcasting Service 2014). Brown people can pass them, but the problem is they are forced to study a culture and history that pretends their ancestry had no history. While the test questions can easily intersect with the lives of the white test-takers, the brown test-takers have no connection, or worse, a connection infused with white domination.

I looked at a recent SAT study guide and this question drew my attention: "The Emancipation Proclamation declared slaves in which of the following areas 'forever free?'"

(A) All areas of the United States
(B) All areas of the Confederacy
(C) Areas in border states loyal to the Union
(D) Confederate areas still in rebellion

(E) Areas in states controlled by Union forces (College Board 2021).

I leave you to figure out the answer. The question above still refers to these people as "slaves" rather than "enslaved people." Even in the formation, it avoids stating that the white people mentioned in the other questions under U.S. History, kidnapped people from civilizations in Africa and forcefully enslaved them in the Americas. Brown and white people need to be taught this in school, and it should be part of scholastic exams. Even the multiple-choice answers make one pause at how they are slanted. All the history should be included, not just selective sterilized versions. By the way, the answer above is D - maybe.

Sadly, many of the SAT questions glorify Eurocentric history. In this way, brown people trying to enter college must subjugate themselves to a series of questions that will subliminally tell them they are inferior. Not one question asks about African kingdoms, rulers, or any great Native American chiefs or touches on their history before European arrival, or invasion, depending on whom you ask.

Even in mathematics and science questions, they could mention ancient African civilizations who developed architecture, and sciences upon which we base modern civilization today. None of the questions take any of this history into account. In the Science section, there is a great opportunity to include a question on who developed the idea of vaccination—using the weak specimen of the virus or bacteria from an infected person injected into healthy people to make them immune. The West Africans had discovered this approach to prevent contagious diseases, and an enslaved person from that region, in 1721, shared the idea with a doctor in Boston who went on to save many people. The enslaved person never received a patent, any foundation, any generational wealth, not even a statue, a line in history books, a plaque in his name, or entered a question on the SAT (Amadi 2020). To help eradicate racism, these tests must account for history to include African, Asian, and Indigenous people's contributions to the planet, not just Europeans.

That means that the writers of these tests must also enrich themselves with a global understanding beyond just Euro-centric knowledge. This must be infused into the school curriculum to cater to all who want to take these tests. A school system should include the total history of the planet, and be inclusive of people from various origins, particularly native peoples, so the resulting educated graduates will have the mental tools necessary to shape a world that is less racist and more stable and productive.

Furthermore, tests to enter the workforce, such as the State Department's Foreign Service Officer Test, and many others, must consider that it's not just white people taking the test. There may be many brown and indigenous people from different parts of the world. Their history must be included, and just as brown people had to learn all about French

Revolution and other European and white American histories, white people should learn about African and indigenous history, culture, and languages.

Ignorance of the real world outside Euro-centric knowledge and history is one of the main contributors to racism. People will always fear what they don't know or understand. If a white kid grows up thinking brown kids in his class have only a history of being enslaved, how can he respect them? He may pity them and become their friend, but never on an equal plain of respect. Meanwhile, the brown child may have a similar thought. He or she may not have the self-esteem or self-confidence to succeed in life. Or he or she may succeed, but not because it's a normal course of action for them or to do well in life. Rather, they may see their success as some abnormal or special effort they have undergone.

I would like to point out some other ideas I have to help eradicate racism in education and to help raise the bar in education so that it too becomes a tool towards our aim. Some of my thoughts on this subject include:

Career mentoring should be a regular part of the corporate culture. The corporate tax code should include incentives that require companies and performance credits given to all staff members who take time at least once per year to promote career day. It's important for community work and to alert students and teachers of the various professions in the world. Many don't know their options, partly because they are discouraged by a myopic educational system, but also because they don't know what's available.

History and I mean real, honest, and all history should be taught to all students regardless of so-called race and ethnic origin.

I truly believe that some white people will suffer emotionally from the awakening of a world they have been denying. The default reaction in many white people is to seek shelter in denial and disillusion themselves that there is no racism, and certainly, they are not racist. They prefer to believe that it is everyone else in the world making a "big deal" about the way the world works. They believe in the adage, "if it isn't broken, don't fix it." Their perception is that the world is not broken, understandably because it works for them. For everyone else, native people, women, and brown people, it has been broken for centuries. But we should not neglect that there is a psychological fragility that governs this behavior, and the education system will have to reorient itself to help those already exposed to the rhetoric of white supremacy. Young white children, unexposed to racist parents or who have progressive parents are fine. The challenge is finding ways to help those already primed for xenophobia. Those willing to go out and shoot innocent people because of some racist fantasy, I have little hope for them. We must change as much of society as possible so that these people are in the minority and are removed from society when they terrorize and murder people. However, in the schools, at primary, secondary, and tertiary levels, students, and teachers, brown, white, or whatever color or race they ascribe to, will all need constant re-enforcement to eradicate racism. To counter centuries of indoctrination, supported by church, state, and monarchy, the racism eradication program must be aggressive. Colleges, universities, and private schools should also have to offer race integration training for all staff and faculty on an annual basis. Also, don't ask brown people to help set up these courses without giving them authority and fair compensation. Racism is not a brown problem. It affects all of society.

Streamline brown people throughout the educational system at every level whether in the government related to regulatory agencies, political level, private sector educational institutions, or public and of course modernize all aspects of the curriculum to be more inclusive and uplifting of all people.

Public school funding should be allocated according to the number of students in a school. No student should have to travel out of their district or county to attend school. As neighborhoods become mixed, so too should the teachers, school board administrators, and everyone in the supply chain, starting at the federal level and mandating it at the state and local government levels. Integration of schools is not just about the students, but every aspect of the school system.

Many elite schools are bloated with endowment funds. In 2019, eight elite colleges in the United States controlled endowments valued at over 140 billion dollars—equivalent to Hungary's Gross Domestic Product with a population of 9.7 million people. Five reported operational surpluses of over $200 million in their financial statement for 2019. Yet, as part of the federal coronavirus stimulus package in 2020, they were geared up to receive almost $62 million of taxpayers' money (Kerr and Olohan 2020). Instead of hoarding these funds for time immemorial, at least fifty percent should go to help students who cannot afford their education but show academic progress. The interest alone, after accounting for inflation, could probably pay for many students' education. A greater proportion should be skewed to those who have been disadvantaged for generations and now must play catch-up. These include Native Americans and brown people. Having more brown people in power and money also means they too can eventually contribute to these endowment funds. By the way, I understand the sleight-of-hand of white-controlled scholastic award systems implementing such a policy and noting "academic progress" to be the brightest, most accomplished, straight-A students. There has been no real evidence in my opinion that a straight-A student will eventually contribute more to the world than a B or even a C student. Measure "academic progress" or proficiency fairly with a long-term view of what they can contribute to the planet once given the tools. Just as we allow privileged, lackluster white students to blunder through and find their way to eventual success, the same treatment should be given to an equally ordinary non-superstar brown student.

Surveys show that eighty percent of students——with average debt loads of $87,500 had annual incomes of $60,000. The student debt prevented them from saving for retirement. Furthermore, fifty-nine percent said they cannot make large purchases because of their student-loan bills and fifty-six percent said they couldn't buy a home. The payments to service their student loan were higher than healthcare insurance, food bill, and other basic needs. As with many of my friends and family, student loans are a "major source of stress" for eighty-six percent of the respondents, and one-third said student debt was the number one cause of their stress (Keshner 2018). Graduates should not have to trade food and basic items for payment of student loans. This has become an industry for investors. The Federal government should forgive at least most loans and provide subsidies for private student loans. It's controversial I know for the investors who not only invest in student loans-back securities but also finance political campaigns. But we spend $721.5 billion on military spending, and ten percent of the global Gross Domestic Product (about $7.6 trillion in 2017) is hidden in offshore tax havens—a little less than ten percent for America's mega-rich (Costa 2017). There is no shortage of money being hoarded either by the government itself or in private hands, yet citizens must decide on food or student loans. Solving racism will also lead to policies that go after these vast inequities. Forgiving student debt would boost America's GDP by about $108 billion annually, likely more when you add a multiplier of improved disposable income of the newly graduated in the economy (Arnold 2019).

Create an easier pathway for foreigners who study at American institutions and desire to stay and gain experience to work or intern for a few years to make connections before returning home. They would likely become ambassadors for their field in connection with their colleagues and friends in the U.S. Educational diplomacy is a win-win for both sides.

This is a principle for any country that colonized another. It is woefully unbalanced to subjugate a people to colonialism, build world-renowned educational institutions from that wealth in the metropole, never in the colony, then further extract money from the poor students to attend the institution with foreign student fees. In 2017, the English government limited domestic students to tuition fees of $12,900, while international students, including those from former colonies, had to pay between $14,000 to $56,000 and sometimes higher per year (Studying-in-UK.org 2020). Students from former colonies are expected to borrow money and put themselves in debt to pay for their education. When former colonizers wonder about how to repair the damage caused by centuries of extraction of resources that enriched themselves at the expense of enslaved or colonized people from the so-called Commonwealth, a reasonable start is to charge any student from a former colony the same as an English student, and in instances where they can't afford it, offer scholarships. These are often the people doing their best to get a tertiary education to develop the tools to repair the mess colonialism left. This principle applies to all former "colonial masters," whether it is France, Belgium, Portugal, Spain, or Great Britain. They should not consider it as development aid. The very term, "aid," suggests heroism from the Global North directed toward Global South countries. They should consider that they are repairing the damage caused by hundreds of years of domination. The damage still occurs today, for example, when a white investor gets easier access to the resources of an independent nation, over its brown local investor. These countries should be bursting with intellectual capacity paid for by their former colonizers.

The same principle goes for the United States. Any country it ever invaded, bombed, extracted resources from, or infiltrated its leadership to overthrow its governments, should automatically be offered scholarships to their nationals of these countries and regions to give these people the tools to repair the damage caused by their imperialism. We know who many of these are and as time goes by, more will come to light as secret government documents are declassified, and evidence is shown by the receiving country.

Eliminate violence in schools. Because there is easy access to guns in America, coupled with the culture of violence, school children will, unfortunately, occasionally shoot people for some frivolous reason. Until unnecessary guns are eliminated from society, which we are a long way off since people prefer their guns to human beings, schools should have metal detectors at entrances and randomly at various locations to alert the school of students carrying weapons. Teachers should never have guns in school. There may be a security officer, but their job is to protect the students and the teachers, not harm students. They similarly should never have a gun among our future labor force, leaders, and makers of families. All children should be treasured and made to understand that school is preparing them for stewardship of the planet they live on. Destroy it, or each other, and the human species will annihilate itself. Where children are unruly, have a social worker, psychiatrist, or other relevantly trained professional available to help rather than hurt the student. Do not call the police unless someone is murdered. I mean that. Don't call the police for stealing, fighting, or any of these common things that happen among kids and teenagers. Criminalizing children for normal human behavior is not going to help society heal. The very occurrence of a police officer apprehending a child scars their emotional well-being, as well as everyone witnessing the kerfuffle, for life. School should feel safe and be a place to learn and welcome each other's differences as part of that learning experience.

Education systems need to be regularly evaluated and publicly reported on the progress of eradicating racism. Open public dialogue on the progress, what's working and what's not, should be discussed. Evaluations should include inputs into the system—teachers, exams, infrastructure and resources, curriculum—as well as outputs—grades, returns of education in terms of jobs and business establishment, and overall sentiment of educated people towards racial harmony.

I know this will take a while, but educational reform must be aggressive and radically out-of-the-box thinking. All the answers are not here, but these are my observations of what needs to happen to get things moving. Others who are educational professionals may realize other means of eradicating racism in education starting in the U.S.

America has the advantage of being a country that many others turn to as a moral leader. This is true despite the violence seen on the global news about how Americans attack and murder their people due to racism. There is still time to regain an image of care for humanity. I know that if America attacks racial discrimination in its educational system, in a steady, consistent and aggressive way, it will break systemic racism from the inside out. Maya Angelou once said, "Prejudice is a burden that confuses the past, threatens the future, and renders the present inaccessible." Even someone holding on to race with a gun pointed at people he (it's usually a "he"), knows in the back of his mind that no matter how many he tries to kill, it's not the world he wants. He is burdening a country he cares about with past beliefs that threaten and roadblock our future to prosperity and peace.

I often wonder what's at the core of racism. In the next chapter, I try to understand the why within the why of a racist mind. What is it they don't understand what's driving their beliefs?

Chapter 9

WHITE PERFORMANCE

*"I can't depend on the American moral credit to
save some of the people whom I love"*

~ JAMES BALDWIN, on The Dick Cavett Show, aired

May 16, 1969

I was speaking to a colleague about a particular boss who, as a white male, had exhibited a behavior many in the organization considered passively racist. To understand what others saw, I asked her why she thought he was hostile to me. She responded that he was accustomed to brown people bending to his will, no matter how asinine. I challenged his white privilege and power by asking, "Why are you doing this?" and even more, making it known that I would not tolerate such behavior or disrespect even if it meant termination. To be fair, the thought had not occurred to me that he was racist until later. I had noticed his reverence for white staff and dismissal of brown, or any minority staff, especially brown women. Again, to be fair, he was also dismissive of the white women in the organization.

My colleagues noted that typically, a brown man, and she cited a few in our company, who was addressed by a white person, especially a white male, would be humble and take whatever unjustified minor reprimand they got. Even though they knew they were being disadvantaged, they would perform in a way to appease the white man. This comes from years of practice to avoid some form of violent retribution. My performance of showing power, driven by a strong sense of self and conviction in what I deserve in life, was foreign to him. Consequently, his performance of superiority was shaken, and to recoup, he avoided me for months until another iterative attempt to discredit my character. Eventually, he decided to engage with me minimally and civilly until he left the organization.

I realize that in both our cases we were performing in a way to influence how we are treated and how we are seen. If I too believed in his fantasy of superiority, then I would be passing him my power, or at least negating mine in favor of his. Dr. Omar Ali, in his TEDx Talk, described Race as a function of power (O. Ali 2016). The notion that I got from his presentation was that we perform to gain power, and sometimes that power is race. A bully will perform an attack only on those he feels he has power over.

We see this performance as a dance for power in various levels of racism. My experience with a white male boss is at the individual micro-level. At a global macro level, England, after extracting resources to enrich its noble class, after the Second World War, agreed with other countries to provide independence, the right for former colonies to self-determine their destiny. We see the right to self-determination of peoples in many international and regional treaties. In international law, it is the basic tenant for human rights and freedom. Somehow, its systems of exploitation—mostly guided by powerful white men, who, after extracting resources—have no more use for the countries or have found new ways to dominate that are less burdensome to them. Brown people do not have the same sense of self-determination as white people do —at least not in an uninterrupted way. Much of that self-determination whether at the national, global, or individual level is the ability for everyone to have access to their resources and for all to benefit from their skill set.

When a brown person decides to get all the requisite qualifications for a job and realizes that her white boss is less qualified than her and less competent, how can she even have a hope of self-determination when she does not have access to the same benefits? Brown people know that they must work multiple times as hard as a white person to get even a measure close to what the white person earns. Having resources stripped away from former colonies, and history before colonialism removed from school curriculum, all help to chip away at the tools needed for self-determination. Furthermore, achieving success despite the attempt to huddle brown people into cages of poverty saps the very idea of self-determination and any notion of real power. The performance of white supremacy is just that, a performance, always with the hope that the abused will perform docile and subjugated.

It, therefore, means that brown people must perform the way they want to be treated. They must perform by letting white supremacists know that their behavior is unpatriotic, ungodly, inhumane, barbaric, uncivilized, violates human rights and dignity, and is destructive to the world over time. Their desire for dominating power from others seeking harmony and peace, plus a fair share of their labor and the world, is unsustainable.

Admittedly, I am after a solution to help both sides, and this journey of discovery about racism is a deep dive into parts unknown. By many indications, racism in America is more open. Similarly, racist forces are driving even more anti-racism from every "race." I was not surprised when white supremacists attacked the U.S. Capitol on January 6, 2021, to overthrow the incoming government. Brown people had witnessed this behavior for centuries from white people bent on keeping their privilege. They broke the doors and windows of the Capitol and searched for government officials to murder, perhaps on the noose they erected outside. Some chanted to hang the Vice President of the United States, also a white man whom they believed had betrayed them.

I wanted to understand more about what happens when someone is awakened from a delusion and made to look at themselves and the world they contribute to. It's hard because no white person will subject themselves to such vulnerability. In January 2021, a white man from the state of Georgia was among those charged with unlawful entry into the U.S. Capitol, a misdemeanor that carries a maximum penalty of up to 180 days in jail and a fine of up to $1,000. Other than what's written in the media, one cannot tell what the motives were, but he took a gun and shot himself in the chest, committing suicide (Lambe 2021).

I wondered what he saw or feared to make him go that far to choose death rather than life. Brown people must face suffering and still go on, often raising children in a world where they see little hope of an awakening of white people. What happens when reality peels into our contrived sight and all the false stories of triumphant discoveries and "self-made" success and privileges are shown to be based on a fabricated premise and are therefore all a delusion? What happens to white people when they realize who they are and where they come from? What happens to a brown person in a similar light? When such a hard reality hit some of us, do we choose death or true spiritual liberty?

The denial of reality is like emotional cancer that is not only destroying brown people but is destructive to society. Racism is also deforming and disfiguring the character of people who embrace it. White supremacy is like a societal leaky ship. It is gradually sinking, taking all of us with it, even as we throw people that don't speak, look, and act like us overboard. Without collaboration and facing the fact that the ship has holes (belief in white supremacy), eventually, we all will perish (NPR 2020).

The challenge for white supremacists having to face these moral demons in their heads. The fantasy has encircled them. Since everyone else, including brown people, accommodates the illusion normally out of fear of being economically or physically murdered, they too get ensnared. Freedom will require absolute openness to be vulnerable. That honesty of character will be tumultuous and often hurt brown people who want more. White people should not negate that they deserve more—look at the real history of perpetual torment to today.

That vulnerability means introspection and examination of your words and actions. A white person who is culturized to be a racist will become defensive and reiterate that they are not racist and feign offense at the suggestion. That is not showing vulnerability, nor is it helping to end racism. Brown people often try their best not to call it out, in terms of racism, despite seeing it, mainly because the people with the delusion have accumulated the power. Remember, there was a time when, if a brown person exhibited any form of confidence, defiance, or outright calling racism what it was, they were rewarded with torture, lynching in public parks like it was a circus show, or just assassinated. These hostile reactions are designed to preserve the illusion to maintain their power.

People who fight for *black* power, whether it's the *Black Lives Matter* (#BLM) movement against police brutality and murder of brown people or the 1960s civil rights movements, were met with the ridicule that "All Lives Matter." This makes a mockery of people being indiscriminately shot and killed by police and not being held accountable.

Non-racist white people have power too. By nature of their origin, they too have the privilege to speak out and be heard. They are often accused of being "liberals," but they are still in a safer place to chip away at the system with every opportunity they get.

Power manifests in many ways. Economically, it's control over the law, politics, land, wealth, control of people's labor supply, and global supply chain pipelines—for example, trade lanes, and sea routes. It's relational also, affecting how we as humans engage with each other. In a project I was working on that required engineering participation, my white engineering colleague refused to work with me on the project because it was originally taken from him a few years before. I noticed he exhibited passive aggression whenever he was asked to perform a task related to the project. I don't believe it was all race issues that guided his actions of non-compliance and non-support, but I can't help but think there was a layer of superiority when he said that the project area did not need public transport because everyone who worked in that area could afford a car. The fact was we were having major issues keeping staff because they were being paid minimum wage and still had to drive to work. Access to public transport was, to me, a temporary fix, until we could elevate the project, so people did not have to earn minimum wage. Over ninety percent of the employees earning minimum wage were non-white.

White advantage, coupled with brown disadvantage, is dynastic. Everyone must work together to tip the scales to allow more of the wealth to flow to compensate for 400 years of ever-growing polarization. An effort to recalibrate the centuries-old broken system would require that brown people get some advantages and white people, or wealthy people, reduce their hoarding for the sake of preserving humankind.

The key word here is ownership. Brown people need to own contributors to wealth. Many own mostly their labor, but that is dispensable because there are more suppliers of labor than demand, depending on one's skills and connections to other wealthy people. Brown people need to own real estate that increases in value, plus access to capital to work it. Wealth growth cannot happen unless everyone has an equal opportunity to own and similarly is allowed the means to gather the resources to do so. Ownership is power, and power spread evenly can help to end racism. If we don't solve the wealth hoarding, also known as inequality, and the gap widens, the people who are hurt will rebel (DW Documentary 2018).

While I refer to solutions as mainly needing to occur in the U.S., they are global problems, and racism induced by resource-hoarding is a global problem. An asset manager of wealthy clients thinks of different countries as a shopping mall of laws that are chosen based on what the client wants to do with an asset. Fund managers direct funds from the wealthy into foreign direct investment portfolios that grow their wealth in a dynastic way. In the DW documentary, there are only white men around a conference room making decisions on what funds and countries they will invest in to maximize their wealth. Reparations mean derailing this dynastic wealth, not in a way that impoverishes them, but in a way that brings balance to a society without hoarding (DW Documentary 2018).

The power derived from wealth hoarding provides political power. In the U.S., Jane Mayer, author of *Dark Money*, illustrates how political power is purchased through a web of rich people using their wealth to influence tax structure, laws, environmental regulations, capital and investment regulations, labor laws, court appointments, trade rules, and distribution of land. They influence even common perceptions of what we think through their tax-exempted charity foundations molding think tanks and university theories about the economy and social aspect of society. The result is that their wealth allows them to buy the tools—a savvy accountant who can help them avoid taxes, asset managers who can form off-shore companies to help them hide their wealth, and politicians to pass laws—to support their wealth gains (Mayer 2017). Racism is one result. Most often when we speak of racism, we ignore the ultimate intersectionality of race—class. Poor white people who are racist, do so in hope of reaching where rich white people are. Notwithstanding, they too are just a cog in an engine of wealth hoarding.

This has been anecdotally known for some time. In church Sunday school, we learned from many parts of the Bible that, "the love of money is the root of evil" (JW.org 2021). Proverbs 28:20 says that "hastening to get rich will not remain innocent." As wealthy people, whether dynastic or self-made rich, grow in their wealth, studies are showing they become more apathetic to the non-wealthy. Furthermore, they may see the people around them—workers, servants, wives, husbands, girlfriends or boyfriends, politicians, laws, regulations, native people, brown people, and poor white people—only as tools that support or create obstacles to their aspirations. A rich oil tycoon sees nothing wrong with paying campaign funds to politicians to remove or defund an environmental department from regulating them. Similarly, a rich capitalist will purchase favor from a low-paid financial regulator to allow them to maximize their ambitions unimpeded (L. Miller 2012).

In an experiment at the University of Minnesota, the results published in the journal *Science* in 2006, a psychologist studied students exposed to or "primed" for money. They behave less helpful when they bumped a student who then dropped all their pencils and books. All these studies show that as humans, regardless of race, money primes us to be less caring for others. Race makes brown people the underclass and whites the class or group with money. It makes sense that the wealthier the white person, the less likely they are to care about brown suffering. The idea is not foreign. While in a supermarket shopping for groceries, or in a park, or anywhere, I notice non-white people wearing masks during the coronavirus pandemic, and white people less so. Furthermore, in the grocery store, they would come right next to me as if I were invisible despite the signs requiring six feet distance. It could be that we are in the same income bracket, but the effect of white superiority and belonging to a made-up group, gives them the power not to care, as if they indeed had lots of money.

Poverty makes people anxious. Even where children have the ambition to escape poverty via tertiary education, they worry that they may have to endure a lifetime of education debt to pay for a chance to be better educated, just to have the tools to better analyze their world. At impoverished levels, there are children with less nutrition, poorer quality food, and parents who cannot help them with their homework because they too had a substandard education. Living in a crime-ridden area—an old friend of mine used to recount occasionally hiding behind cars to get to school in Washington DC in the 1980s to avoid crossfire from rival gangs—also creates social desperation. Constant anxiety creates a feeling of hopelessness and fear of not having a viable future.

Wealth makes you more strategic, better health, calmer decision-making, and a horizon to move into the future knowing that you are entitled to be successful. That knowledge of the future makes people save and invest more. One study showed that people who are upper class, in the upper-income bracket, and in American society, a proxy for white, are not as attuned to the suffering of others as are those who are of a lower income bracket or lower class. Brown people allude to this phenomenon often. They are aware of micro-aggressions, and implicit biases, and understand the impact of racial discrimination for centuries, while many white people use their privilege to ignore it. In various studies, it is a combination of some lacking compassion due to the need to use the underclass to build themselves up—pay workers a minimum wage while the top owners and executives can afford to go skiing in Aspen every year.

Psychologists have shown that prosperous people value individuality—uniqueness, separation, individualism, triumph—whereas people lower down on the social hierarchy tend to emphasize homogeneity, healthy personal relationships, kindness, and group attachment. Rich people tell their kids they are number one and the world is their oyster. They also have the resources to make that true. Most poorer people teach their children to look out for family, love, and cherish people around and help others in need. I taught my children empathy, family togetherness, and being kind to people around them. However, when I started to study societal deficiencies like racism, I wondered if I should have taught them to be apathetic and ruthless. Ultimately, we all genuflect between these feelings of dominance and humanity. Some rich people worry that their children may be too ruthless because they too will suffer when those devil-for-children grow up. Plus, they want to be seen as good, often Christian people, always being the heroes of the world.

You see this bifurcation in our collective societal mentality being manipulated in commercials. A commercial of a sporty BMW M5, i8, or any of the sports cars almost always features a white male, and they are usually somewhere on a lonely road or in a desert driving way past any existing road speed limit, never attracting a traffic police stop (Autoport Magazine 2014). In one commercial I watched, the police cleared the street for their reckless driving, then drove off with them at the end (The Car Media 2018). It signals that they make their own rules given their individualism, and given uniqueness, the system will adapt to suit their desires. Price is rarely if ever, mentioned. As a friend of mine used to say regarding the price, "If you have to ask, you can't afford it."

In comparison, commercials in both Spanish and English language, featuring Toyota, Nissan, Hyundai, and Honda, typically feature a family, a group, or a couple, and display the car on the street with even more people, or, in a dealership as a backdrop, with balloons and families browsing around. They are also more likely to feature happy-wide-eyed people being thrilled at the low cash deposits and payments for a car. Contrary to uniqueness, these commercials also include other "smart" people with the same car (The Library of Old Car Ads 2 2022).

I happen to know a female Latinx mother and wife who drives a BMW M5, and she is not represented anywhere in any of their commercial that I have ever seen. The point is marketing and capitalism prey on our mental images of ourselves and others. They subconsciously reinforce stereotypes and prejudices. Those reinforced perceptions are so strong that even though anyone can buy a BMW or any other fill-in-the-blank luxury car, my Latinx friend gets harassed, mostly by white men, about owning her car. She once had a Mercedes-Benz S-Class and a white male asked her, after she parked her car in the same parking lot as him, how she could afford a car like that. With a straight face, she said with a Latinx accent, "Oh, I am a high-class escort."

Brown people get harassed by the police for driving luxury cars. It may stem from the need for white people to control the mobility of enslaved people. The intersection of the prejudices the commercials are banking on is not lost here. The origin of police and law enforcement vigilantes comes from the need to protect property and those white people who seek to control enslaved people through slave patrols. Mobility gives people the freedom to explore their environment, live wherever they want and be free to escape violent cities and the low wages of sharecropping. During the Great Migration (from 1916 to 1970), six million brown people fled the rural South for the cities of the North, Midwest, and West to improve their livelihoods, despite the xenophobia they met upon arrival (History.com 2021).

It is that free mobility that allowed white Europeans to explore the world and find new resources owned and unowned. Their mobility was subsidized and incentivized by the Doctrine of Discovery, by their monarch to encourage them to pillage any possessions found and further enrich their countries. Mobility leads to progress. It opens one's mind to new possibilities and discovery of new ways of life, people, and new ideas that can create economic and social growth. For brown people, it also gave them the ability to live in the suburbs. Efforts to curtail this new mobility of brown people come in the form of stop and search guided by racial profiling, especially if, like my Latinx friend, you are driving a vehicle that white people believe you should not be able to afford because of their white supremacy beliefs.

There is a phrase, "driving while *black*," that signifies the discrimination and harassment by police, often leading to jail time, injury, or even death from a traffic stop. It means driving in fear for your life, not dissimilar from enslaved people who were prohibited from moving around outside of a mile of their place of labor (PBS 2020). Without mobility, brown people cannot organize, meet, and orchestrate their actions toward freedom. I wondered if this psychology of mobility is one of the main reasons most white people felt the need to move about, meet in groups, socialize, and generally be out during the coronavirus pandemic starting in 2020. While out for exercise, I often saw mostly white people outside, including in groups, and few had protective masks.

Since there is nothing a brown person can do to guarantee their lives will be saved if they perform in a particular way while being mobile, and since white people are not equally assaulted by the police, then the reason is control and restriction of mobility. The change must come from the police and from the system that controls them. Keep in mind it is not just the police who believe they need to curtail the movement of brown people.

Generally, civilian white people also try to enforce restrictions on the progress of brown people. Where the police fail to control mobility, white people will fill in. My partner and I drove through a neighborhood, just outside of Atlanta's perimeter in Georgia, looking for places where we would like to purchase a new home. I looked in my rearview mirror and realized a big GMC van was following us almost on my bumper in a quiet neighborhood. I could not believe this was happening in 2017, so I kept turning different roads, only to have the vehicle follow me. It was a white male at the wheel, seemingly alone. We pulled into a small parking lot. When he followed us there and just remained behind us, I knew we may be in trouble. In America, there is no assumption of well-meaning intention when someone follows you around for twenty minutes in a quiet neighborhood. Our vehicle had no tint, so it was easy to tell our complexion.

I am grateful for my maturity at the time because a younger, more egotistical *I* would have exited my car to confront this stalker and likely been shot in the head. I assumed he was armed and confident he was more armed than he thought I would be. I also assumed he had no job, a family that cared for him, or a stimulating hobby, since he had time to follow people—this may be his hobby—seeking a confrontation so he could do some killing to protect what he considered his territory. We set our GPS to take us back to the Interstate highway and headed out of there. He followed us until we were on the exit to the highway.

I often hear of brown Americans who have never left the country, or sometimes, even their county. One older brown lady I met at a party said she has never left the county she grew up in. When I asked why she said it was not safe. People—I later realize she meant white people—would kill you. I felt like I was back in the 1700s. Mentally, many poorer brown people felt the need to stay where they are, especially if they were from the South, to ensure they stayed safe. When I mentioned to my colleagues that I would spend a weekend going on hikes in the forest, walking the streets, and generally exploring, they warned me that I could get murdered by violent white people.

I did not believe it at first. Then I started reading the stories of brown people being murdered. Ahmaud Arbery, while jogging in a Georgia suburb in 2020, videos of an attempted lynching of a brown man while camping in an Indiana forest also in 2020. Then I was shocked to see an old-fashion noose hanging of five brown men in 2020: hanged from a tree near the community city hall, twenty-four-year-old Robert Fuller in Palmdale, California, thirty-eight-year-old Malcolm Hersch in Victorville California some fifty miles from Fuller's murder, twenty-seven-year-old Dominique Alexander in a Manhattan public park, New York, a seventeen-year-old in a Spring, Texas, elementary school playground, a Latinx man in Houston, Texas. In all five cases, the authorities—police, government, all white, jumped to a conclusion labeling them as suicide, until there was a public outcry to investigate (Democracy Now 2020).

The fact that law enforcement exhibited disinterest in even investigating their deaths is a racism problem in itself. Any white person dying for any reason, including suicide, is investigated to determine why they would even consider suicide. The aim is to prevent losing more of a valuable life. The same principle should be applied to brown people. Even if it was suicide, there should be an investigation to determine the reason and attempts to avoid replication to save a valuable life.

Between 2010 and 2015, I went on numerous solo hikes in the forest parks of Lancaster, Pennsylvania, and swamp tours in Okefenokee camp in South Georgia, without much consideration for where I was living and what was happening to other brown people. My grandmother used to say that "God protects children and fools." I think it was lucky because as a brown man, I may not have always seemed like a pushover.

When poor white people realize the foundations of white supremacy are false, it's like burning the wings off a butterfly. Not only can't they fly through life on white advantage, but they are also suddenly equal to, and more often suffering worse off than brown people. White people come to realize this through long periods of unemployment, struggle, poverty, and hopelessness, which in turn leads to alcoholism, and drugs fueled by opioid availability (Villarosa 2019).

The knowledge that there have been seventy-nine hangings of brown men between 2000 and 2016, all unsolved, with no real and transparent move to solve them by our elected officials, attorney generals, and prosecutors, shows the cancer we have allowed fester in America (Democracy Now 2020). To end racism, all of these must be investigated, and the murderers brought to trial and sentenced fairly. "Sentenced fairly" means treatment equivalent to that, as if they were brown people who hanged a white person. That's how we prove that "all lives matter."

If one considers the government's quick conclusions that brown men are hanging themselves, you would believe brown men have a high suicide rate. However, the Center for Disease Control studies in 2018 shows that rates of suicide among *black* men are 12.0 per 100,000, while that for white men is 30.4 per 100,000. Hispanics are also around 12.1 per 100,000 and only American Indians are higher than white males at 34.8 per 100,000. For *black* and Hispanic women, it's even lower at 2.9 per 100,000 and for white women 8.3 per 100,000 (National Institute of Mental Health 2019).

The rates add even more weight to the need to investigate these deaths and bring the criminals to justice. American history is riddled with uninvestigated cases of murder of brown people and children with no one ever being held to account. That's what happens when the lawmakers and enforcers are mostly white supremacists. Brown people who have suffered are usually endowed with a healthy surplus of resilience to a difficult life. Even brown people who grew up wealthy, know that because of their skin color, they are not far from a wrongful arrest, or worse, entanglement with law enforcement that could be fatal. One wonders, if white people, especially white men, are on top of the food chain, why are they most likely to commit suicide?

In a discussion with a white Dutch friend of mine about her perception of racism, she confessed, that she never considered herself white. In the Netherlands, she is just a Dutch woman. I told her I knew Western society considered me *black*, but it was not a marker of my destiny, at least I was not sure it was until I moved to America. Our discussion made me realize that there is an original lie about a falsely made-up community called white people.

Europeans, before they landed in America, were English or British, German, Italian, Scottish, French, Spanish, and so on. When they came to America, they became white. Whiteness necessitated the rejection and subjugation of brown culture. I have already alluded to the genocide of Native Americans, enslavement, and so on. Those acts of violence and false historical storytelling to cover up the shame of such crimes must be perpetuated to maintain the advantage. Even when not violent, they prefer to fill seats of power with mediocre white men and women, rather than consent to someone brown to rule. Being white, with all the advantages, requires a moral death of the conscience. As James Baldwin pointed out in his essay, "On Being White . . . And Other Lies," striving to be white, with all its societal and environmental destructive depravities to every other people and itself, is a moral choice (Baldwin 1994).

We see men today still willing to erode their morality just to gather resources or what they perceive or have been fooled into thinking is profit. The storming of the U.S. Capitol on January 6, 2021, is such an example of chasing a belief to the detriment of their moral compass. When they sense the evaporation of the scheme of whiteness, they become bitter, and panic that the reality outside their belief should allow some brown people to prosper, to the zenith of a brown president to reign for two terms— President Barack Obama. I saw the panic as mainly white men were willing to overthrow the government and ignore election results for a party they did not support. I worried that I would see even more murders of brown people by white supremacists out of desperation. Their belief in white supremacy was so great, they were willing to oust democracy.

The bitter panic of white people comes from a real place of erosion. Despite 400 and counting years of oppression and murder to maintain "whiteness," brown people survive and even thrive. Demographic evolution is changing one of the original vestiges of white supremacy—the number of white people versus everyone else. The U.S. Census Bureau reported that in 2020, the growth rate over the last ten years for Asians was thirty percent, Hispanics, twenty percent, and *black* people twelve percent. Meanwhile, people who claimed they were white grew by 4.3 percent (Staff, News One 2020).

Apart from demographic changes, you have other triggers of a white bitter panic—obesity, health challenges, lack of easy-to-afford health care for all, globalization which moves lower-level jobs to countries of the Global South, higher skills jobs require tertiary education, often unattainable to not just brown people, but poor white people as well. Even when attainable, student debt allows you to be educated enough to realize you can intellectually participate in society but cannot prosper financially. The new global companies shun unions, and despite what one of our former U.S. presidents—number forty-five—said about his opponents exporting jobs, my ex-mother-in-law bought me one of his branded ties that were made in China.

Since "maintaining the myth of whiteness and white superiority requires a certain amount of disassociation, including the ability to dehumanize entire groups of people," the constant push by brown people, and the downward economic mobility of some white people, often in support of rich white people, leads to "deaths of despair" (Daniels 2018).

Research shows that there is an increasing mortality rate, from drugs, alcohol, and suicide, among middle-aged white people, especially those without a bachelor's degree, and not just those from Appalachia. This is at a time when globally, white mortality rates are falling. When people lose their status of whiteness and belonging, as associated with prosperity, they become bitter as the falsities and trappings of being white strip away. One reaction is the attacks we observe on non-whites, including mass shootings. (Boddy 2017).

One reaction that fascinates me even further is not so much the white people who realize their lives may be worse off than brown people despite their choice of whiteness, it's the ones who are well-to-do, are educated, claim not to be racist, but still hold fast to their choice of whiteness. An example of holding on to whiteness portrays itself can be seen in a panel discussion I once witnessed. The white male moderator asked the brown panelist how they felt about the murder of George Floyd by a white police officer. The panelist replied, "I feel the same way I hope you feel about the death of any human being in such a barbaric way." The point is, he should be expressing how he feels and joining that feeling of hurt with everyone else including the panelist. The fact that he believed he feels differently, and the question is addressed to a brown person is already pointing to a direction of his choice, as if he is an outsider to the hurt of a brown community.

White people who chose all the trappings of whiteness, also select to be inhumane and to benefit from an economy and social status built on the genocide and un-homing of Native Americans, kidnapping, forced migration, then imprisonment on a plantation, enslavement, and continuous abuses today. Educated, Christian, good, "I-am-not-a-racist" people, chose whiteness.

The brand of "whiteness" has become so well-marketed, that even brown people aspire to be white. Colorism, where lighter skin brown people get more privileges than darker skin people, is a result of white branding. Another is skin bleaching, where brown people use skin creams and other chemicals to lighten their complexion, often with devastating and cancerous effects, not to mention mental health deterioration. In the Caribbean, some mothers used to put clothes pegs on their children's noses in hope that the squeezing pressure would make them more pointed like the white brand. I recall my mother and other women, hot ironing their hair—heating a metal comb on the stove and combing their hair with it to get it straight. The house would smell of burned hair. Every brown woman I know went through the age of relaxing their hair with caustic lye and non-lye chemicals, often burning their scalp, and leaving scabs around the edges where the chemical stayed too long on the skin.

In Caribbean banks, before the 1980s, mostly lighter skin women got jobs as tellers because the managers, often white or light skin themselves, believed the people with money, mainly white people, only wanted to see their group handling their money. Straight hair, signifying white people's hair, was so glamorized that even if a woman was light-skinned she was unlikely to get a job in the bank if her hair was left naturally curly. Anything African was frowned upon—braided hair was considered not feminine, poor, and associated with *blackness*. African pictures and symbols were considered evil and ungodly. In America, studies show that brown women are thirty percent more likely to be called out for violations of workplace appearance policy. These policies are often drafted by white people in celebration of white imagery only. Furthermore, they are eighty-three percent more likely to be judged more harshly because of their looks, dress, and attire (Akutekha 2020).

As a teenager, I found myself brainwashed by my upbringing, often thinking that beauty was linked to lighter skin and long, straight hair. The brand and marketing of whiteness are seen everywhere. In commercials, only recently have we been seeing a resurgence of non-white model advertisements. In consumerism among countries in the Caribbean, it's often believed that food, clothes, and styles, from the metropole, are superior.

People who sport styles from the metropole are considered cooler than those wearing local brands. Children grow up seeing their parents battle over hair, and stress over them their hair never pleased that it does not stay straight. Hair badgering causes erosion of mental health from an early age. Instead of concentrating on solving higher-order global problems, or just enjoying their lives, these young people are crippled with thoughts that they need their hair to look like white people's.

Protecting the brand of whiteness is debilitating for brown people. It's like trying to juggle a cloud. The choice of whiteness is deeply damaging to society and everyone's mental capacity. I love to see the freedom that children have in a kindergarten, all complexions playing together, enjoying each other's company, and learning life skills before they are corrupted with lessons on racism. They have freedom. The choice of whiteness is like mental enslavement for anyone who believes in it. They can never truly see the world for its brilliance, and never reach their optimal lives because there is this wall of whiteness where you are either in or out.

Recently, many brown women have been cutting off their relaxed hair and going natural. Some even reject the idea that long hair is beautiful via the big chop—they cut it all off. I commend their newfound freedom. Others adopt sisterlocks, an interlocking method that resembles micro locks or microbraids allowing the hair to be natural without chemicals. This technique was invented by an African American Studies professor named Dr. JoAnne Cornwell (Haupt 2017).

Brown men used to be among the cool folks that Jerry Curled their hair just like women. This was a chemically straightened hairstyle from the 1980s and 1990s. Few, if any, do that now. I did a version of this, called S-curl, during Summer vacation during the 1980s. When I returned to college and the tropical sun of the Caribbean hit my hair, the chemical reaction turned it bright orange. My friends laughed at me. Admittedly, I laughed at myself, because it looked ridiculous. I cut them off in less than a month. I rejected whiteness even then.

Women who adopted natural hairstyles and mentally embrace them always talk about how freeing it is to be able to wash their hair in a quick time, go to the pool or beach, exercise and not worry about sweating, or not running from the rain because a few drops of unwelcomed water on processed hair will ruin the style. Also, pursuing whiteness is expensive for brown people. The base price for a "virgin relaxer" is typically $100, and $90 for relaxing re-growth, that new hair that grows out the scalp later. Depending on how fast your hair grows, or how well it is treated with the maintenance chemicals, which themselves are also hundreds of dollars, you may have to return every few weeks for touch-ups.

Despite the fuss about hair, brown women are still challenged by jobs headed by white managers, or even brown managers who have chosen whiteness. They are still shunned from certain careers often seen as the realm for whiteness—the stock market and financial sector, corporate world, basically anywhere where many white people have chosen to be fragile in their whiteness. By fragile, I mean they are so fickle in the fiction of whiteness that they believe that if too many brown people are added, especially brown people that have not humbled themselves to whiteness, then that very whiteness could be in jeopardy of erosion.

I always make it my duty to tell women, or young girls, of course without being creepy, that their hair looks nice, or I like their hairstyle, or I like how they keep their hair. One of the reasons is that people want to feel confident that they are attractive. There are so many forces telling us that unless we embrace whiteness, we are not beautiful. Breaking away can be scary. We think, that if we don't embrace whiteness, no one will like us. I think we need to counter that and tell men and women, who have embraced their image rather than that prefer by white choice, that they are beautiful. Each compliment fills their emotional bank account such that maybe when they hear the put-downs, they can wash them away as ignorance and move on to people who believe in reality.

Here are some of my recommendations to address some of these racial issues outlined in this chapter. As with other chapters, I don't have solutions for everything, and racism is so intertwined in various aspects of the fabric of society, that it's almost impossible for one person to come up with every single solution. But these go in the right direction and help others, including white progressive people, develop solutions to help heal and move America, and maybe the world forward.

Brown women, girls, and boys should not be asked to embrace a false premise of whiteness to keep a job or go to school. Pass the Crown Act. CROWN in this case stands for "Creating a Respectful and Open World for Natural hair." It's a law that prohibits race-based hair discrimination, something that brown people experience. People are denied jobs and educational opportunities because of their hair texture or protective hairstyles including braids, locks, twists, or Bantu knots. If we aim to eradicate the imagination of whiteness, we have to embrace other cultures and peoples as beautiful and deserving of being in spaces and thought of as glamorous. While many brown lawmakers lead the movement to make the Crown Act national, I encourage all legislators to join in, and for people who write their legislators to tell them that this is important to them. So far, eight states have signed. Mississippi is the only state that rejected it (The Crown Act 2020). Other states should think of the investments that they will attract them as the states are seen to be modern and progressive.

Companies that are genuinely interested in profits more than perpetuating a false ideology focus on talent regardless of their candidates' skin color, hair, accent, origin, gender identification, or sexual orientation. "Best places to work" measurements and publications like Indeed, Glassdoor, and Fortune.com should all add a measurement of a company's openness to focus on talent. They should be measured according to how well they increase and integrate the talent pool with ethnic and gender diversity, including at leadership and decision-making levels.

When white people drive along a road and see a policeman beating, manhandling, or ill-treating anyone, regardless of their skin complexion, they should stop their car a little distance so that the police do not feel threatened, but make sure the police are aware that they are being monitored and they will be held accountable for their actions. Record them with a camera. If they are using lethal force, publish it on social media and report it to your local politicians, television news networks, pastors, or anyone in leadership. But whatever you do, never just gawk and pass the scene. Also, it does not matter if others have stopped and are recording the event, the more people stop and hold them accountable, the better you are making your society by bringing transparency to law enforcement. Finally, don't just record the abuse. Warn law enforcement to stop. Remind them we do not allow this savage behavior in America. Make it your business to follow up on the incident to make sure the person made it out of the arrest safely. Often, the murders are done in the confines of a patrol vehicle or jail. We must hold law enforcement accountable.

For white people, instead of panicking because they are losing the majority in terms of the population, embrace it. Perhaps the big fear is losing political power in a democracy. It could be why many white supremacists-supported political parties are so bent on restricting brown people from voting—the last-breath effort to hold on to control and maintain the whiteness. We see the desperation and anger in white supremacist marches across America. I understand they believe what they do and, like a religion, their attachment to privilege appears like it's being eroded—it's not—so violent attacks and chants about "reclaiming America" go on. These people need to be monitored by the federal government. Reeducation is vital for adults and children in these groups. The only people that have a right to reclaim America are Native Americans. Everyone else came from someplace else. America is not a white country, because whiteness is not a real thing. It will take generations to get this idiocy out of the heads of protestors and KKK-like people, or even normal people who still see the need to protect whiteness. But it must be done to save the country and to save them.

The ability for anyone to record and share videos has helped showcase the effect of whiteness on the social fabric of society. It's a vital tool that has helped expose the violence that many brown people have been talking about for ages. We should eliminate police attacks and wrongful arrests, white neighborhood vigilantes' assaults, and white hate groups making public speeches and attacking people. The television showed video images of police beating and using attack dogs on men, women, and children in a peaceful march in Selma, Alabama, in 1965. White people were appalled at the behavior, and it led to more white progressives getting involved in bringing civilizing behavior to violent white people. Today, we see the same thing since everyone has a video recorder on their phone and broadcasts tools via social media. Brown and white people need to record any act of violence and broadcast it to the world. People who believe in whiteness want to be secretly violent, to hang brown men and escape. If it was a cause worth fighting for, they would be willing to go public and die for it. Intrinsically, they know it's fake. But they insist on preserving whiteness to gain resources and power. Record every act of racial aggression and make it public.

Earlier, I mentioned a white guy in a GMC van following me and my wife to chase us out of town or killing us. At the time, I thought of myself in his shoes—to an extent. I would unlikely get in my vehicle to drive around looking for brown people to harass. I would be too busy playing with my kids, working on my house, reading a book, watching a good movie, being occupied with my hobbies, having drinks with friends, and a plethora of other activities. So, I assumed he had none of those things to occupy his time. People like him need to be studied and educated. Our education system should help him find usefulness and purpose beyond hunting brown people to potentially murder them. He may have a mental health issue or be on drugs. Who knows? To make sure I spared my life and body from injury, I never stopped to confront him. I, after all, have things in life to occupy my time, and I want to live to continue to do these things rather than be shot for whiteness. Social systems, and social work, ignore racism and adults who teach their children racism. We cannot do that and expect them to come out on top.

Every aspect of the preservation of whiteness must be challenged by the church, state, private sector, non-governmental organizations, and international government organizations. It cannot be one-off solutions and half-hearted attempts. It cannot be white executives wearing pins on their $3,000 suits that say, "*Black* Lives Matter," or people staking signs in their front yard with the same message. It must be a full onslaught against whiteness and all the destruction it stands for and has stood for in history. Racism cannot end with just brown people protesting every time some injustice is inflicted on another person. We wait for a justice system to punish murderous policemen, for example, only for a white supremacy system to free them or give them minimal jail time. Remember, the "government," and the "system" is made up of white supremacists. They must be replaced by normal people who want peace and harmony in this adopted country we all call home. Politically, the executive, legislative and judicial branches must be diverse, just like the private sector. Religion must play its part in the reeducation of white and brown people who want to uphold whiteness.

Departing from whiteness also means treating Africa and any other continent with predominantly non-white people, with the same level of respect that is provided to Europe. Just as America does not pillage Europe, nor does Europe, anymore, plunder America, Africa should not be ransacked anymore. Africa and other formally and some still colonized people have made America and Europe wealthy for eons into the future. What is the solution? Stop. Invest in Africa and the Caribbean just as European companies have invested in America. Africa should have car plants, research and development, aerospace companies, and high-end technology sectors, especially since many of the raw materials come from there. I commend countries like Ghana and Rwanda which are taking bold steps to control their destiny. All Asian, Latin American, African and Caribbean countries should go this route towards their development. They all have people smart enough to help them develop. Admittedly, many are caught in the chase for whiteness—stolen wealth from their people, self-enrichment, and political corruption. Much of that mentality comes from following the white hoard mentality. That too will take time to re-educate, even the politicians in these countries that are pillaging their people. An America that has shunned whiteness will be much better equipped to help other countries grow in their moral leadership. An America that seeks to participate in their growth, rather than just plunder raw materials and ship them to the metropole for processing, will lead to progress against whiteness. Any forest left untouched will regrow, once not devastated. Similarly, if countries of the global north stop stealing resources from countries in the continent that is the raw material capital of the world, Africa, then it will save itself. In the end, America too will benefit from a stable, safer world.

Action requires long-term planning and implementation. It must be a long game, with little worry about momentary failures, setbacks, or factions. It also means working together and building trust among people from all ethnic groups. Some factions will try the old "divide and conquer" tactics to split groups and movements that are successful. We are individuals, all smart with great, but pedagogically different ideas that we sometimes believe are too fundamental to enable us to work together. Those who want to maintain the status quo will take advantage of real and perceived differences to slit and weaken movements. To soothe their guilt, they want brown people to be accomplices to their murder—like one of my bosses tried to get me to incriminate myself so he would be free of the guilt from his assault. As I did, speak out and say exactly what is happening. Don't keep such behavior a secret. Report it to the world that there is a traitor to the cause of destroying whiteness. It will take bravery, and in the early days, you may lose as the attacks against your integrity, in their effort to keep whiteness. Point the guilt where it belongs. Turn divide and conquer on its head. Then offer to help them heal and move to a phase where they don't need whiteness anymore. They may resist and deny, but offer the olive branch, anyway. At least cover your credibility and make it public if they try to hurt you.

It can only work if we focus on the big picture. The big picture is something that James Baldwin suggested, America is not the summit of human civilization. It cannot be because of a lack of moral credit. Saying so is not sacrilege to be delegitimized. It's the truth. Whiteness is a lie, and too many brown sacrificial lambs—people's lives—are required to keep that lie going. That is a falsehood white people have pronounced to themselves and the world and brown people have also embraced it just to get crumbs. If we don't eradicate the presence of whiteness in this world, we will all slowly and imperceptibly perish.

Chapter 10

HOW TO END ECONOMIC RACISM

"Hope is invented every day."

~ JAMES BALDWIN, novelist, playwright, essayist, poet, and activist

A friend and colleague said I depressed her with my talk about how the world is, and the way racism destroys both its believers and the oppressed. Her next question was always, "Well, what is the solution?" I believe we must know the problem before we can solve it. I also know that sometimes, the problems are so enormous, that we mull them over a lot before we come up with a solution, especially if we are the ones facing these tribulations. Furthermore, the answers may seem so fundamentally against the reality we face, such that they seem impossible. However, if we understand racism to be profoundly distant from our ideal human values, then radically sweeping solutions may be perfectly reasonable.

Economic Racism is one of those big problems that I see as a market externality. In economics, an "externality" is the consequence of consumption, production, or any decision on an individual group who did not have an option or choice in the market-driven event and whose interests were never taken into consideration. These externalities can be positive or negative. For illustration, imagine a factory that produces luxury fur coats that dump waste from the rabbits onto the land and pollutes the air from burning rabbit corpses; a beautiful neighborhood with mansions that pipes its sewage into the river polluting drinking and groundwater downstream closer to a lower-income neighborhood; mining gold in a river to make beautiful necklaces that lead to mercury poisoning of a local native tribe; or building a new airport opening-up the region to global travel, thus adding noise pollution, jet fumes in the neighborhood air, and hearing deterioration of nearby residents. These positive productive efforts all resulted in a negative externality. Similarly, enslavement, Jim Crow, the

Black Code, redlining, lack of voter rights, land grabs, mass incarceration, and economic racism all lead to negative externalities. They benefited one group of people at the expense of another and eventually negatively affects our entire civilization.

A positive externality is where a public good like education is accessible to all regardless of income, class, or so-called "race," resulting in a more productive, harmonious, and motivating nation that is better equipped to solve their problems whether personal or societal. Public goods that are available to everyone mean that a larger, more inclusive society is more equipped to solve problems. In the case of the coronavirus global pandemic that hit us starting in 2020, white Americans realized that due to hundreds of years of deeply entrenched racism in every aspect of society, not only were brown people more likely to die or become seriously ill from the virus, they were also the ones most difficult to vaccinate due to lack of simple facilities like nearby pharmacies, health insurance, or trust in a vaccine developed mainly by white people, notorious for secretly experimenting on brown people (Golden, Coronavirus in African Americans and Other People of Color 2020).

In the case of a positive externality like education, some governments decide to subsidize to ensure that everyone benefits as equally as possible. Then they spend fewer resources on combating crime and dealing with social problems. Studies by the National Bureau of Economic Research show that "an additional four years of education lowers five-year mortality by 1.8 percentage points; it also reduces the risk of heart disease by 2.16 percentage points and the risk of diabetes by 1.3 percentage points." Education has the positive externality of improved health and earnings, just to name two benefits (Picker 2007). This is why, in Scandinavian countries, tuition fees for tertiary education are either very low or sometimes free for nationals. These countries have a higher quality of life due to more focus on supporting positive externalities and taxing negative externalities.

The "Cap and trade" policy of the United States is a method to tax and incentivize companies that pollute the environment to account for their negative externalities. The "cap" reduces greenhouse gas emissions with limits on pollution, and the "trade" is a market that allows companies to buy and sell allowances in a mechanism that makes pollution-resulting production more expensive, and non-polluting processes cost-effective (Keohane and Kizzier 2021). Cap and trade have reduced sulfur dioxide pollution, thus, reducing acid rain.

Racism is similarly a positive and negative externality in its results. Of course, much of the negatives go to the poor white people, and brown people, while the other white people—sometimes unwittingly, as if these results were normal to all lives—benefit positively from the system. The destructive producing practices are linked to the racism that deprives a group of people of possessions and freedom to prosper uninhibited. Attempts to right the resource grab attract confrontation from white people. Just as pollutants cause harm to everyone, so too does racism. Moreover, these negative externalities are triggered by the very wealthy, hoarding economic growth among a few people—the top one percent, the *raison d'être* for exploitation of people including *via* racism (Matthews 2017).

As a negative externality, racism and its accompanying wealth hoarding should also be taxed and regulated to redistribute resources to support the positive externality or equity in all aspects of society. Civil rights laws are passive and weak in their anti-racism, and more importantly, anti-hoarding effects. Anti-racism must be incentivized via a system of taxes and subsidies at the institutional level. The movement towards anti-racism requires access to grow brown wealth and power, to own their rural and urban lands, small businesses, and large corporations. Brown people do not need meager handouts to assuage the guilt of white supremacists.

For starters, some of the inequality is coming from the tax structure America has today. The tax structure is supposed to be progressive, meaning that as your income increases, you pay more tax. Wealthier households should pay a larger share of their income than the middle class and the poor. In the 1970s, the richest Americans paid more than fifty percent (seventy percent in 1950) of their income in taxes. Today, due to successive tax cuts by governments entrenched with the influence of rich folks, the 400 richest people pay a twenty-three percent tax rate while middle- and lower-income people pay 24.2 percent (Picchi 2019). Although the top one percent pay about thirty percent, the tax loopholes mean they too pay a smaller tax rate than middle and poorer people. Warren Buffett brought attention to this when he said he paid a lower tax rate than his secretary, courtesy of the loopholes and deductions that benefit the wealthy (Leonhardt 2019).

The problem is even more exasperating because the tax rates do not account for the real problem of poverty. We are in such an "it's-all-about-me-and-to-hell-with-everyone-else" culture that our society cannot see the destruction of its selfishness. The pursuit of whiteness further exasperates this self-centeredness. I came across a comment to a story about tax rates that read, "Last year we made $220K between two self-employed people and paid a total of $105K in Federal, State, and local taxes. That's a 48 percent tax rate, about half. Someone making $35K takes home about 75 percent of that, for a 25 percent tax rate" (Buchheit 2017).

That is all true. The disposable income of the first household was $115,000. They are self-employed, meaning they are already in an opportunity to guide their destiny and increase their income. The statement expressed annoyance that the poor household got to pay a smaller tax rate than they did, amounting to a disposable income of $26,250, more than four times less than theirs. Both households must buy goods and services at the same prices and often with the same regressive sales tax. Who is worse off despite the progressive tax structure? The selfishness is deep-seated.

According to a *Washington Post* article, the same 400 richest Americans own more wealth than the bottom 150 million people. These are the top 0.00025 percent of the population. Brown people need to have an opportunity to increase their wealth. By wealth, I mean net worth: the value of assets a family owns, minus the value of liabilities. Assets such as homes, rental real estate ownership, land possessions, stock holdings, business equity, intellectual property, and bank accounts are included. Liabilities include outstanding amounts on loans, credit cards, business expenses, and taxes (Ingraham 2019).

Real tax reform will require that we return to an era where the rich paid a progressively higher tax rate than middle and poorer people. Furthermore, someone making an income of $35,000 or less should have social services that help them to be more productive and earn more, benefiting from their added productivity, instead of the rich owner hoarding the gains. This is especially true for brown families because they are often supporting many people—parents, a sibling, a niece or nephew, and more children—unlike white people who are often just supporting themselves because their parents and family are growing on successional wealth.

When I was growing up, I believed, like many people in the lower to middle class today, that getting a tertiary education would increase my income and pull me and my family out of poverty. It did for the most part, and I was lucky to have been educated outside America, if not, I would have acquired hefty student loans. That loan leads those entering the workforce, to be well-educated, but with a negative net worth. The expectation they tend to have at first is that their education leading them to become fill-in-the-blank high earning professionals will pay off the student loan and launch them into positive net worth before they need the next loans for adult needs like a home, car, and spending to make sure their kids get an even better education than they did.

Indeed, their higher education has led to productivity increases, but without the proportional increases in real net earnings. The situation is worse for those without tertiary education. They may harbor a mentality of poverty—shame, anxiety, and victimhood about money—perhaps caused by their impoverished environment growing up. They could make it up, but without hereditary wealth, they must borrow without much help even for the deposit. Financial institutions will lend, which is good, because they have a future income stream almost guaranteed by their education, and really to get a loan, you mostly need a steady job. During payments of their student loans, they then need another advance for a car for transportation, while they pay rent, sometimes to the top rich one percent. To escape rent, and to improve their security, they get a mortgage.

A lack of real pay increases can be painful. I told the stories of being overlooked for promotions and salary increases myself. The same is true for colleagues, family, and friends due to racism. Hoarding power requires that those who provide employment, get more out of laborers without reciprocating with commensurate rewards. When I joined my company, I spent three years asking for a raise and promotion, while the organization said it was on a wage freeze, during an upturn in the economy. They used the 2008 crisis to freeze wages but never did unfreeze them after the economy rallied and inflation eroded our real income by close to five percent annually. I met colleagues who had been working for about ten years without a pay increase. Meanwhile, their productivity increased with experience, training, and added technology. Demand for their products and services had also increased. As their disposable income shrank, they had to cut back on spending to survive.

The fact is that many companies hoarded their productivity gains and increased the earnings of the top-tier staff and shareholders or owners of private companies. Much of the smaller increase in wages of mid-to lower-tier staff is eroded by inflation, leaving real wages flat or declining as happened during the COVID-19 economic slowdown and inflation due to fuel price hikes. Wealthy people and the politicians that serve them will note how hourly wages have increased by 2.8 percent from 2009 to 2018 (Watson 2018).

Unfortunately, politicians tend to ignore deflating these increases by Consumer Price Index (CPI) because nominal numbers make them, the politicians, look like they are achieving success for their voters. CPI is measured by a basket of goods, looking at the rate of increase of a sample of these goods (and services depending on the methodology) across different regions in a country. For illustration, in February 2021, the U.S. Bureau of Statistics reported that the CPI-U (the "U" means all urban consumers), was 0.4 percent, an increase on top of a 0.3 percent increase in January. Gasoline index in that CPI basket increased by 6.4 percent. If you are dependent on your car to drive to work, with no increases in your wages, you are made poorer (U.S. Bureau of Labor Statistics 2021).

Because I inherited no family trust fund, stock options, life insurance payouts, or gift of assets, I still incurred student debt paying for my children's education, still in the belief that the income earned would lift them out of poverty. To be responsible adults with our finances, we learn that we should have savings and emergency funds and prepare for retirement. We should properly manage our 401(k), Roth IRA, and Health Savings Accounts, and eliminate credit card debts, and other consumer loans. The aim should be to gather enough resources to be secure. I often hear my colleagues talk about their retirement funds and some older colleagues who still have a pension as their security blanket to serve them until death.

Theirs and my offspring must start again to repeat that cycle, having an income, but never really growing in wealth and power. One of my cousins revealed she just needed to reach $1,000,000 in time for her retirement to be in a secure place. She was referring to today's money, not future value—taking into consideration inflation, nor leaving a trust for her children to have a successful lift in their wealth.

In the education chapter, I outlined my viewpoints on how to address student debt. No one should leave their tertiary education with a negative net worth before they get their first paycheck. That is a market failure again, where U.S. educational institutions hoard their endowment funds and charge exorbitant tuition fees outside what's normal in many other industrialized countries.

The belief and pursuit of whiteness have also gnarled our democracy like a dog to a rag doll. Democracy, according to Merriam-Webster dictionary, is "a government in which the supreme power is vested in the people and exercised by them directly or indirectly through a system of representation usually involving periodically held free elections." For this reason, we believe, as citizens, we live in a democracy where we control our politicians via elections. One other definition in Merriam-Webster caught my eye. It stated that democracy is "the absence of hereditary or arbitrary class distinctions or privileges."

Yet, our electoral system depends on financing from outside sources, normally those with most of the wealth—the top one percent. The executive, legislative, and judiciary branches of government, meant to be a check-and-balance for the people, are often installed in office via campaign financing from the wealthy. High net-worth individuals exchange their money for power and influence, ensuring that laws and government policies, all sway to preserve and increase their affluence. Consequently, politicians train their attention closely to the policy desires of the already rich—not the less prosperous voters they campaign to help. Wages that do not keep up with inflation, student loan debts, exploitation of labor, environmental degradation, and many of the negative externalities of economic growth are rarely addressed in any adequate way because doing so may hurt the net worth of the wealthy and mostly white people. Despite endless studies, the public outcry of inequity, racism, and people unhoused, the wealthy use their monetary power to buy politicians, who pass government policies and laws—which guide the judiciary—to protect their fortunes.

Based on the definition above, America is not a democracy. The top one-percenters use their "hereditary or arbitrary class distinctions or privileges" to re-enforce their "hereditary or arbitrary class distinctions or privileges." Vehicles to funnel money include rich donor sponsors, corporations, foundations such as 501(c) that represent wealthy people, and Super PACs—Political Action Committees with a mercurial means of the unlimited campaign and special interest financing that claims not to be in control of the party of candidates they support, although the PAC can also donate money to the candidate it supports (Ballotpedia 2020).

According to the Center for Responsive Politics, the estimated total cost of the 2020 political cycle was about $14 billion. Many Americans contribute to their favorite party or candidates, but more than half of that cost is covered by white, wealthy, right-leaning, donors bent on hoarding wealth, even as they watch, and encourage the struggle of fellow human beings (L. Savage 2021).

It is bewildering to me that a nation, founded on Christianity, promoted the American dream, the leading democracy of the world, could spend $14 billion to ensure that it is indeed not a democracy. Elections have become their industry with a complete ecosystem that many people parasitically feed on. Meanwhile, we have seventeen of every 10,000 people unhoused or homeless, a student debt of $1.7 trillion, and many more externalities caused by the hoarding and preservation of beliefs in whiteness. The United States is behind other countries in areas of fast-rail train service, universally available technology like 5-G telecommunications, universal education, and healthcare, as well as having a system of racial reconciliation (Hess 2020).

I like the solution that one of my friends told me. He said to make all contributions to politicians illegal. We need to revamp the entire monetary-based political system—no more super PACs, donors, corporations, lobby groups—just cancel all means of candidates and parties receiving money from anyone. The question then remains, well how do we ensure the candidates are known and promote themselves according to what their electorate needs are?

Political candidates should get money allocated from and by taxpayers. At all levels, federal, state, county, and city, all campaign financing should be a set sum designated by the government, where all qualified parties and opposing candidates are allocated an equal and non-exorbitant amount to the campaign. Transparency will help guide voters on the integrity of the politician they are voting for. The expenses should be audited to determine how the funds are used, as it is public money, to make sure spending is not excessive. Here, since taxpayers are funding the campaigns, the candidates will be incentivized to focus on the electorate's needs rather than that of a rich benefactor. This approach is a first step to returning to democracy where the "supreme power is vested in the people."

There is another major form of corruption that the elimination of private donors would help with—the crisis of rewarding donors with jobs and access. These are typically the mid-tiered private individual donors—if you can consider amounts like $3 million as mid-tiered. Once in their government job, usually at the top decision-making positions, they then have to repay the favor of those wealthy connections who helped them get there. For instance, if one of these donors is a manufacturer of some widget, they may need to pass regulations that encourage output and discourage environmental protection. Once in office, they use their authority to defund or sideline the department that protects the environment. Often, these people are not hired on their merit, just their donor status, and interest. The recommendation from my friend would eliminate the need to hire unqualified people just because they donated money to a campaign. Part of democracy is having government, well suited and well-represented in the population they serve (Arnsdorf 2016).

Another practice of power hoarding that erodes democracy is gerrymandering. Gerrymandering is an underhand way to ensure votes for a particular party are maximized, thus solidifying a win come election season. It's a periodic re-drawing of the electoral boundary lines in a way skewed to favor districts containing majority Republicans or Democrats, thus ensuring a partisan slant for election season. It consolidates the party to power in election after election, creating a one-party rule system. When a candidate is almost guaranteed she or he will win due to the majority of the people in that district being of her or his party, there is no need to care what the electorate needs are. The focus can be again on the donors to maximize whatever policies or future jobs the politicians will move to after their political life. Additionally, the politician can focus on issuing government contracts to family, friends, and influencers to protect their next cycle of electoral campaign financing and winnings. The solution here is simple, make all gerrymandering illegal. Eventually, as people move, and citizens with varying political interests start living together, the electoral system will even out to be more democratic.

That leaves one more political tool that promotes white hoarding of resources—the paradoxical electoral college system. This too is built on a system of white hoarding and insistent on full control of all branches of government. The electoral college was designed 250 years ago to protect the property of America's landed class, giving them more voting power than the landless. We have already seen that white people own most of the land and property. America markets itself as one of the leading representative democracies founded on the standard that all votes are enshrined in every citizen. Since every citizen is equal, their vote is also equal. The candidate who wins the most votes should win the elections.

This is not so as can be seen when a popular minority party wins the election. This happened in 2016 to the then-presidential candidate Hillary Clinton. She won roughly three million more votes than her opponent, Donald Trump—more than two percentage points. Yet she lost the presidency due to fewer than 80,000 Republican votes in three states (Wegman 2020). The same scenario happened in the 2000 elections between Al Gore, a Democrat, who won the popular vote by about 543,895 votes. In the end, the election results were determined by the U.S. Supreme Court to award George W. Bush the Presidency giving him Florida's twenty-five electoral votes (Bellano 2021).

The highest office is supposed to represent all Americans equally and should be won by the selection of the numerical majority of all Americans, regardless of the state in which they live. Doing otherwise is to segment the value of votes, and therefore the value of citizens. The electoral college renders citizens' votes, and therefore, the citizens themselves, as unequal people with unequal rights. It's the reason many citizens believe the system is so rigged, their votes would not count, so they feel less interested in even bothering.

Another way to allow for greater democracy and eradication of racism is to allow a system for multiple parties to vie for political power. Americans are diverse, and multi-everything: religion, ethnicities, and beliefs about where the country should go. As a result, the two parties are becoming more and more out of step with the needs of their electorate. Furthermore, they tend to coalesce around some major policies. Both parties typically vote to increase the budget for military spending or at least keep it steady, despite what polls suggest that fifty-seven percent of Americans prefer a reduction of military spending, and diversion of those savings towards social development. Together, both parties tend to nitpick on any legislation to support small businesses, racial equality, rehabilitative justice, women's issues, indigenous people's rights, LGBTQIA parity, the poor, or providing universal healthcare. They agree on foreign intervention in other countries' politics and avoiding heavy financial regulations on Wall Street companies, even when corporate greed triggers a recession (Benedetti 2021).

The two-party system leaves us rooted in the same quagmire of the past, Democratic and Republican parties that offer little innovations as they aim to stay close to their professed ideals. Both parties have supported political and Economic Racism that protects white landowners and a status quo lasting over 400 years—one that does not serve all citizens. It forces candidates and voters alike with new ideas to soften their ultimate ideals of freedom and progress to fit the molds of both parties, rendering them far from representative of the majority needs of the citizens. Running as an Independent or third-party candidate just means running as an outsider to the established and recognized parties. They need a certain number of signatures to get on a general election ballot, while the Democratic and Republican parties essentially have automatic ballot access. Even where candidates join the duopolistic party system and aim to change it from the inside, they are still labeled progressives, left or right-leaning, ultra-liberal, conservative-liberal, and so on. The aim is to "other" anyone, candidate, or citizen, who wants anything outside the framework of the two parties.

The process of voting in the primaries is one bottleneck for any third party. When I request a ballot for voting in primaries, I am asked which one I want, Republican or Democratic. I have no choice but to say I want a third party. I can never understand why I don't get a ballot with the full slate of candidates so I could choose based on the person and how they market themselves, rather than the party. There are instances when I want to select a Republican candidate for Senate, a Democratic candidate for president, a Green Party candidate for Congress, and a Libertarian for some other fill-in-the-blank office. I choose my candidates based on what they bring to the table, not party affiliations since I know both parties' collective ideals do not match mine or most Americans. Yet, during primaries, I have no choice. I must vote for the lesser of two evils, instead of someone that represents my values.

One reform I am proposing is during primaries, we should eliminate the either-or-party ballots and vote for the candidate. Let the candidate, based on the support she or he gets, choose the best party platform they believe they can win. This focuses the electorate on policies offered by the candidates rather than on the tribalism of the party. We would have new parties emerging like the People's Party, among others, with real improvements, many of which are different from our present white-aspiration and protection parties (People's Party 2021).

Some pundits for electoral reform tout the multi-party democracies of Ireland, New Zealand, and Australia, as examples America should follow (leaving out the monarchy part, of course)—putting away its exceptionalism and being open to learning from others who are doing something better (Drutman 2019).

Of the top ten democracies ranked in the 2015 Global Democracy Ranking, the U.S. is not listed. America is ranked number 16. The Democracy Ranking model looks at the quality of democracy on the political dimension, as well as five non-political dimensions covering civil liberties; gender; the economy; knowledge-based information society, research, and education; health status and the health system; and environmental sustainability.

A reformed American system that required the candidates to form coalitions to shape a government would give more voices in policy and allow for easier innovations than the regular deadlock we now have with a two-party system. Among the toolbox of measures to end racism, we should present a system in favor of the mixed member proportional system or MMP, allowing even small parties like our Green and Libertarian parties among others to enter government. In some minor instances when we have one or two Independent seats in the Senate, they tend to caucus with one of the other dominant parties, thus diluting the reason their electorate voted for them.

Chapter 11

FINAL THOUGHTS

"Now is the time to make real the promises of democracy. Now is the time to rise from the dark and desolate valley of segregation to the sunlit path of racial justice. Now is the time to lift our nation from the quicksands of racial injustice to the solid rock of brotherhood. Now is the time to make justice a reality for all of God's children."

~ MARTIN LUTHER KING, JR.

A few years ago, I took a weekend vacation in Jamaica for a friend's wedding. While visiting a museum at Konoko Waterfalls, the tour guide taught us about a bear trap. They had an old rusty one for us to see. It was like a giant rat trap with big metal teeth, but the sign on it said, "man trap." It was indeed designed to capture bears in America. However, it was used during enslavement to catch enslaved people who tried to escape their predicament. Plantation owners laid these traps around the perimeter of the estates and covered them in leaves and bushes as camouflage. Captives bled to death in their menacing, rusted, iron teeth.

Among the group were white tourists. They were having fun on their vacation, climbing the refreshing waterfalls, enjoying the views of the tropical gardens, and the accent of their brown tour guide while taking selfies. The tour guide explained what the man trap was, and how it was used. I watched as the white tourists averted eye contact with brown people in the group and fidgeted during this very matter-of-fact description from our tour guide. Then for the cherry on the cake, our tour guide said, "This picture on the wall has the words to Bob Marley's *Redemption Song*, and we will all now sing it: 'Emancipate yourselves from mental slavery, none but ourselves can free our mind . . .'" A fitting end. I gave her a nice tip and thanked her.

For a brown person, these mantraps are still present, albeit in other forms. They include mass incarceration, systematic arrests or actual murder by police, and catch and release of white people who get captured for killing a brown person—in Atlanta in March 2021, a mass shooter murdered women, mainly Asians after planning and driving to three spas around the metropolitan city, said he did it because he was addicted to porn, not because he is a racist. I thought, even something so obviously intersectional as racism and misogyny, his belief in his whiteness gives him authority to murder people and decide he is still a "good," porn-loving person, and not horrible racist. Society decides he is only mentally ill (Diaz 2021).

The mantrap here is the guy himself since he is just as deadly. However, here is the real fear. I went out to get food at a local Asian restaurant and found myself facing the door in case of a potential attack, as well as being extra alert when I see a white male walking alone around the establishment, making sure to watch for any bulge of a weapon. To me, that is analogous to hiding the mantrap under bushes to capture unsuspecting enslaved people.

The entire system designed for hoarding resources by the few is protected by this symbolic mantrap. There is still so much unraveling and reteaching of the truth that must be accomplished. I also maintain that we cannot end racism overnight, nor can we end it by doing some and not all of the recommendations proposed. There are many more that I have not proposed because, like many who are finding solutions, I don't know all the stumbling blocks created to block brown people.

Some are not even intentional. I learned recently that medical devices impact brown people disproportionately. An Economist report shows that devices are biased against people of different skin color—for example, an oximeter pulse examiner, a device that clips onto your finger like a clothespin. During the COVID-19 pandemic, it was used to triage patients. Those with oxygen levels above a certain level were sent home to self-monitor, while those below oxygen levels were admitted to the emergency room. Studies showed that the pulse examiner misread brown patients by around four points about twelve percent of the time. The device pulses a laser light through the finger to determine the level of oxygen in the patient. Since browner skin absorbs more light, the device could suggest that they are okay to go home, if this is the only or main source of a medical practitioner making an informed decision. This could account for some of the brown people who did not get sufficient medical care during peak infection periods of the coronavirus pandemic. The design of the device was based on white patients (Cukier 2021). There are similar issues with algorithms trained on societal biases typically based on white males from the 1970s.

Brown people should develop a set of diversity empowerment principles. I would like to see chairs and CEOs of major companies, heads of international organizations, major film executives, and heads of states and agencies, lead a global campaign to take action to increase race diversity at board and senior management levels, in film productions, and governments. This campaign should be perpetual and have at the top *black*, brown, and non-racist white leaders. Progressive companies, countries, governments, and international institutions that become members would get extra recognition as open non-racist entities. That means their products and service should be purchased by people of color and non-racist white people because they have leadership and staff who cater to those markets.

These are tools that would ultimately lead to a country with more success. America could become more prosperous and powerful while enjoying social stability. In 2018, America was an estimated twenty-trillion-dollar economy. Think how much that could grow if the entire population could prosper. There is an economic case for dismantling racial discrimination. Racism expends a toll on a country amounting to trillions of dollars in squandered productivity, innovations, and legacy family progress. When there is racism, brown men and women are frequently denied work and promotions commensurate with their skills. Racism also encourages the misallocation of the immigrant workforce. How often have you met a taxi driver from some foreign country in New York who is more qualified than his passengers? Wasting human resources is where immigrants are earning lower wages below their education level. There is a clear need for better qualification recognition treaties and greater transparency in regulations of foreign credentials so that qualified people can work in the area they are trained.

Some white people agree to some reparations for the public relations of it but muddle the discussion when they talk about giving money to brown people. They know if you were to give money to a poor desperate family who has never had a relationship with money, they won't have the tools or system around them to make that money beneficial, or generational. Besides, the system is geared for them to spend most of that money back on white-owned corporations.

This is an ongoing discussion now in the Caribbean. These countries, and Africa, have been pillaged by colonizers for centuries. The resources taken are still legacy wealth for white families today. These families are descendants of these colonizers. Research on reparations has connected most brown people's names with plantation owners and their descendants. The Caribbean people want reparation. They have set up a non-profit commission made up of academics and bi-partisan politicians to discuss its implementation. In the Caribbean, reparations do not only have elements of monetary compensation. It also has aspects of investment treaties, educational programs, and scholarships, infrastructural donations, trade treaty connections that do not just require these countries to produce raw materials, but finished goods too, with guaranteed market access in the metropole. Great Britain and other colonizers should support ending racism rather than their present tactics to avoid the discussion or muddle it with talk of monetary compensation.

In 1996, I visited an aluminum plant in Washington, D.C., that sourced its bauxite from Jamaica and Guyana. I asked them why they, the aluminum plant in D.C., did not just produce aluminum at the source of the raw material and ship that to the U.S. They ignored my question and continued the tour. Producing aluminum, the finished product, for local consumption and export, would have led to the evolution of an economic structure in both Guyana and Jamaica that would have boosted their prosperity. They would likely develop research and development institutions and companies, educational systems, and clean manufacturing methods to support this production. All that knowledge base would have supported these countries' development, and spilled over into other sectors, creating an innovation-driven community. They would have been encouraged to practice clean mining because people there who suffer from poor mining practices can vote and would let their politicians and legislators know they need environmental protection. Other industries would develop around this sector, augmenting their creativity.

In Trinidad and Tobago, we see something similar where there are many engineers because methanol and oil production are major components of their economy. These are the types of collaborative investments that benefit the nation over the long term to bring equity. It is not a handouts, reparations, or development aid, but sustainable business connections. Allow and support countries of the Global South, or developing countries, to produce finished goods, or at least intermediary goods, from their raw materials. The Caribbean realizes that dismantling the effects of colonialism is not just about money. It is about building a society able to sustain itself in the long term.

In America, the same needs to happen, starting at the community level. All brown children should go to schools where teachers are well qualified, paid a decent income with benefits, and respected by their community through programs, as well as national and state awards that showcase teaching excellence. These "good" schools should be everywhere, not just in white-segregated communities. Education should be free and at least subsidized at the tertiary level. With that education, there is no reason to deny them jobs.

Inside the schools, racist practices would have to change. I realize that many brown people in the U.S. who go to underprivileged schools do not know how to speak in public and debate or express their opinions. They come from a school system where the white kids were mostly chosen for the debating team, current affairs competitions, and spelling "B" competitions. One friend told me the only time she ever made it on stage in front of the school was when she was dancing. This was despite her role as head of many school bodies. The teachers always asked her white counterpart to do the speeches. This discrimination happens because the such teachers are mainly people who pursued whiteness.

To support this, the federal and state governments should then put effective laws in place to take positions of power away from white people still bent on racism and racist behavior. Use the media, and entertainment industry, including Hollywood, Bollywood, Nollywood, and other production centers, to produce brown content, not just brown movies and shows where they seem to suffer. They should also produce positive, uplifting content highlighting brown people are inventors and producers, they give to their communities, and they are heroes. Show these movies instead of white people shooting at or incarcerating mostly brown people in a skewed system. Schools should have a real history going back to African kingdoms, showing their rise and fall, their greatness, and their innovations. Embrace the truth about enslavement to both white and brown children.

Take a closer look at companies that have boards solely of white people. Look at those that have never had a brown CEO, CFO, or anyone at the top. This includes those that have a token *black* person often too afraid to make a difference and speak because they know they will be quickly lynched and booted out. Whenever you enter a room and see all or mostly white people, especially white males, that is a sick and racist organization. If you are brown or a white progressive, they will give you a hard time. These, too, need reform.

There are solutions for racial discrimination. Society can benefit white, and brown people. The world is not a zero-sum game. Many white people believe that if we end discrimination, they will get less. That is false. All of society will benefit, and all people will get more. In America, we think of most things in terms of money. The health of a society should be more about human happiness, satisfaction, legacy, stability, and progress. Brown people need to support each other and recognize where the discrimination lies. If brown people understand there is more to gain for them and their families, they will not be desperate and despondent. Anyone who truly cares about their family, and their country, will work for the stability and progress of all, not just themselves. They know the current racist systems are unsustainable. We must progress from the primitivity of racial discrimination.

As such, peaceful protests are only a start. Brown people must gain access to positions of empowerment. They must become politicians and legislators to change laws. Brown people must be heads of major conglomerates and be on boards. They must become scientists and leaders in their communities. They must also be "their brother's keeper," working to solve racial power dynamics together. An education that teaches ancient history is vital to building pride and self-esteem.

Frances Ellen Watkins Harper, a poet, lecturer, and civil rights activist, addressed the Eleventh National Women's Rights Convention in New York on May 10, 1866. There are many great parts to her speech where she highlights the dilemma that hoarding power and greed could lead to the creation of leaders like President Andrew Jackson, who ends up on the wrong side of history. But the most profound part is this:

> *We are all bound up together in one great bundle of humanity, and society cannot trample on the weakest of its members without receiving the curse in its soul. You tried that in the case of the negro. You pressed him down for two centuries, and in so doing you crippled the moral strength and paralyzed the spiritual energies of the white men of the country. When the hands of the black were fettered, white men were deprived of the liberty of speech and the freedom of the press. Society cannot afford to neglect the enlightenment of any class of its members (Harper 1866).*

I hope you take away a few things from this book. Whether you are religious or secular, whether you consider yourself *black*, mixed-race, brown, white, or identify with any specific group, you deserve to also "inherit the earth." The racial slights, emotional cuts, wounds, and outright verbal attacks like "go back to where you came from," are uttered by someone who believes in a fantasy they know is in their head only—superiority and whiteness.

Don't be afraid to call it what it is and shame it and the person as being from a more primitive age devoid of reason. White non-racist people should also stand up to that when it's happening and let them know we want a better society, not the unstable one they want to create with their primeval ways. We should not tolerate racism of any kind. Don't worry about those who say you are going overboard. They want the status quo due to fear of change.

We have the tools, the momentum in society now, and a generation of *black*, brown, white, and a diverse group of people of various origins who have concluded they want a better, more stable world to live in and they will do something about it today. The call to action is for all of us to start the dialogue and implement solutions to end Economic Racism.

EPILOGUE

Let's take the time to analyze why racist behavior is so anathema to our peace of mind, regardless of how we are racially categorized or self-identify. We understand that it is not natural as we feel it in our souls. The law of nature tells us that we must practice piety in our daily lives in speech and deeds to maintain harmony. A racist mind is a wild mentality enslaved to imaginations of superiority and grandeur with no realization of peace. Its aim is always to commit harm to others and to blame others for its failures. In harming others, it instantly hurts itself. In simple terms, a racist mind is a sinful mind.

I had the opportunity to attend a 10-day Vipassana course recently. While studying the approach to meditation, it occurred to me that this could be helpful to so many others suffering from the misery created by racism. It has introduced me to tools to clear my mind and detox much of the hurt and anger I felt facing people burdened by their racist speech and behavior. It helped clarify my thoughts when authoring this book. While my practice remains challenging since I am back in the real world, I continue to try. I can still restore my harmony, knowing that I can reject the gifts of misery wrapped in the package of racism offered to me by whoever utters words or actions that try to harm. It has fortified my self-confidence to refuse them by allowing me to control my reaction to their diatribe. It is the art of living to constantly seek harmony and peace in one's mind to alleviate misery.

I encourage white people who realize they struggle with harmful energy to pursue a course in Vipassana. Vipassana meditation allows one to see the truth—your reality in your subconscious and offers tools for self-observation and self-purification. There are many Dhamma meditation centers across America and in other countries. If you maintain the practice, it promises to help you find compassion you never imagined you had. Finally, I also encourage brown people, suffering like open wounds provoked by a pursuit of whiteness, whether in themselves or others, to try a ten-day course. Some courses in the U.S. also offer all-black students with a black assistant teacher, which I suspect relieves the anxiety of seeing people that look like your oppressor around you while becoming vulnerable during meditation. I hope readers of this book take the opportunity to find the peace that gives them the strength to execute recommendations to end racism.

ABOUT THE AUTHOR

Martin Kush is an economist and author who writes about the intersection of economic development and social issues. He is an American of Caribbean origin, thus his affinity to the region. Martin is passionate about hard issues like racism, politics, effective government, sensible economic policies, poverty reduction, global governance, and magnificent and innovative infrastructure. Martin believes that these cannot function well without global open-mindedness, and social harmony in both family and work life, and he ponders much about the shortfalls caused by cultural non-acceptance. He is a fervent lover of people of all backgrounds. He is fascinated with human behavior and its historical origins. Martin has worked as a diplomat on trade policy and international treaties, with governments on logistics, support agencies for encouraging manufacturing, trade, export, developing service industries, and training on trade policy. He is a frequent speaker on these topics at conferences and lectures on trade policy.

Martin's work takes him around the world where he engages with various cultures. While traveling, he usually takes the time to delve into the country's history. He has written various articles and journals about trade policy, international affairs, social justice, and economic development. Economic Racism is his inaugural work on the impact of racism on an economy and its people based on his experience. He presently lives in Atlanta, Georgia, USA.

Martin has three children, Rosita, Xaine, and Xavier. He has lived in the Caribbean, Europe, New York, Pennsylvania, Florida, and Georgia.

You can find out more about this book at www.economicracism.com. Order copies on the website or Amazon.com. Thank you for reading.

BIBLIOGRAPHY

McIntyre, Niamh, Pamela Duncan, and Haroon Siddique. 2021. *Conditions that led to 2011 riots still exist today, experts warn.* July 30. Accessed April 23, 2022. https://www.theguardian.com/uk-news/2021/jul/30/conditions-2011-uk-riots-still-exist-today-experts-warn.

Abdulbaki, Mae. 2021. "Why Lovecraft Country Was Cancelled (& What Season 2 Would've Been About)." *Screen Rant.* August 18. Accessed April 24, 2022. https://screenrant.com/lovecraft-country-season-2-cancelled-reason-story-details/.

Adachi, Jeff. 2021. "Police Militarization and the War on Citizens." *American Bar Association.* February. Accessed March 2021. https://www.americanbar.org/groups/crsj/publications/human_rights_magazine_home/2016-17-vol-42/vol-42-no-1/police-militarization-and-the-war-on-citizens/.

Adamson, Christopher R. 1983. "Punishment After Slavery: Southern State Penal Systems, 1865-1890." *Social Problems.* June 1. Accessed March 2021. https://academic.oup.com/socpro/article-abstract/30/5/555/2925199?redirectedFrom=fulltext.

Ahmed, Nadia B., and Asifa Quraishi-Landes. 2019. "Five Myths About Hijab." *The Washington Post.* March 15. Accessed January 2021. https://www.washingtonpost.com/outlook/five-myths/five-myths-about-hijab/2019/03/15/d1f1ea52-45f6-11e9-8aab-95b8d80a1e4f_story.html.

Ahmed, Tufayel. 2016. "TV Star Salaries Reveal Pay Gap Between White and Minority Actors." *Newsweek.* October 5. Accessed November 27, 2020. https://www.newsweek.com/leaked-tv-star-salaries-reveals-big-pay-gap-between-white-and-minority-actors-506585.

Akpan, Nsikan. 2018. "Police Militarization Fails to Protect Officers and Targets Black Communities, Study Finds." *PBS.* August 21. Accessed February 2021. https://www.pbs.org/newshour/science/police-militarization-fails-to-protect-officers-and-targets-black-communities-study-finds.

Akutekha, Esther. 2020. "How The Natural Hair Movement Has Failed Black Women." *Huffington Post.* March 16. Accessed April 2021.

https://www.huffpost.com/entry/natural-hair-movement-failed-black-women_l_5e5ff246c5b6985ec91a4c70.

Alec MacGillis, ProPublica. 2016. "The Original Underclass." *The Atlantic.* September. Accessed January 2021. https://www.theatlantic.com/magazine/archive/2016/09/the-original-underclass/492731/.

Alfonsi, Sharyn. 2021. "How Curtis Flowers, Tried Six Times for the Same Crime, Was Saved From Death Row." *CBS News - 60 Minutes.* January 3. Accessed February 2021. https://www.cbsnews.com/news/curtis-flowers-in-the-dark-60-minutes-2021-01-03/.

Ali, Omar. 2016. *Race: A Function of Power.* April 14. Accessed March 2021. https://youtu.be/CxkCxEDnt2E.

Ali, Safia Samee. 2020. "Homeless but Hidden, Some Americans Families are Disqualified From Crucial Aid." *NBC News.* December 18. Accessed March 2021. https://www.nbcnews.com/news/us-news/homeless-doubled-families-living-other-households-may-fall-aid-blind-n1251446.

Allcock, Beth. 2020. "RACE CARD Piers Morgan Erupts With Fury After Being Called a 'Racist' During Meghan Markle Debate on Good Morning Britain." *The Sun.* January 13. Accessed November 27, 2020. https://www.thesun.co.uk/tvandshowbiz/10725531/piers-morgan-racist-meghan-markle-gmb/.

AlterNet. 2015. "Why White People Freak Out When They're Called Out About Race." *AlterNet.org.* March 10. Accessed November 27, 2020. https://www.alternet.org/2015/03/why-white-people-freak-out-when-theyre-called-out-about-race/.

Amadeo, Kimberley. 2021. "U.S. Education Rankings Are Falling Behind the Rest of the World." *The Balance.* February 28. Accessed March 2021. https://www.thebalance.com/the-u-s-is-losing-its-competitive-advantage-3306225.

Amadi, Osa. 2020. *Isabel Wilkerson's Caste: How a Black Slave Introduced Immunisation in America.* August 24. Accessed March 2021. https://www.vanguardngr.com/2020/08/isabel-wilkersons-caste-how-a-black-slave-introduced-immunisation-in-america/.

American Commissioners. 1786. *American Commissioners to John Jay, 28 March 1786.* March 28. Accessed December 2020. https://founders.archives.gov/documents/Jefferson/01-09-02-0315.

Angyal, Chloe. 2016. "Affirmative Action is Great for White Women. So why do They Hate it?" *Huffington Post.* January 21. Accessed December 2020. https://www.huffpost.com/entry/affirmative-action-white-women_n_56a0ef6ae4b0d8cc1098d3a5.

Anonymous. 2019. "What Happens After Rich Kids Bribe Their Way Into College? I Teach Them." *The Guardian.* March 25. Accessed March 2021. https://www.theguardian.com/us-news/2019/mar/25/what-happens-after-rich-kids-bribe-their-way-into-college-i-teach-them.

Armstrong, Jeremy, and Damien Fletcher. 2012. "Olympic 100m Hero Usain Bolt Powered by Chicken Nuggets and Yams." *The Mirror.* February 3. Accessed November 25, 2020. https://www.mirror.co.uk/news/uk-news/olympic-100m-hero-usain-bolt-328610.

Arnold, Chris. 2019. "Forgiving Student Debt Would Boost Economy, Economists Say." *NPR.* November 25. Accessed April 2021. https://www.npr.org/2019/11/25/782070151/forgiving-student-debt-would-boost-economy.

Arnsdorf, Isaac. 2016. *Trump Rewards Big Donors With Jobs and Access.* December 12. Accessed April 2021. https://www.politico.com/story/2016/12/donald-trump-donors-rewards-232974.

Asiedu, Kwasi Gyamfi. 2017. "A Speech by Ghana's President Calling for Africa to End its Dependency on the West is a Viral Hit." *Quartz Africa.* December 4. Accessed April 2021. https://qz.com/africa/1145953/ghanas-president-akufo-addo-shocks-frances-macron-with-africa-non-dependent-speech/.

Autosport Magazine. 2014. *BMW i8 - Powerful Idea Commercial.* May 9. Accessed June 9, 2022. https://youtu.be/CD47O_Rob3A.

Axner, Marya. 2020. *Understanding Culture and Diversity in Building Communities.* Accessed February 2021. https://ctb.ku.edu/en/table-of-contents/culture/cultural-competence/culture-and-diversity/main.

Bailey, Lily. 2020. "Challenging Racism in the Workplace." *Psychology Today.* November 12. Accessed December 2020. https://www.psychologytoday.com/us/blog/because-we-are-bad/202011/challenging-racism-in-the-workplace.

Baldwin, James. 1994. *On Being White...And Other Lies.* April. Accessed April 2021. https://sacred.omeka.net/items/show/238.

Ballotpedia. 2020. *PACs and Super PACs.* Accessed April 2021. https://ballotpedia.org/PACs_and_Super_PACs.

Barnes, Patricia. 2019. "Is The EEOC Protecting Workers Or Discriminatory Employers?" *Forbes.* September 4. Accessed January 2021. https://www.forbes.com/sites/patriciagbarnes/2019/09/04/is-the-eeoc-protecting-workers-or-discriminatory-employers/?sh=67fb9fa85407.

BBC. 2022. *America's gun culture - in seven charts*. May 25. Accessed June 6, 2022. https://www.bbc.com/news/world-us-canada-41488081.

—. 2003. "God on the Brain." *BBC*. April 17. https://www.bbc.co.uk/science/horizon/2003/godonbrain.shtml.

Beckett, Lois. 2019. "A History of Recent Attacks Linked to White Supremacy." *The Guardian*. March 15. Accessed November 25, 2020. https://www.theguardian.com/world/2019/mar/16/a-history-of-recent-attacks-linked-to-white-supremacism.

Bell, Carl C. 1980. "Racism: A Symptom of the Narcissistic Personality." *Journal of the National Medical Association* (Jackson Park Hospital,) 72 (7): 661-5.

Bell, Carl C. 1980. "Racism: A Symptom of the Narcissistic Personality Disorder." *The Journal of the National Medical Association* 72 (7): 661-665.

Bellano, Anthony. 2021. "'Democracy Prevailed' In Electoral College Vote, Norcross Says." *MSN News*. January 7. Accessed April 2021. https://www.msn.com/en-us/news/politics/democracy-prevailed-in-electoral-college-vote-norcross-says/ar-BB1cyGN8.

Benedetti, Jakob. 2021. "Why America Needs More Than Two Political Parties." *The University News*. March 11. Accessed April 2021. https://unewsonline.com/2021/03/why-america-needs-more-than-two-political-parties/.

Biography.com. 2021. *John Lewis Biography*. January 12. Accessed February 2021. https://www.biography.com/political-figure/john-lewis.

Black, Rachel, and Aleta Sprague. 2016. "The Rise and Reign of the Welfare Queen." *New America*. September 22. Accessed April 24, 2022. https://www.newamerica.org/weekly/rise-and-reign-welfare-queen/.

BlackPast. 2021. *Racial Violence In The United States Since 1660*. Accessed February 2021. https://www.blackpast.org/special-features/racial-violence-united-states-1660/.

Blake, John. 2008. *Why Many Americans Prefer Their Sundays Segregated*. August 06. http://edition.cnn.com/2008/LIVING/wayoflife/08/04/segregated.sundays/index.html.

Blakemore, Erin. 2018. "California Once Tried to Ban Black People." *History Stories*. February 9. Accessed December 2020. https://www.history.com/news/california-once-tried-to-ban-black-people.

—. 2020. "California's Little-Known Genocide." *History Stories*. December 4. Accessed December 2020. https://www.history.com/news/californias-little-known-genocide.

Blay, Zeba. 2015. "Watch Muhammad Ali's Perfect Response To 'Not All White People Are Racist' — In 1971." *Huffington Post.* November 4. Accessed January 2021. https://www.huffpost.com/entry/muhammad-ali-on-not-all-white-people_n_563a5e9ee4b0307f2cabb2e6.

Bloomenthal, Andrew. 2020. "Race and Income Inequality." *Investopedia.* November 11. Accessed December 2020. https://open.lib.umn.edu/principleseconomics/.

Boddy, Jessica. 2017. "The Forces Driving Middle-Aged White People's 'Deaths Of Despair'." *NPR.* March 23. Accessed April 2021. https://www.npr.org/sections/health-shots/2017/03/23/521083335/the-forces-driving-middle-aged-white-peoples-deaths-of-despair.

Borresen, Kelsey. 2020. "6 Things White People Say That Highlight Their Privilege." *Huffington Post.* June 10. Accessed December 2020. https://www.huffpost.com/entry/things-white-people-say-highlight-privilege_l_5edeafafc5b637b87e22cee0.

Boyle, Alan. 2014. *10 Shocking Ways The West Abuses Developing Countries.* February 14. Accessed March 2021. https://listverse.com/2014/02/14/10-shocking-ways-the-west-abuses-developing-countries/.

Branson, Richard. 2007. *Losing My Virginity: How I Survived, Had Fun, and Made a Fortune Doing Business My Way.* New York: Crown Publishing Group.

Brooks, Khristopher J. 2019. "Disparity in Home Lending Costs Minorities Millions, Researchers Find." *CBSNews.* November 15. Accessed January 2021. https://www.cbsnews.com/news/mortgage-discrimination-black-and-latino-paying-millions-more-in-interest-study-shows/.

Brooks, Kristopher J. 2019. "Disparity in home lending costs minorities millions, researchers find." *CBS News.* November 15. Accessed November 27, 2020. https://www.cbsnews.com/news/mortgage-discrimination-black-and-latino-paying-millions-more-in-interest-study-shows/.

Brown, Emma. 2016. "Yale Study Suggests Racial Bias Among Preschool Teachers." *The Washington Post.* September 27. Accessed March 2021. https://www.washingtonpost.com/news/education/wp/2016/09/27/yale-study-suggests-racial-bias-among-preschool-teachers/.

Browne, Chris, Clare Codling, Leo Musyoki, Richard Page, and Craig Russell. 2005. "Community Cohesion: SEVEN STEPS A Practitioner's Toolkit." *Office of the Deputy Prime Minister.* March. Accessed February 2021.

http://www.tedcantle.co.uk/publications/015%20Community%20
cohesion%20seven%20steps%20%20Community%20Cohesion%2
0Unit%20.pdf.

Brownlee, Clint. 2016. *The Battle of Kennesaw Mountain - Civil War Reenacting.*
June 27. Accessed April 2021.
https://warwashere.com/category/civil-war-reenacting/.

Buchheit, Paul. 2017. *The Rich Pay Fewer Taxes Than The Poor, And Get More
Services.* March 26. Accessed April 2021.
https://www.salon.com/2017/03/25/the-rich-pay-fewer-taxes-
than-the-poor-and-get-more-services/.

Cane, Clay. 2020. "Not Just Tulsa: Race Massacres That Devastated Black
Communities In Rosewood, Atlanta, and Other American Cities."
BET. July 19. Accessed November 25, 2020.
https://www.bet.com/news/national/2019/12/17/not-just-tulsa--
five-other-race-massacres-that-devastated-black.html.

Centers For Disease Control and Prevention. 2020. *Data and Statistics About
ADHD.* November 16. Accessed March 2021.
https://www.cdc.gov/ncbddd/adhd/data.html.

Chami, Pablo A. 2000. "Estatutos de Limpieza de Sangre." *Pachami.com.*
October. http://pachami.com/Inquisicion/LimpiezaSangre.html.

Chappet, Marie-Claire. 2020. "Why White People May Feel Uncomfortable
Right Now - And Why That's A Good Thing." *Glamour Magazine.*
June 11. Accessed November 27, 2020.
https://www.glamourmagazine.co.uk/article/white-people-
discomfort.

Chen, Kelly. 2017. "Charleston Church Shooting: White Gunman Kills 9 At
Historic Black Church." *Huffington Post.* December 6. Accessed
November 25, 2020. https://www.huffpost.com/entry/charleston-
shooting-churc_n_7608738.

Clarke, Alexis. 2019. *How the History of Blackface Is Rooted in Racism.* February
15. Accessed January 2021.
https://www.history.com/news/blackface-history-racism-origins.

Cline, Austin. 2018. *When Christianity Is Used to Justify Violence.* July 27.
Accessed December 2020.
https://www.learnreligions.com/christianity-and-violence-249551.

College Board. 2021. *Subject Test U.S. History.*
https://collegereadiness.collegeboard.org/sat-subject-
tests/subjects/history/us-history/sample-questions/19.

Collins, Keith. 2017. *Tech is overwhelmingly white and male, and white men are just
fine with that.* March 29. Accessed June 6, 2022.
https://qz.com/940660/tech-is-overwhelmingly-male-and-men-
are-just-fine-with-that/.

Community Toolbox. 2020. *Section 8: Creating Good Places for Interaction.* Accessed March 2021. https://ctb.ku.edu/en/table-of-contents/implement/physical-social-environment/places-for-interaction/main.

Costa, Pedro Nicolaci da. 2017. "The Ultrawealthy Have 10% Of Global GDP Stashed In Tax Havens — And It's Making Inequality Worse Than It Appears." *Business Insider.* September 13. Accessed April 2021. https://www.businessinsider.com/wealthy-money-offshore-makes-inequality-look-even-worse.

County of Oneida v. Oneida Indian Nation . 1985. 83-1065 (United States Supreme Court, Fine Law March 4).

Cruz, Anjana. 2017. *Europeans Invented the Concept of Race as we know it.* July 21. Accessed January 2021. https://timeline.com/europeans-invented-the-concept-of-race-as-we-know-it-58f896fae625.

Cukier, Kenneth. 2021. "Finger on the pulse of bias—why do some medical devices work less well for non-white people?" *The Economist.* April 7. Accessed April 2021. https://www.economist.com/podcasts/2021/04/07/finger-on-the-pulse-of-bias-why-do-some-medical-devices-work-less-well-for-non-white-people.

Curtin, Melanie. 2013. "Want A Fulfilling Relationship? Science Says The Happiest Couples Have These 13 Characteristics." *Inc.com.* December 31. Accessed February 2021. https://www.inc.com/melanie-curtin/science-says-happy-couples-have-these-13-characteristics.html.

Daniels, Jesse. 2018. "White Supremacy Is Deadly For Everyone headshot Jessie Daniels." *Huffington Post.* April 19. Accessed April 2021. https://www.huffpost.com/entry/opinion-white-suicide-addiction-death_n_5b903737e4b0511db3dea162.

DeCapua, Joe. 2015. "Study Examines Racial Bias in US Sports Reporting." *VOA News.* June 5. Accessed November 25, 2020. https://www.voanews.com/usa/study-examines-racial-bias-us-sports-reporting.

Delaney, Arthur, and Alissa Scheller. 2015. "Who Gets Food Stamps? White People, Mostly." *Huffington Post.* February 28. Accessed February 2021. https://www.huffpost.com/entry/food-stamp-demographics_n_6771938.

Democracy Now. 2020. *Five Black & Brown Men Have Been Recently Found Hanged in Public. Were Some of Them Lynched?* June 22. Accessed April 2021. https://www.democracynow.org/2020/6/22/us_public_hangings _lynching_history.

Devereaux, Ryan. 2021. "Storming Of The Capitol Was Openly Planned But Ignored By Law Enforcement." *The Intercept.* January 7. Accessed March 2021.
https://theintercept.com/2021/01/07/capitol-trump-violence-law-enforcement/.

DiAngelo, Robin J. 2018. *White Fragility: Why It's so Hard for White People to Talk About Racism.* Boston: Beacon Press. Accessed December 2020.

DiAngelo, Robin. 2015. "Why It's So Hard to Talk to White People About Racism." *Huffington Post.* April 30. Accessed November 27, 2020.
https://www.huffpost.com/entry/why-its-so-hard-to-talk-to-white-people-about-racism_b_7183710.

Diaz, Jaclyn. 2021. "8 People, Many Of Them Asian, Shot Dead At Atlanta-Area Spas; Man Arrested." *NPR.* March 17. Accessed April 2021.
https://www.npr.org/2021/03/16/978024380/8-women-shot-to-death-at-atlanta-massage-parlors-man-arrested.

Digital Chicago Lake Foerst College. 2021. *Racial Restriction and Housing Discrimination in the Chicagoland Area.* Accessed March 2021.
https://digitalchicagohistory.org/exhibits/show/restricted-chicago/other/redlining.

Dowling, Tim. 2015. "'This is Not Who we Are' is American For: 'This is Sort of Who we Are'." *The Guardian.* March 10. Accessed January 2021.
https://www.theguardian.com/commentisfree/2015/mar/10/this-is-not-who-we-are-american-lindsay-graham.

Drutman, Lee. 2019. *Let a Thousand Parties Bloom.* October 19. Accessed April 2021. https://foreignpolicy.com/2019/10/19/us-democracy-two-party-system-replace-multiparty-republican-democrat/.

DW Documentary. 2018. *Inequality – How Wealth Becomes Power (1/3) | DW Documentary.* August 18. Accessed March 2021.
https://youtu.be/AFIxi7BiScI.

Eisenberg, Richard. 2018. "Why Minority Financial Planners Are Nearly Nonexistent — And How To Fix It." *Forbes.* June 12. Accessed February 6, 2020.
https://www.forbes.com/sites/nextavenue/2018/06/12/minority-financial-planners-nearly-nonexistent/?sh=549511fed9cb.

Elliott, Debbie. 2020. "5 Years After Charleston Church Massacre, What Have We Learned?" *NPR.* June 17. Accessed February 2021.
https://www.npr.org/2020/06/17/878828088/5-years-after-charleston-church-massacre-what-have-we-learned.

Encyclopedia.com. 2020. *European Migrations to American Colonies, 1492–1820.* November 28. Accessed November 28, 2020.
https://www.encyclopedia.com/history/encyclopedias-almanacs-

transcripts-and-maps/european-migrations-american-colonies-1492-1820.

Ephesians 2:11-22 New International Version. n.d.

Ephesians 6:5 New International Version. n.d.

Epstein, Ethan. 2019. "America is a Violent Country, With or Without Guns." *The Washington Times.* August 8. Accessed March 2021. https://www.washingtontimes.com/news/2019/aug/8/america-is-a-violent-country-with-or-without-guns/.

Equal Justice Initiative. 2017. *Black Children Five Times More Likely Than White Youth to Be Incarcerated.* September 14. Accessed March 2021. https://eji.org/news/black-children-five-times-more-likely-than-whites-to-be-incarcerated/.

—. 2019. "Racial Double Standard in Drug Laws Persists Today." *Equal Justice Initiative.* December 9. Accessed November 28, 2020. https://eji.org/news/racial-double-standard-in-drug-laws-persists-today/.

Evelyn, Kenya. 2020. "How TV Crime Shows Erase Racism and Normalize Police Misconduct." *The Guardian.* January 25. Accessed February 2021. https://www.theguardian.com/media/2020/jan/25/law-and-disorder-how-shows-cloud-the-public-view-of-criminal-justice.

2015. *Wilmington on Fire.* Directed by Christopher Everett. Produced by Blackhouse Publishing. http://wilmingtononfire.com/about.

Exploring Your Mind. 2020. *Chaos and Narcissists: How Disorder Favors Narcissists.* September 26. Accessed February 2021. https://exploringyourmind.com/chaos-narcissists-disorder-favors-narcissists/.

—. 2018. *Narcissism: 5 Causes of Narcissistic Personality Disorder.* July 26. Accessed February 2021. https://exploringyourmind.com/narcissism-5-causes-of-narcissistic-personality-disorder/.

FBI. 2020. *Don't be a Puppet.* Accessed February 2021. https://www.fbi.gov/cve508/teen-website/what-are-known-violent-extremist-groups.

Foot, John, and Christopher Hibbert. 2020. *Benito Mussolini.* July 25. Accessed January 2021. https://www.britannica.com/biography/Benito-Mussolini.

Fottrell, Quentin. 2019. *White Workers are More Likely than Black or Latino Americans to Have a Good Job — Even With the Same Level of Education.* October 21. Accessed November 25, 2020. https://www.marketwatch.com/story/white-workers-are-more-likely-than-black-or-latino-americans-to-have-a-good-job-even-with-the-same-level-of-education-2019-10-17.

Fox, Justin. 2019. "Broken Windows' Theory Was Right … About the Windows." *Bloomberg.* October 16. Accessed December 2020. https://www.bloomberg.com/opinion/articles/2019-10-16/what-broken-windows-theory-got-right-about-crime.

Freeman, Hadley. 2018. "What does Hollywood's reverence for a child rapist Roman Polanski tell us?" *The Guardian.* January 30. Accessed April 24, 2022. https://www.theguardian.com/film/2018/jan/30/hollywood-reverence-child-rapist-roman-polanski-convicted-40-years-on-run.

Fuchs, Erin. 2014. "6 Reasons Why Prison Is Better In Europe Than America." *Business Insider Australia.* May 31. Accessed February 2021. https://www.businessinsider.com.au/vera-institute-european-american-prison-report-2014-5.

Gee, Michael. 2018. "Why Aren't Black Employees Getting More White-Collar Jobs?" *Harvard Business Review.* February 28. Accessed December 2020. https://hbr.org/2018/02/why-arent-black-employees-getting-more-white-collar-jobs.

—. 2018. "Why Aren't Black Employees Getting More White-Collar Jobs?" *Harvard Business Review.* February 28. Accessed November 28, 2020. https://hbr.org/2018/02/why-arent-black-employees-getting-more-white-collar-jobs.

GH Admin. 2017. *What is Doxing and How it is Done?* May 17. Accessed February 2021. https://www.gohacking.com/what-is-doxing-and-how-it-is-done/.

Gilbert, Stanley W., David T. Butry, Jennifer F. Helgeson, and Robert E. Chapman. 2015. "Community Resilience Economic Decision Guide for Buildings and Infrastructure Systems." *National Institute of Standards and Technology.* December 15. Accessed March 2021. https://nvlpubs.nist.gov/nistpubs/SpecialPublications/NIST.SP.1197.pdf.

Gino, Francesca. 2017. "Another Reason Top Managers Are Disproportionally White Men." *Scientific American.* September 12. Accessed January 2021. https://www.scientificamerican.com/article/another-reason-top-managers-are-disproportionally-white-men/.

Glaun, Dan. 2019. "'A Rigged System:' Here's How Rich Parents Allegedly Spent up to $6.5 Million to Bribe and Cheat their Children into Elite Colleges." *MassLive.* March 12. Accessed March 2021. https://www.masslive.com/news/2019/03/a-rigged-system-heres-how-rich-parents-allegedly-spent-up-to-65-million-to-bribe-and-cheat-their-children-into-elite-colleges.html.

Gold, Ashley, and Michael Southall. 2020. "Why 'Stop-and-Frisk' Inflamed Black and Hispanic Neighborhoods." *The New York Times.* February

19. Accessed February 2021. https://www.nytimes.com/2019/11/17/nyregion/bloomberg-stop-and-frisk-new-york.html.

Golden, Sherita Hill. 2020. *Coronavirus in African Americans and Other People of Color.* April 20. Accessed April 2021. https://www.hopkinsmedicine.org/health/conditions-and-diseases/coronavirus/covid19-racial-disparities.

—. 2020. *Coronavirus in African Americans and Other People of Color.* April 20. Accessed December 2020. https://www.hopkinsmedicine.org/health/conditions-and-diseases/coronavirus/covid19-racial-disparities.

Goluboff, Risa. 2016. "The Forgotten Law That Gave Police Nearly Unlimited Power." *Time.* February 1. Accessed March 2021. https://time.com/4199924/vagrancy-law-history/.

Goodwin, Morgan Taylor. 2018. *Racial Battle Fatigue: What is it and What are the Symptoms?* December 7. Accessed January 2021. https://medium.com/racial-battle-fatigue/racial-battle-fatigue-what-is-it-and-what-are-the-symptoms-84f79f49ee1e.

Grabmeier, Jeff. 2004. *When Europeans Were Slaves: Research Suggests White Slavery Was Much More Common Than Previously Believed.* May 7. Accessed January 2021. https://news.osu.edu/when-europeans-were-slaves--research-suggests-white-slavery-was-much-more-common-than-previously-believed/.

Graham-LoPresti, Jessica R., Tahirah Abdullah, Amber Calloway, and Lindsey M. West. 2017. "The Link Between Experiences of Racism and Stress and Anxiety for Black Americans: A Mindfulness and Acceptance-Based Coping Approach." *Anxiety.org.* March 16. Accessed December 2020. https://www.anxiety.org/black-americans-how-to-cope-with-anxiety-and-racism.

Gray, Alex. 2018. "Here's How Finland Solved its Homelessness Problem." *World Economic Forum.* February 13. Accessed March 2021. https://www.weforum.org/agenda/2018/02/how-finland-solved-homelessness.

Gray, Aysa. 2019. "The Bias of 'Professionalism' Standards." *Stanford Social Innovation Review.* June 4. Accessed January 2021. https://ssir.org/articles/entry/the_bias_of_professionalism_standards.

Green, Emma. 2020. "The Unofficial Racism Consultants to the White Evangelical World." *The Atlantic.* July 5. Accessed December 2020. https://www.theatlantic.com/politics/archive/2020/07/white-evangelicals-black-lives-matter/613738/.

Griffin, Tamerra. 2015. "14 Words That Carry A Coded Meaning For Black People." *Buzz Feed.* February 10. Accessed December 2020.

https://www.buzzfeed.com/tamerragriffin/loaded-words-coded-meanings-black-people.

Gupta, Sujata. 2020. "Why African-Americans May Be Especially Vulnerable To COVID-19." *Science News.* April 10. Accessed December 2020. https://www.sciencenews.org/article/coronavirus-why-african-americans-vulnerable-covid-19-health-race.

Hales, Larry. 2009. "Oppression Breeds Resistance." *Workers World.* March 14. Accessed January 2021. https://www.workers.org/2009/us/oppression_0319/.

Hall, Martin. 2020. *South Africa.* November 22. Accessed November 27, 2020. https://www.britannica.com/place/South-Africa.

Harari, Yuval Noah. 2015. *Sapiens: A Brief History of Humankind.* New York: HarperCollins Publishers.

Harper, Frances Ellen Watkins. 1866. *We Are All Bound Up Together - May 1866.* May 1. Accessed February 2021. https://awpc.cattcenter.iastate.edu/2017/03/21/we-are-all-bound-up-together-may-1866/.

Harriot, Michael. 2017. "Is the South More Racist Than Other Parts of the US?" *The Root.* December 4. Accessed January 2021. https://www.theroot.com/is-the-south-more-racist-than-other-parts-of-the-us-1820893655.

Haupt, Petrina. 2017. *Everything You Need to Know About Sisterlocks.* August. Accessed April 2021. https://www.naturalhairqueen.net/everything-you-need-to-know-about-sisterlocks/.

Head, Tom. 2020. *Interracial Marriage Laws History and Timeline.* July 4. Accessed November 27, 2020. https://www.thoughtco.com/interracial-marriage-laws-721611.

Healthline. 2019. *What is Stockholm Syndrome and Who Does it Affect?* November 11. Accessed June 5, 2022. https://www.healthline.com/health/mental-health/stockholm-syndrome.

Heath, Dreisen. 2021. "H.R. 40: Exploring the Path to Reparative Justice in America." *US House Committee on the Judiciary Subcommittee on the Constitution, Civil Rights, and Civil Liberties.* Washington, DC: Human Rights Watch. 18.

Hegewisch, Ariane. 2020. *The Gender Wage Gap: 2019 Earnings Differences by Race and Ethnicity.* March. Accessed November 25, 2020. https://iwpr.org/wp-content/uploads/2020/07/2020-Weekly-Wage-Gap-2020-FINAL.pdf.

Helsel, Carolyn B. 2018. "Ten Myths White People Believe About Racism." *The Christian Century.* December 27. Accessed December 2020.

https://www.christiancentury.org/article/critical-essay/ten-myths-white-people-believe-about-racism.

Henson, Hunter. 2017. *Top 10 US Government Experiments Done On Its Own Citizens.* June 01. Accessed March 2021. https://listverse.com/2017/06/01/top-10-us-government-experiments-done-on-its-own-citizens/.

Hess, Abigail Johnson. 2020. "U.S. Student Debt has Increased by More Than 100% Over the Past 10 years." *CNBC.* December 22. Accessed April 2021. https://www.cnbc.com/2020/12/22/us-student-debt-has-increased-by-more-than-100percent-over-past-10-years.html.

Hinchey, Marcus. 2018. *Come Sunday.* Netflix. Directed by Joshua Marston. Produced by Marc Forster, Ira Glass, Alissa Shipp, James D. Stern and Julie Goldstein. Performed by Chiwetel Ejiofor. Netflix.

HipLatina. 2018. *10 States in The U.S. That Were Once A Part of Mexico.* November 12. Accessed April 09, 2022. https://hiplatina.com/10-states-in-the-u-s-that-were-once-a-part-of-mexico/.

History.com. 2020. *Charleston Church Shooting.* June 8. Accessed December 2020. https://www.history.com/this-day-in-history/charleston-ame-church-shooting.

—. 2020. *Columbus Reaches the "New World".* A&E Television Networks. October 12. Accessed January 2021. https://www.history.com/this-day-in-history/columbus-reaches-the-new-world.

—. 2020. *Emmett Till is Murdered.* August 28. Accessed December 2020. https://www.history.com/this-day-in-history/the-death-of-emmett-till.

—. 2019. *Loving v. Virginia.* June 10. Accessed November 27, 2020. https://www.history.com/topics/civil-rights-movement/loving-v-virginia.

—. 2020. *Native American Cultures.* October 28. Accessed February 2021. https://www.history.com/topics/native-american-history/native-american-cultures.

—. 2020. *Rafael Trujillo.* January 29. Accessed March 2021. https://www.history.com/topics/1960s/rafael-trujillo.

—. 2021. *The Great Migration.* January 26. https://www.history.com/topics/black-history/great-migration.

—. 2018. *U.S. Immigration Timeline.* December 21. Accessed January 2021. https://www.history.com/topics/immigration/immigration-united-states-timeline.

—. 2021. *Voting Rights Act of 1965.* January 26. Accessed February 2021. https://www.history.com/topics/black-history/voting-rights-act.

Hodgetts, Rob. 2020. "Eliud Kipchoge's Record-Breaking Nike Shoes to be Banned." *CNN*. January 31. Accessed November 25, 2020. https://edition.cnn.com/2020/01/31/sport/nike-world-athletics-vaporfly-alphafly-ban-spt-intl/index.html.

Holt-Gimenez, Eric. 2014. "We Already Grow Enough Food For 10 Billion People — And Still Can't End Hunger." *Huffington Post*. December 18. Accessed February 2021. https://www.huffpost.com/entry/world-hunger_b_1463429.

Hongbo Yu, Yunyan Duan, Xiaolin Zhou,. 2017. "Guilt in the Eyes: Eye Movement and Physiological Evidence for Guilt-Induced Social Avoidance." *Journal of Experimental Psychology* 71: 128-137.

Hoover Institution. 2018. *Discrimination and Disparities with Thomas Sowell*. May 3. Accessed December 2020. https://youtu.be/U7hmTRT8tb4.

Hosenball, Mark. 2021. *U.S. report warns of threats from white supremacists, militias*. March 17. Accessed June 5, 2022. https://www.reuters.com/world/us/us-spy-agencies-warn-growing-domestic-terrorism-threat-2021-03-17/.

IHI Multimedia Team . 2017. *How to Reduce Implicit Bias*. September 28. Accessed February 2021. http://www.ihi.org/communities/blogs/how-to-reduce-implicit-bias.

Ingraham, Christopher. 2019. "Wealth Concentration Returning to 'Levels Last Seen During the Roaring Twenties,' According to New Research." *The Washington Post*. February 8. Accessed April 2021. https://www.washingtonpost.com/us-policy/2019/02/08/wealth-concentration-returning-levels-last-seen-during-roaring-twenties-according-new-research/.

International Criminal Court. 2021. *Towards Stability and Lasting Peace*. Accessed March 2021. https://www.icc-cpi.int/about.

Investopedia Staff. 2020. "Guide to Economics." *Investopedia*. September 11. Accessed December 2020. https://www.investopedia.com/terms/e/economics.asp.

Jackson, Greg. 2011. *How did Native Americans' View of Land Use Differ From That of European Colonists?* August 20. Accessed February 2021. https://www.enotes.com/homework-help/how-did-native-americans-view-of-land-use-differ-273443.

James Scott Farrin. 2010. *$1.25 Billion Settlement for Black Farmers*. Accessed June 5, 2022. https://www.farrin.com/black-farmers/.

Johnson, Spike. 2018. "Arming Teachers in America." *The Washington Post*. August 16. Accessed March 2021. https://www.washingtonpost.com/graphics/2018/national/amp-stories/arming-american-teachers/.

Johnson, Umar. 2016. *Wilmington on Fire*. Christopher Everett. June 11. Accessed November 25, 2020. https://www.pbs.org/video/black-issues-forum-wilmington-fire/.

Jones, Edward W. 1986. "Black Managers: The Dream Deferred." *Harvard Business Review*. May. Accessed November 27, 2020. https://hbr.org/1986/05/black-managers-the-dream-deferred.

Jordan, Mike. 2021. *Black US farmers dismayed as white farmers' lawsuit halts relief payments*. June 22. Accessed June 5, 2022. https://www.theguardian.com/us-news/2021/jun/22/black-farmers-loan-payments.

JW.org. 2021. *Is Money the Root of All Evil?* https://www.jw.org/en/bible-teachings/questions/money-root-of-evil/.

Kaleem, Jaweed. 2016. "They Dared to Register Blacks to Vote, and the KKK Killed Them: A 52-year-old Case is Closed & Unsolved." *The Los Angeles Times*. June 21. Accessed February 2021. https://www.latimes.com/nation/la-na-doj-civil-rights-20160621-snap-story.html.

Kariuki, Thuku. 2019. *Deutsche Welle (DW)*. September 9. Accessed November 25, 2020. https://p.dw.com/p/3PGMt.

Katyal, Calder. 2020. *Racist Algorithms: How Code Is Written Can Reinforce Systemic Racism*. October 6. Accessed June 5, 2022. https://www.teenvogue.com/story/racist-algorithms-testing-policing.

Keaten, Jamey. 2021. "US to Seek Seat on UN Human Rights Body, After Trump Pullout." *ABC News*. February 24. Accessed March 2021. https://abcnews.go.com/US/wireStory/us-seek-seat-human-rights-body-trump-pullout-76082403.

Keith, Caver A., and Ancella B. Livers. 2002. "'Dear White Boss…'." *Harvard Business Review*. Accessed December 2020. https://hbr.org/2002/11/dear-white-boss.

Keohane, Nathaniel, and Kelley Kizzier. 2021. *How Cap and Trade Works*. Accessed March 2021. https://www.edf.org/climate/how-cap-and-trade-works.

Kerr, Andre, and Mary Margaret Olohan. 2020. "America's Ivy League Schools Sit Atop $140 Billion In Endowments, And They're About To Get Millions More In Coronavirus Aid." *NewportBuzz*. April 22. Accessed March 2021. http://www.thenewportbuzz.com/americas-ivy-league-schools-sit-atop-140-billion-in-endowments-and-theyre-about-to-get-millions-more-in-coronavirus-aid/23445.

Keshner, Andrew. 2018. *How Student-Loan Debt Affects the Rest of Your Life (It's Not Pretty)*. November 20. Accessed April 2021.

https://www.marketwatch.com/story/what-student-debt-does-to-people-its-not-pretty-2018-11-14.

Kirkpatrick, Nikola. 2022. *The Truth About Why Do Bullies Bully.* April 6. Accessed June 8, 2022. https://www.betterhelp.com/advice/trauma/the-truth-about-why-do-bullies-bully/.

Klein, Christopher. 2015. "How Selma's 'Bloody Sunday' Became a Turning Point in the Civil Rights Movement." *History.* March 6. Accessed December 2020. https://www.history.com/news/selma-bloody-sunday-attack-civil-rights-movement.

Klein, Cristopher. 2018. *DNA Study Finds Aboriginal Australians World's Oldest Civilization.* August 22. Accessed February 2021. https://www.history.com/news/dna-study-finds-aboriginal-australians-worlds-oldest-civilization.

Knafo, Saki. 2013. *When It Comes To Illegal Drug Use, White America Does The Crime, Black America Gets The Time.* September 18. Accessed April 8, 2022. https://www.huffpost.com/entry/racial-disparity-drug-use_n_3941346.

Labode, Modupe. 2020. "John Lewis' Storied History of Causing 'Good Trouble'." *SmithsonianMag.* July 21. Accessed February 2021. https://www.smithsonianmag.com/smithsonian-institution/john-lewis-storied-history-causing-good-trouble-180975368/.

Lambe, Jerry. 2021. *Georgia Man Dead Days After Being Arrested for Attempting to Enter Capitol Grounds.* January 12. Accessed March 2021. https://lawandcrime.com/2020-election/georgia-man-christopher-stanton-georgia-dead-days-after-being-arrested-for-attempting-to-enter-capitol-grounds/.

Lee, Alicia. 2020. "Why Christopher Columbus Wasn't the Hero we Learned About in School." *CNN.* June 12. Accessed January 2021. https://www.cnn.com/2020/06/12/us/christopher-columbus-slavery-disease-trnd/index.html.

Lee, Kien. 2020. *Building Inclusive Communities.* Accessed February 2021. https://ctb.ku.edu/en/table-of-contents/culture/cultural-competence/inclusive-communities/main.

Leonhardt, David. 2019. "The Rich Really Do Pay Lower Taxes Than You." *The New York Times.* October 6. Accessed April 2021. https://www.nytimes.com/interactive/2019/10/06/opinion/income-tax-rate-wealthy.html.

Levine, Sam. 2019. "Georgia City Under Fire For Moving Polling Location To Police Station." *Huffington Post.* October 10. https://www.huffpost.com/entry/jonesboro-georgia-polling-location_n_5d9e0979e4b06ddfc51272f0.

Love, David A. 2010. *Racially Biased SAT System Speaks to a Broken Education System.* July 8. Accessed November 27, 2020. https://blackcommentator.com/383/383_col_sat.php.

Love, David. 2018. "Black People Are the Most Religious People In America, But What Are They Getting Out Of It?" *Atlanta Black Star.* March 11. Accessed December 2020. https://atlantablackstar.com/2018/03/11/black-people-religious-people-america-getting/.

Ludden, David. 2015. "Your Eyes Really Are the Window to Your Soul, Pupils never lie." *Psychology Today.* December 31. Accessed January 2021. https://www.psychologytoday.com/us/blog/talking-apes/201512/your-eyes-really-are-the-window-your-soul.

Lumen. n.d. *Organizational Behavior and Human Relations.* Accessed January 2021. https://courses.lumenlearning.com/wm-organizationalbehavior/chapter/group-vs-individuals/.

MacAskill, Ewen. 2017. "The CIA Has a Long History of Helping to Kill Leaders Around the World." *The Guardian.* May 5. Accessed March 2021. https://www.theguardian.com/us-news/2017/may/05/cia-long-history-kill-leaders-around-the-world-north-korea.

Mahmood, Parvez. 2019. "When North Africa Traded in European Slaves." *The Friday Times.* December 20. Accessed January 2021. https://www.thefridaytimes.com/when-north-africa-traded-in-european-slaves/.

Matthew 19:24 New International Version. n.d.

Matthews, Dylan. 2017. *You're Not Imagining it: The Rich Really are Hoarding Economic Growth.* August 8. Accessed April 2021. https://www.vox.com/policy-and-politics/2017/8/8/16112368/piketty-saez-zucman-income-growth-inequality-stagnation-chart.

Mayer, Jane. 2017. *Dark Money.* New York: Penguin Random House.

McClintock, Pamela. 2019. "Box Office: 'Black Panther' Makes SAG Awards History With Best Ensemble Win." *Hollywood Reporter.* January 27. Accessed November 27, 2020. https://www.hollywoodreporter.com/heat-vision/sag-awards-black-panther-makes-history-best-ensemble-win-1180023.

McIntosh, Kriston, Emily Moss, Ryan Nunn, and Jay Shambaugh. 2020. *Examining the Black-Wealth Gap.* February 27. Accessed June 13, 2020. https://www.brookings.edu/blog/up-front/2020/02/27/examining-the-black-white-wealth-gap/.

Merriam-Webster Dictionary. 2021. https://www.merriam-webster.com/.

Merriam-Webster. n.d. "Trust." *Merriam-Webster Dictionary and Thesaurus.* Accessed January 2021. https://www.merriam-webster.com/dictionary/trust.

Mesnards, Fanny Guénon Des. 2020. "The 11 best Parisian chocolatiers of 2020." *Vogue*. December 21. Accessed April 2021. https://www.vogue.fr/lifestyle-en/article/the-10-best-parisian-chocolatiers-of-2019.

Metzl, Jonathan M. 2020. "The Politics of White Anxiety." *Bostom Review*. October 23. Accessed February 2021. http://bostonreview.net/race/jonathan-m-metzl-politics-white-anxiety.

Miller, Arianne, and Lawrence Josephs. 2013. "Whiteness as Pathological Narcissism." *Contemporary Psychoanalysis* (Taylor and Francis Online) 45 (1): 93-119. Accessed February 2021. https://doi.org/10.1080/00107530.2009.10745989.

Miller, Joshua Rhett. 2020. "Bank Calls Cops on Black Man Trying to Cash Check From Discrimination Lawsuit." *New York Post*. January 23. Accessed January 2021. https://nypost.com/2020/01/23/bank-calls-cops-on-black-man-trying-to-cash-check-from-discrimination-lawsuit/.

Miller, Lisa. 2012. "The Money-Empathy Gap - How Money Makes People Act Less Human." *New York Magazine*. June 27. Accessed March 2021. https://nymag.com/news/features/money-brain-2012-7/.

Milton, Giles. 2004. *White Gold*. New York: Farrar, Straus, and Giroux.

Minnesota Gun Rights. 2022. *Will You Fight in 2022? - Renew Your Membership*. December 18. Accessed April 24, 2022. https://www.minnesotagunrights.org/will-you-fight-in-2022/.

Mmoujeke, Chinwendu. 2018. "Top 10 Most Corrupt Leaders That Ever Lived - All You Should Know." *BuzzNigeria*. May 23. Accessed March 2021. https://buzznigeria.com/corrupt-leaders-world/.

Mock, Brentin. 2018. "The Great Migration: The First Moving-to-Opportunity Project." *Bloomberg*. January 25. Accessed February 2021. https://www.bloomberg.com/news/articles/2018-01-25/what-happened-when-blacks-moved-north-during-the-great-migration.

Moiz, Mahwish. 2020. *List of Tent Cities in America*. July 14. Accessed March 2021. https://caufsociety.com/list-of-tent-cities-in-america/.

Moore, Abby. 2020. *How Narcissism & Racism Are Connected, According To Research*. July 2. Accessed February 2021. https://www.mindbodygreen.com/articles/link-between-narcissism-and-racism.

Moore, Antonio. 2017. "#BlackWealthMatters: The 5 Largest U.S. Landowners Own More Land Than All of Black America Combined." *Huffington Post*. December 6. Accessed February 2021. https://www.huffpost.com/entry/ted-turner-owns-nearly-14_b_8395448.

Myers, Barton. 2020. *Sherman's Field Order No. 15.* September 25. Accessed March 2021. https://www.georgiaencyclopedia.org/articles/history-archaeology/shermans-field-order-no-15.

Nagesh, Ashitha. 2020. "What Exactly is a 'Karen' and Where Did the Meme Come From?" *BBC News.* July 30. Accessed December 2020. https://www.bbc.com/news/world-53588201.

Nakrani, Sachin. 2020. "Groundbreaking Report Reveals Racial Bias in English Football Commentary." *The Guardian.* June 29. Accessed November 25, 2020. https://www.theguardian.com/football/2020/jun/29/groundbreaking-report-reveals-racial-bias-in-english-football-commentary.

National Alliance to End Homelessness. 2020. *State of Homelessness: 2020 Edition.* Accessed March 2021. https://endhomelessness.org/homelessness-in-america/homelessness-statistics/state-of-homelessness-2020/.

National Geographic. n.d. *Hijab: Veiled in Controversy.* Accessed January 2021. https://www.nationalgeographic.org/media/hijab/print/.

National Institute of Mental Health. 2019. *Suicide is a Leading Cause of Death in the United States.* Accessed April 2021. https://www.nimh.nih.gov/health/statistics/suicide.shtml.

Nero, Dom. 2018. "Star Wars Fans Fundamentally Misunderstand Star Wars." *Esquire.* June 7. Accessed February 2021. https://www.esquire.com/entertainment/movies/a21205523/star-wars-kelly-marie-tran-harassment-controversy/.

Newman, Jonah. 2016. "Trauma of Witnessing Police Violence is Not Lost on Children." *The Chicago Reporter.* August 22. Accessed March 2021. https://www.chicagoreporter.com/trauma-of-witnessing-police-violence-is-not-lost-on-children/.

News 1130. 2016. *Video: California Neighbourhood Officially Has 'Whites Only' Rule.* August 25. Accessed March 2021. https://youtu.be/lT-W8y6Ib_E.

Nicholls, Sallyann, Alice Tidey, and Emma Beswick. 2019. "How Does Europe Compare With the US on Gun Ownership?" *Euronews.* June 8. Accessed March 2021. https://www.euronews.com/2019/08/05/which-european-country-boasts-the-most-guns-.

Niesse, Mark. 2019. "Groups Oppose Moving Voting Precinct to Jonesboro Police Station." *Atlanta Journal-Constitution.* October 8. Accessed February 2021. https://www.ajc.com/news/state--regional-govt--politics/groups-oppose-moving-voting-precinct-jonesboro-police-station/rgeerwVyqS17uDWs0bp5vL/.

Nittle, Nadra Kareem. 2020. *Persistent Racial Stereotypes in TV Shows and Movies.* December 14. Accessed February 2021. https://www.thoughtco.com/common-racial-stereotypes-in-movies-television-2834718.

—. 2020. *The Roots of Colorism, or Skin Tone Discrimination.* January 30. Accessed January 2021. https://www.thoughtco.com/what-is-colorism-2834952.

NPR. 2011. *Parents Cross Lines To Get Kids Into Good Schools.* January 26. Accessed June 9, 2022. https://www.npr.org/2011/01/26/133246495/Parents-Cross-Lines-To-Get-Kids-Into-Good-Schools.

—. 2020. "The Fire Still Burning." *NPR.* December 30. Accessed March 2021. https://www.npr.org/2020/12/29/951152424/the-fire-still-burning.

—. 2019. "White Lies." *NPR.* May. Accessed February 2021. https://www.npr.org/podcasts/510343/white-lies.

Nzongola-Ntalaja, Georges. 2011. *Patrice Lumumba: the most important assassination of the 20th century.* January 17. Accessed April 9, 2022. https://www.theguardian.com/global-development/poverty-matters/2011/jan/17/patrice-lumumba-50th-anniversary-assassination.

Ogusola, David. 2015. "The Roots of European Racism Lie in the Slave Trade, Colonialism — and Edward Long." *The Guardian.* September 8. Accessed January 2021. https://www.theguardian.com/commentisfree/2015/sep/08/european-racism-africa-slavery.

Oluo, Ijeoma. 2018. *So You Want to Talk about Race.* New York: Seal Press.

Ortiz, Erik. 2019. "Inside 100 Million Police Traffic Stops: New Evidence of Racial Bias." *NBC News.* March 13. https://www.nbcnews.com/news/us-news/inside-100-million-police-traffic-stops-new-evidence-racial-bias-n980556.

Own. 2020. *Jane Elliott's "Blue Eyes/Brown Eyes" Anti-Racism Exercise | The Oprah Winfrey Show | OWN.* June 5. https://youtu.be/ebPoSMULI5U.

Parker, Charlie. 2019. *JUSTICE FOR JAMES White supremacist executed for dragging black man behind truck for 3 miles until his head ripped off in 'worst hate crime in history'.* April 25. Accessed June 2, 2022. https://www.thesun.co.uk/news/8934585/racist-executed-dragging-man-truck-miles-head-ripped-off-hate-crime/.

Paul, Andrew. 2020. "'Cops' Fed a Racist Mythology to Americans. How Did it Survive This Long?" *NBC News.* June 10. Accessed November 27, 2020. https://www.msn.com/en-us/news/us/cops-fed-a-racist-mythology-to-americans-how-did-it-survive-this-long/ar-BB15jpz5.

PayScale. 2020. "The Racial Wage Gap Persists in 2020." *PayScale.* Accessed December 2020. https://www.payscale.com/data/racial-wage-gap.

PBS. 2020. "Driving While Black: Race, Space, and Mobility in America." *Public Broadcasting Service.* October 13. Accessed March 2021. https://www.pbs.org/video/driving-while-black-race-space-and-mobility-in-america-achvfr/.

PBS Frontline. 2011. *The Silent Majority: Adult Victims of Sexual Exploitation by Clergy.* April 19. Accessed December 2020. http://www.adultsabusedbyclergy.org/psychological_impacts.html.

Peeler, Travis. 2019. *Suing For Emotional Distress.* April 2. Accessed January 2021. https://www.legalmatch.com/law-library/article/how-to-sue-for-emotional-distress.html.

People's Party. 2021. *Movement For A People's Party.* Accessed April 2021. https://peoplesparty.org.

Philimon, Wenei. 2020. "Not Just George Floyd: Police Departments Have 400-year History of Racism." *USA Today.* June 7. Accessed November 27, 2020. https://www.usatoday.com/story/news/nation/2020/06/07/black-lives-matters-police-departments-have-long-history-racism/3128167001/.

Phillips, Patrick. 2016. *The Year Black People Were Hounded Out of Forsyth County, Georgia.* October 16. Accessed February 2021. https://historynewsnetwork.org/article/163743.

Picchi, Aimee. 2019. *America's richest 400 families now pay a lower tax rate than the middle class.* October 17. Accessed April 2021. https://www.cbsnews.com/news/americas-richest-400-families-pay-a-lower-tax-rate-than-the-middle-class/.

Picker, Les. 2007. *The Effects of Education on Health.* March 3. Accessed March 2021. https://www.nber.org/digest/mar07/effects-education-health.

Powell, Colin, and Tony Koltz. 2012. *It Worked For Me — In Life and Leadership.* New York: HarperCollins.

Prison Policy Initiative. 2019. *United States Incarceration Rates by Race and Ethnicity, 2010.* December 5. Accessed November 25, 2020. https://www.prisonpolicy.org/graphs/raceinc.html.

Psychology Today. 1982. "Broken Windows Theory." *Psychology Today.* Accessed December 2020. https://www.psychologytoday.com/gb/basics/broken-windows-theory.

Public Broadcasting Service. 2014. *The Test Score Gap.* Accessed March 2021. https://www.pbs.org/wgbh/pages/frontline/shows/sats/etc/gap. html.

Quinn, Melissa. 2020. "Stand Back and Stand By": Trump Declines to Condemn White Supremacists at Debate." *CBS News.* September 30. Accessed February 2021. https://www.cbsnews.com/news/proud-boys-stand-back-and-stand-by-trump-refuses-to-condemn-white-supremacists/.

Rae, Noel. 2018. "How Christian Slaveholders Used the Bible to Justify Slavery." *Time.* February 23. Accessed December 2020. https://time.com/5171819/christianity-slavery-book-excerpt/.

Rand, Ayn. 1957. *Atlas Shrugged.* New York: Random House.

Refinitiv. 2020. *Diversity & Inclusion Ratings From Refinitiv.* September. Accessed January 2021. https://www.refinitiv.com/content/dam/marketing/en_us/docu ments/methodology/diversity-inclusion-rating-methodology.pdf.

Reynolds, Kim. 2018. "How White People Have Reacted to Black Success Over Time in the United States." *TeenVogue.* July 20. Accessed March 2021. https://www.teenvogue.com/story/how-white-people-have-reacted-to-black-success-over-time-in-the-united-states.

Rinderle, Susana. 2017. "How Racism Hurts White People Too." *Huffington Post.* May 10. Accessed December 2020. https://www.huffpost.com/entry/the-dirty-secret-of-racism-it-hurts-white-people-too_b_59133f53e4b0e3bb894d5c93.

Rogers, Dexter. 2017. "Tiger Woods: Does the Lack of Media Diversity Contribute to Biased Coverage?" *Huffington Post.* June 2. Accessed November 25, 2020. https://www.huffpost.com/entry/tiger-woods-does-lack-of-media-diversity-contribute_b_592f6877e4b017b267ee000f.

Romano, Christina, Nick Schifrin, and Katrina Yu. 2020. *China Power and Prosperity.* https://www.pbs.org/newshour/series/china-power-and-prosperity. Directed by Koju Boateng, Travis Daub, and Vanessa Dennis. Produced by Dan Sagalyn and Christina Romano. Performed by Nick Schifrin. PBS. Accessed March 2021. https://www.pbs.org/newshour/series/china-power-and-prosperity.

Rosales, John. 2018. *The Racist Beginnings of Standardized Testing.* April 24. Accessed March 2021. https://www.nea.org/advocating-for-change/new-from-nea/racist-beginnings-standardized-testing.

Roy, Eleanor Ainge, and Lisa Martin. 2019. "49 Shot Dead in Attack on Two Christchurch Mosques." *The Guardian.* March 15. Accessed November 25, 2020.

https://www.theguardian.com/world/2019/mar/15/multiple-fatalities-gunman-christchurch-mosque-shooting.

Safdar, Khadeejar. 2020. "Racial-Discrimination Settlements Usually Came With an NDA. That's Changing." *The Wall Street Journal.* October 20. Accessed January 2021. https://www.wsj.com/articles/racial-discrimination-settlements-usually-came-with-an-nda-thats-changing-11603208180.

Safier, David. 2019. "Wilmington, Tulsa, Orangeburg And The Blackout of Black History." *Tucson Weekly.* November 8. Accessed November 27, 2020.
https://www.tucsonweekly.com/TheRange/archives/2019/11/08/wilmington-tulsa-orangeburg-and-the-blackout-of-black-history.

Sammis, John Henry, and Daniel Brink Towner. 1887. "Hymn: Trust and Obey." *Hymnalnet.* Accessed December 2020.
https://www.hymnal.net/en/hymn/h/582.

Savage, Audra. 2019. *The Religion of Race: America's First Religion (Dr. Audra Savage).* April 30. Accessed April 2020.
https://youtu.be/fF1FoI3epYk.

Savage, Luke. 2021. *Campaign Finance Reform by Itself Won't End Elite Control of Politics.* March 3. Accessed April 2021.
https://jacobinmag.com/2021/03/campaign-finance-reform-canada-united-states-politics.

Schmidt, William, Andy Henion, and Nicole Geary. 2015. *Schools Worsen Inequality, Especially in Math Instruction.* Accessed March 2021.
https://research.msu.edu/schools-worsen-inequality-especially-in-math/.

Schnell, Lindsay, and Sam Ruland. 2019. "Thousands of Catholic Priests Were Accused of Sexual Abuse, Then What Happened? An Investigation Reveals Most Have Become the Priest Next Door." *USA Today.* November 13. Accessed December 2020.
https://www.usatoday.com/in-depth/news/nation/2019/11/11/catholic-sexual-abuse-accused-priests-arent-sex-offender-registry/4012206002/.

Schweitzer, Jeff. 2015. "Founding Fathers: We Are Not a Christian Nation." *Huffington Post.* February 26. Accessed December 2020.
https://www.huffpost.com/entry/founding-fathers-we-are-n_b_6761840.

Scott, Gary. 2012. "Prison Is Too Violent for Young Offenders." *The New York Times.* June 5. Accessed February 2021.
https://www.nytimes.com/roomfordebate/2012/06/05/when-to-punish-a-young-offender-and-when-to-rehabilitate/prison-is-too-violent-for-young-offenders.

Scott-Clayton, Judith, and Jing Li. 2016. *Black-White Disparity in Student Loan Debt More Than Triples After Graduation.* October 20. Accessed November 27, 2020. https://www.brookings.edu/research/black-white-disparity-in-student-loan-debt-more-than-triples-after-graduation/.

Seltzer, Leon F. 2013. "Anger: How We Transfer Feelings of Guilt, Hurt, and Fear." *Psychology Today.* June 14. Accessed January 2021. https://www.psychologytoday.com/us/blog/evolution-the-self/201306/anger-how-we-transfer-feelings-guilt-hurt-and-fear.

Shoppe Black. 2021. *Black Farmer's Are Fighting to Be Saved As The Number of Black Owned Farms Grows Smaller.* September 13. Accessed June 5, 2022. https://shoppeblack.us/2021/09/black-farmers-fighting-to-be-saved/.

Shropshire, Terry. 2020. "White Woman Plays Victim, Calls Cops on Black Man Even Though She Broke Rules." *Rollingout.* May 26. Accessed December 2020. https://rollingout.com/2020/05/26/white-woman-plays-victim-calls-cops-on-black-man-even-though-she-broke-rules/.

Sicroff, Albert A., and Yom Tov Assis. 2020. "Limpieza de Sangre." *Encyclopedia.com.* December 12. https://www.encyclopedia.com/religion/encyclopedias-almanacs-transcripts-and-maps/limpieza-de-sangre.

Sifferlin, Alexandra. 2017. "Degenerative Brain Disease Found In 87% of Former Football Players: Study." *Time.* July 25. Accessed March 2021. https://time.com/4871597/degenerative-brain-disease-cte-football/.

Slisco, Aila. 2020. "'Cops' Resumes Production After Being Cancelled, New Episodes Won't Air in U.S." *Newsweek.* October 2. Accessed November 27, 2020. https://www.newsweek.com/cops-resumes-production-after-being-cancelled-new-episodes-wont-air-us-1535833.

Smedley, Audrey. 2004. *Race.* December 17. Accessed January 2021. https://www.britannica.com/topic/race-human.

Smith, Alex Duval, and Joanna Walters. 2015. "Roman Polanski 'very happy' US extradition rejected." *The Guardian.* October 30. Accessed April 24, 2022. https://www.theguardian.com/film/2015/oct/30/polish-court-rejects-us-request-to-extradite-roman-polanski.

Smith, David Michael. 2016. *Counting the Dead: Estimating the Loss of Life in the Indigenous Holocaust, 1492-Present.* Accessed November 25, 2020. https://www.se.edu/native-american/wp-content/uploads/sites/49/2019/09/A-NAS-2017-Proceedings-Smith.pdf.

Smith, Gregory A., Alan Cooperman, Besheer Mohamed, Elizabeth Podrebarac Sciupac, Becka A. Alper, Kiana Cox, and Claire Gecewicz. 2019. "In U.S., Decline of Christianity Continues at Rapid Pace." *Pew Research Center - Religion & Public Life.* Travis Mitchell. October 17. Accessed December 2020. https://www.pewforum.org/2019/10/17/in-u-s-decline-of-christianity-continues-at-rapid-pace/.

Smith, Jamil. 2020. "What We All Had to Lose." *Rolling Stone.* August 19. Accessed February 2021. https://www.rollingstone.com/politics/political-commentary/what-we-all-had-to-lose-with-trump-1047008/.

Souli, Sarah. 2020. "Does America Need a Truth and Reconciliation Commission?" *Politico.com.* August 16. Accessed March 2021. https://www.politico.com/news/magazine/2020/08/16/does-america-need-a-truth-and-reconciliation-commission-395332.

Sowell, Thomas. 2005. *Black Rednecks and White Liberals.* San Francisco: Encounter Books.

Staff, News One. 2020. "Fear Of A Black Planet: White People Becoming Minorities In America Sooner Than Expected, New Census Data Confirms." *NewsOne.* June 25. Accessed April 2021. https://newsone.com/3965535/white-people-american-minorities-census-data/.

St-Amant, Michèle. 2016. *150 Years of Hate: The Resurgence of the Ku Klux Klan.* May 29. Accessed June 9, 2022. https://www.culteducation.com/group/1015-ku-klux-klan/29444-150-years-of-hate-the-resurgence-of-the-ku-klux-klan.html.

Starling, Frank. 2020. "The Intersections Of Anti-Racism And Anti-Sexism In The Workplace." *Forbes.* September 29. Accessed January 2021. https://www.forbes.com/sites/frankstarling/2020/09/29/the-intersections-of-anti-racism-and-anti-sexism-in-the-workplace/?sh=362c8caf632c.

Stevens, Matt. 2019. "Joe Biden Says 'Poor Kids' Are Just as Bright as 'White Kids'." *New York Times.* August 9. Accessed February 2021. https://www.nytimes.com/2019/08/09/us/politics/joe-biden-poor-kids.html.

Stone Mountain Park. 2022. June 9. Accessed June 9, 2022. https://www.stonemountainpark.com/.

Studying-in-UK.org. 2020. *UK Tuition Fees 2020 Guide.* Accessed March 2021. https://www.studying-in-uk.org/uk-tuition-fees/.

Summers, Juana. 2020. "Black Patriotism: When Love Of Country Means Holding It Accountable." *NPR.* July 3. Accessed November 28, 2020. https://www.npr.org/2020/07/03/886535795/for-some-black-americans-love-of-country-means-holding-it-accountable.

Taberski, Dan. 2020. *Headlong: Running From Cops.* June 5. Accessed November 27, 2020. https://www.himalaya.com/society-culture-podcasts/headlong-running-from-cops-1062949.

Taiwo, Caroline. 2020. *White Supremacy in the Workplace.* Accessed January 2021. https://www.pollenmidwest.org/stories/confronting-white-supremacy-in-the-workplace/.

Taylor, Steve. 2018. "The Psychology of Racism." *Psychology Today.* January 28. Accessed February 2021. https://www.psychologytoday.com/us/blog/out-the-darkness/201801/the-psychology-racism.

The Car Media. 2018. *Top 10 BMW Advertisements.* April 5. Accessed June 9, 2022. https://youtu.be/4tJwMMVbnKc.

The Crown Act. 2020. *Creating a Respectful and Open World for Natural Hair.* Accessed April 2021. https://www.thecrownact.com/.

The Dick Cavett Show. 1969. *James Baldwin Discusses Racism | The Dick Cavett Show.* May 16. Accessed April 2021. https://youtu.be/WWwOi17WHpE.

The Free Dictionary. n.d. *Human.* Accessed December 2020. https://www.thefreedictionary.com/human.

The International Organization for Standardization. 2021. "International Organization for Standardization." *ISO.org.* https://www.iso.org/home/about-us/strategy-2030/priorities.html.

The Library of Old Car Ads 2. 2022. *2013 - 2019 Nissan Sentra Commercials Compilations (Part 7, END).* February 18. Accessed June 9, 2022. https://youtu.be/TMzstcx1tuw.

The Oak Park Regional Housing Center. 2013. *Diversity vs. Integration.* October 28. Accessed June 3, 2022. https://oprhc.org/2013/10/diversity-vs-integration/.

Time. 2001. "When The Boss Is Black." *Time.* June 24. http://content.time.com/time/magazine/article/0,9171,151404,00.html.

Trapasso, Clare. 2020. *The Surprising Ways Race Remains a Factor in Mortgage Lending.* July 20. Accessed March 2021. https://www.realtor.com/news/trends/black-communities-higher-mortgage-rates/.

Tucker, Josh. 2016. "Black History: A History of Permanent White Oppression, from 1619 to 2016." *Medium.com.* March 1. Accessed February 2021. https://medium.com/the-new-standard/black-history-a-history-of-permanent-white-oppression-from-1619-to-2016-8bcfa38dfce.

U.S. Bureau of Labor Statistics. 2021. *Consumer Price Index Summary*. March
10. Accessed April 2021.
https://www.bls.gov/news.release/cpi.nr0.htm.

U.S. Department of Labor. 2020. "Usual Weekly Earnings of Wage and
Salary Workers - Third Quarter 2020." *Bureau of Labor Statistics -
U.S. Department of Labor*. October 16. Accessed December 2020.
https://www.bls.gov/news.release/pdf/wkyeng.pdf.

United States Holocaust Memorial Museum. 2019. *Nuremberg Race Laws*.
September 11. Accessed November 27, 2020.
https://encyclopedia.ushmm.org/content/en/article/nuremberg-
laws.

University of Minnesota Libraries Publishing. 2016. "Principles of
Economics." *Factors of Production*. June 17. Accessed December
2020. https://open.lib.umn.edu/principleseconomics/.

Urban Dictionary. 2014. *Welfare Queen*. November 2. Accessed April 24,
2022.
https://www.urbandictionary.com/define.php?term=welfare%20q
ueen.

Villarosa, Linda. 2019. "Myths About Physical Racial Differences Were
Used To Justify Slavery - And Are Still Believed By Doctors
Today." *The New York Times Magazine*. August 14. Accessed April
2021.
https://www.nytimes.com/interactive/2019/08/14/magazine/raci
al-differences-doctors.html.

Villegas, Tim. 2017. *A Brief History of Special Education*. June 29. Accessed
March 8, 2021. https://www.thinkinclusive.us/brief-history-
special-education/.

Vinopal, Courtney. 2021. *What we know about the Atlanta spa shootings that
killed 8, including 6 Asian women*. March 19. Accessed April 09, 2022.
https://www.pbs.org/newshour/nation/what-we-know-about-the-
atlanta-spa-shootings-that-killed-8-including-6-asian-women.

Vogell, Heather. 2014. *Violent and Legal: The Shocking Ways School Kids Are
Being Pinned Down, Isolated Against Their Will*. June 19. Accessed
March 2021. https://www.propublica.org/article/schools-
restraints-seclusions.

Waldrop, Theresa, and Jamiel Lynch. 2021. *Nation's largest Confederate
memorial to get new exhibit telling the 'whole story' of Georgia's Stone
Mountain*. May 25. Accessed June 9, 2022.
https://www.cnn.com/2021/05/24/us/stone-mountain-georgia-
confederate-memorial-changes/index.html.

Watson, Patrick W. 2018. "Real Wage Growth Is Actually Falling." *Forbes*.
September 25. Accessed April 2021.

https://www.forbes.com/sites/patrickwwatson/2018/09/25/real-wage-growth-is-actually-falling/?sh=2af236b67284.

Wegman, Jesse. 2020. "The Electoral College Will Destroy America." *The New York Times*. September 8. Accessed April 2021. https://www.nytimes.com/2020/09/08/opinion/electoral-college-trump-biden.html.

Whack, Errin. 2015. "Who Was Edmund Pettus?" *Smithsonian Magazine*. March 7. Accessed February 2021. https://www.smithsonianmag.com/history/who-was-edmund-pettus-180954501/.

White & Case. 2017. *Algorithms and Bias: What Lenders Need to Know*. January 20. Accessed April 2021. https://www.whitecase.com/publications/insight/algorithms-and-bias-what-lenders-need-know.

Wilkerson, Isabel, interview by Terry Gross. 2020. "It's More Than Racism: Isabel Wilkerson Explains America's 'Caste' System." *Fresh Air*. NPR, (August 04).

Williams, Eric. 1970. *From Columbus to Castro: The History of the Caribbean 1492-1969*. New York: Andre Deutsch Limited.

Williams, Marco, and Maia Harris. 2006. *Banished: How Whites Drove Blacks Out of Town in America*. Directed by Marco Williams.

Williams, Yohuru. 2018. *The Most Damaging Myths About Slavery, Debunked*. May 3. Accessed January 2021. https://www.history.com/news/debunking-slavery-myths.

Wilson, Valerie. 2016. "African Americans are Paid Less Than Whites at Every Education Level." *Economic Policy Institute*. October 4. Accessed November 27, 2020. https://www.epi.org/publication/african-americans-are-paid-less-than-whites-at-every-education-level/.

Wingfield, Adia Harvey. 2015. "Being Black—But Not Too Black—In The Workplace." *The Atlantic*. October 14. Accessed January 2021. https://www.theatlantic.com/business/archive/2015/10/being-black-work/409990/.

Wise, Carl, and David Wheat. 2016. *African Laborers for a New Empire: Iberia, Slavery, and the Atlantic World*. Accessed February 2021. https://ldhi.library.cofc.edu/exhibits/show/african_laborers_for_a_new_emp/pope_nicolas_v_and_the_portugu.

Woodward, Aylin. 2019. "European Colonizers Killed so Many Indigenous Americans that the Planet Cooled Down, a Group of Researchers Concluded." *Business Insider*. February 9. Accessed December 2020. https://www.businessinsider.com/climate-changed-after-europeans-killed-indigenous-americans-2019-2?op=1.

Woolf, Christopher. 2015. "A Brief History of America's Hostility to a Previous Generation of Mediterranean Migrants — Italians." *The World.* November 25. Accessed January 2021. https://www.pri.org/stories/2015-11-26/brief-history-america-s-hostility-previous-generation-mediterranean-migrants.

Worstall, Tim. 2020. "So Afua Hirsch Is Ignorant Of History As Well Then." *Continental Telegraph.* May 07. Accessed November 27, 2020. https://www.continentaltelegraph.com/2020/05/so-afua-hirsch-is-ignorant-of-history-as-well-then.

Yadav, Sameer. 2018. *How Has Christianity Contributed to Racism? Part II.* Westmont College. October 31. Accessed December 2020. https://youtu.be/UBWps5j1-dw.

Zappa, Frank. 1966. "Trouble Every Day." *Freak Out!* Cond. The Mothers Of Invention. Comp. Frank Zappa.

www.ingramcontent.com/pod-product-compliance
Lightning Source LLC
Chambersburg PA
CBHW071018280326
41935CB00011B/1401